Praise for *Save the Humans?*

"This is a remarkable book: part personal story, part intellectual history told in the first person by a skilled writer and assiduous historian, part passionate but clearly and logically argued plea for pushing the potential of collective action to preserve the human race. Easy reading and full of useful and unforgettable stories. . . . A medicine against apathy and political despair much needed in the US and the world today."
    —Peter Marcuse, author of *Cities for People, Not for Profit: Critical Urban Theory*

"Over the last decades, Jeremy Brecher has known how to detect the critical issues of a period, to sort the many realities of suffering and injustice, and to emerge with a clear, short, powerful description. He does it again in this important book—a book about people: about how our system devalues people and what needs to be done."
    —Saskia Sassen, author of *Territory, Authority, Rights*

"The most important story of the past half century is that of ordinary people organizing to transform the way society looked at workers, unjust war, women, people of color, and the environment. Jeremy Brecher's life and book tell this story with a passion and comprehensiveness that make this a must-read for fans of justice."
    —John Cavanagh, director of the Institute for Policy Studies and author of *Development Redefined: How the Market Met Its Match* and *The Field Guide to the Global Economy*

"Indispensable. . . . A fascinating blend of political autobiography and manual for social change, giving cogent primacy to the stark goal of human preservation. With species survival at stake, what Jeremy Brecher writes is at once frightening and inspiring."
    —Richard Falk, author of *Palestine's Horizon: Toward a Just Peace* and *Power Shift: On the New Global Order*

"One of America's most admired activist-scholars shines his light on the path forward, reminding us that social change is both possible and urgent."
    —Mike Davis, author of *City of Quartz: Excavating the Future in Los Angeles*

"It is an amazing piece of work indeed, accomplishing the unimaginable, to paraphrase the Port Huron Statement. The blend of personal experience, collective memories, social analysis, and indications of possible ways out of our current disastrous state is impressive."
    —Ferdinanda Fasce, professor of contemporary history at the University of Genoa and author of *An American Family: The Great War and Corporate Culture in America*

"A breathtaking manuscript. I am overwhelmed and beginning to think about how I can integrate this into my teaching. An enormous contribution to the advancement of know-how for common preservation."
    —Frieder Otto Wolf, professor of philosophy at the Free University of Berlin and former member of the European Parliament for the German Greens

"Jeremy Brecher's work is astonishing and refreshing—and, God knows, necessary."
    —Studs Terkel

Save the Humans?

Save the Humans?
Common Preservation in Action

Jeremy Brecher

PMPRESS

Save the Humans? Common Preservation in Action
Jeremy Brecher

PM Press
PO Box 23912
Oakland, CA 94623
www.pmpress.org

Cover design by John Yates/stealworks.com
Layout by Jonathan Rowland

ISBN: 978-1-62963-798-3
ebook ISBN: 978-1-62963-816-4
Library of Congress Control Number: 2019946099

10 9 8 7 6 5 4 3 2 1

Printed in the USA

Contents

This book is dedicated to the memory of Tim Costello, my friend, collaborator, and writing partner of forty years.

ACKNOWLEDGMENTS

This book reflects what I've learned from innumerable friends and colleagues over the past half century. I thank them all, especially those who have led me to question my own ideas. As William Blake said, "Opposition is true friendship."

Jill Cutler has sustained me through the long travails of making this book, as well as providing me the luxury of an in-house editor. Without Michael Pertschuk's faith in it this book might never have seen the light of day. Essential support also came from Anthony Arnove, Nando Fasce, Charles Lindblom, Michael Ferber, Frances Fox Piven, and Frieder Otto Wolf. My editor Jennifer Knerr's vision was essential to the realization of this project.

My colleagues Becky Glass, Brendan Smith, and Joe Uehlein at the Labor Network for Sustainability have provided a context of thought and action that has informed the final shaping of the book.

Thanks to those who have read part or all of the manuscript at one stage or another, including Michael Ames, Michael Athay, Jill Cutler, Josh Dubler, Sharon Hammer, Charles Lindblom, Peter Marris, Brendan Smith, Dan Sofaer, Michael Pertschuk, and Frieder Otto Wolf.

Many of the ideas in this book were worked out over four decades in collaboration with the late Tim Costello.

WHAT I DID WHILE I WAS WAITING FOR DOOM

۶۰

WHEN *SAVE THE HUMANS?* WAS FIRST PUBLISHED IN 2012, THE
Doomsday Clock, which measures the world's vulnerability to catastrophe from nuclear weapons, climate change, and other threats, was set at
five minutes to midnight. In 2020, it reads 100 seconds to midnight—the
closest to midnight it has ever been.

The statement explaining the setting of the Doomsday Clock for 2020
warns, "Humanity continues to face two simultaneous existential dangers—nuclear war and climate change." Civilization-ending nuclear war
is "a genuine possibility." Climate change that could devastate the planet
is "undeniably happening." Institutions that should be working to address
these threats have "failed to rise to the challenge."[1]

Save the Humans? is the story of my search for ways to counter doom
by encouraging a shift from mutual destruction to common preservation. It uses history and my own experience to explore how people shift
from strategies based on greed and self-aggrandizement to strategies that
pursue self-interest by promoting common interests. I hope my answers
to this question may contribute to halting our drive toward doom. Over
the past decade, I have continued to explore those questions. This new
preface updates that story.

Save the Humans? was published in the aftermath of the historic failure of the 2009 Copenhagen climate summit. Meant to set humanity on
the path to climate safety, instead it revealed greedy, self-aggrandizing
governments and corporations unable or unwilling to protect humanity even to preserve themselves. Governments didn't approach climate
change as the biggest threat we face but rather with an eye to advantages that might be gained by economic and political rivals. Fossil fuel

corporations and their allies ladled out cash to persuade politicians and the public to reject policies that might threaten the profits they made from oil, coal, and gas. Copenhagen unveiled the war of all against all among domineering power centers that makes it so difficult to set back the hands of the Doomsday Clock.

Before Copenhagen, climate protection advocates worked closely with national governments that appeared to be putting the world on the road to climate safety. There had been few large climate demonstrations and even less confrontational direct action. After Copenhagen, a transformed climate movement began blocking the construction of pipelines and shutting down coal-fired power plants.[2]

When activists launched a campaign against the Keystone XL Pipeline, I joined the first sit-ins at the White House. I wrote a book titled *Climate Insurgency: A Strategy for Survival* that applied ideas in *Save the Humans?* to the climate crisis. It called for a global nonviolent insurgency—much along the lines of the "human preservation movement" proposed in part 5 of *Save the Humans?*

As the climate crisis deepened, the kind of movement I had envisioned began to emerge. Direct actionists and their allies blocked dozens of fossil fuel pipeline projects. Much of the traditional environmental movement supported such direct action and called for an end to new fossil fuel infrastructure—a "fossil freeze." A wave of direct-action civil disobedience in dozens of locations around the globe demanded that we "Break Free from Fossil Fuels." It was a prefiguration of a climate insurgency. I wrote *Against Doom: A Climate Insurgency Manual* to argue that the climate insurgency had begun and to suggest how it could reverse the momentum toward climate doom.[3]

Much of my own climate action was focused on organized labor and the American working class. I helped found the Labor Network for Sustainability, which built a movement for climate protection within unions and other working-class constituencies. I wrote *Climate Solidarity: Workers vs. Warming* to explain why climate protection was such a hard sell for unions and to lay out a strategy for transforming labor's climate policy by transforming the labor movement itself.[4] Embedding climate protection in a worker-friendly economic program became a central theme of the rapidly emerging movement for a Green New Deal.[5] Despite these efforts, there continued to be an increase in the greenhouse gases added to the atmosphere.

The Doomsday Clock was at its previous low of two minutes to midnight in the depths of the Cold War arms race. Early in *Save the Humans?*

I tell the story of the movement for nuclear disarmament and how it contributed to a ban on nuclear testing, the emergence of Cold War detente, and an 80 percent reduction in strategic nuclear weapons. But as the "2020 Doomsday Clock Announcement" warns, the threat of nuclear catastrophe is now as serious as ever. The treaties that reduced nuclear weapons are now being abrogated, and a new generation of nukes is rolling off the assembly lines.

Human existence is threatened by a world order controlled by rival political, military, and economic power centers willing to put the future of humanity at risk in pursuit of their own wealth and power. To "save the humans" will require a devolution of power both downward and upward. It requires devolving the power of governments and corporations downward to forms of democratic accountability and upward to forms of cooperation that represent the common interests of humanity—first and foremost our common preservation against doom. And that requires a global human survival movement along the lines proposed in part 5 of *Save the Humans?*

I recently completed a companion volume to *Save the Humans?* called *Common Preservation in a Time of Mutual Destruction.*[6] The two were originally part of a single manuscript that I have been working on since the early 1970s. *Save the Humans?* approaches common preservation based on my own experience and historical research. *Common Preservation in a Time of Mutual Destruction* represents a complementary approach that draws on a variety of thinkers to develop a heuristic for exploring common preservation in a wide range of historical and contemporary situations. It shows how our human capabilities make possible shifts from strategies based exclusively on self-preservation and self-aggrandizement to strategies of common preservation—and how the movements that result could develop the power to realize our common goals.

Self-preservation may be life's deepest instinct, but today we can only realize self-preservation through common preservation. Individual strategies can no longer protect us against mutual destruction; none of us can ward off doom by ourselves. The condition of human survival is a global insurgency for common preservation that denies the legitimate authority of those who are leading us on the path to doom—and instead asserts our right and obligation to protect our common life.

Can we save the humans? The answer may be uncertain, but one thing is certain—*we can refuse to consent to doom.* And if enough of us withdraw our consent, we can gain the power to overcome the forces generating doom.

Notes

1. John Mecklin, "It Is 100 Seconds to Midnight: 2020 Doomsday Clock Statement," Bulletin of the Atomic Scientists, accessed January 23, 2020, https://thebulletin.org/doomsday-clock/current-time/.
2. The history of the climate movement is told in part 1 of my *Climate Insurgency: A Strategy for Survival* (Boulder, CO: Paradigm Publishers, 2015) and part 3 of *Common Preservation in a Time of Mutual Destruction* (Oakland, CA: PM Press, 2020).
3. Jeremy Brecher, *Against Doom: A Climate Insurgency Manual* (Oakland, CA: PM Press, 2017).
4. Jeremy Brecher, *Climate Solidarity: Workers vs. Warming* (Takoma Park, MD: Labor Network for Sustainability/Stone Soup Books, 2017), accessed January 12, 2020, https://www.labor4sustainability.org/wp-content/uploads/2017/06/Climate-Solidarity.pdf.
5. I helped support the emergence of the Green New Deal by consulting with leaders from the Sunrise movement and by writing articles collected on the Labor Network for Sustainability website, accessed January 12, 2020, https://www.labor4sustainability.org/green-new-deal/.
6. Brecher, *Common Preservation in a Time of Mutual Destruction* (Oakland, CA: PM Press, 2020).

MARCH LIKE AN EGYPTIAN

ൟ

Why in the world were protesters occupying the Wisconsin statehouse wearing King Tut headdresses? And why were orders for pizza coming into Madison, Wisconsin, from Cairo, Egypt?

The story begins around 1500 BC when Egyptian workers at Deir el-Medina hadn't been paid for three weeks by their notoriously corrupt supervisors. They stopped working and walked out. It may be history's first recorded strike.

Fast-forward thirty-five hundred or so years to the end of 2006 AD. Another group of Egyptian workers, angered at the denial of their promised year-end bonuses and the corruption of their managers, quit working and shut down their workplaces. This strike by Mahalla el-Kubra textile workers startled the Egyptian people and apparently the government and the government-owned employer as well.

The strike started with night-shift workers who were enraged at the company's decision not to pay bonuses that had been promised by Egypt's Prime Minister Ahmed Nazif. The next day they were joined by the day-shift workers, who occupied the plant and a nearby street in protest. Government security forces surrounded the area and cut off electricity to the plant. Eventually twenty-seven thousand workers were involved, including four thousand women, who said they were "standing up for their children."

After five days, the government retreated and offered to restore the bonuses. An employee reported that upon returning to work, "The cashiers were sitting to greet the workers" with their back pay "the minute they walked into work."

In 2006 I was helping start a tiny NGO called Global Labor Strategies (GLS). We called it a "bridge building" organization; our purpose was to help workers and their allies connect across the borders of an ever-more globalizing world. While the Mahalla strike was virtually unreported in the US media, I discovered information about it on the web and wrote about it on the GLS blog.[1]

A couple of years later there was another strike in Mahalla. This time a small organization of student and youth activists formed to support the strikers. They set up a Facebook page and called a demonstration on April 6. Thereafter they began referring to themselves as the April 6 Youth Movement. After the strike was over they continued their social networking website with lively debates on freedom of speech, government nepotism, and economic stagnation. By 2010 they had seventy thousand Facebook friends.

On December 17, 2010, an impoverished Tunisian fruit seller named Mohamed Bouazizi, after repeated police harassment, doused himself with kerosene and set himself on fire to protest the economic and political conditions to which he and his country were subjected. Within a week, seven other Tunisians had done the same. What seemed like futile acts of despair inspired massive protests. With hundreds of thousands of protesters refusing to let business as usual go on, Zine El Abidine Ben Ali, Tunisia's ruler for a quarter of a century, was forced to flee and a transitional government made preparations to hold elections under a new, democratic constitution.

Egyptians watched the unfolding events in Tunisia with fascination. They too faced grinding poverty and a tyrannical government supported from abroad that used violence and torture to repress opposition while looting billions of dollars by means of corruption. A few small groups, including the April 6 Youth Movement, began calling for Egypt to undergo a democratization like that in Tunisia. They used Facebook and other new social media to get out the word. They started holding street meetings in Cairo neighborhoods. To their surprise, large numbers came out in the poor neighborhoods and supported the idea of an "Egyptian Tunisia." They began holding daily demonstrations in Cairo's central Tahrir Square (Arabic for "Liberation Square") calling for Hosni Mubarak, Egypt's autocratic president for thirty years, to go.

Over the course of two weeks the demonstrations swelled. Men and women— Sunni, Shia, and Christian—marched side by side. Initially the established opposition parties and organizations stayed aloof from the protests, but gradually they began to join in. Meanwhile the hated security police launched repeated attacks on the demonstrators. The army began to roll into Liberation Square with its troops and tanks while its airplanes flew overhead. Then suddenly the police withdrew and the army high command issued a statement that it would not fire on the protesters.

The United States, which had provided Mubarak's regime with more than sixty billion dollars over the previous thirty years and maintained a close relationship with Mubarak and the Egyptian military, expressed strong support for Mubarak. But as the number of demonstrators multiplied, the United States began to distance itself from the regime. Within a week, US Secretary of State Hillary Clinton was declaring, "Mubarak must go."

Meanwhile, the protests continued to swell, not only in Cairo but throughout the country. The army troops fraternized with the demonstrators; a young woman told reporters that demonstrators in Liberation Square were arranging a football match with the soldiers. As the police disappeared from the streets, people in Cairo neighborhoods began organizing their own neighborhood watches. Workers throughout the country began to conduct strikes, some seeking to establish unions and gain wage increases, others calling for the removal of the regime.

On February 1, 2011, a "Million Man March" indeed produced something like a million protesters in Liberation Square calling on Mubarak to leave. It was widely reported that he was about to do so. Instead, he went on television and gave a speech making a few concessions but pledging that he would fill out his term and that he would "die on Egyptian soil." Commentators observed that he should be careful what he said.

The protestors felt betrayed; a wave of rage pervaded the entire country. Within six hours the senior officers of the army announced that Mubarak had "resigned" and that an officer's council had taken power. They also announced that they would establish a transitional government that would put into place a new democratic constitution and hold democratic elections. Large demonstrations continued in Liberation Square and throughout the country insisting that they follow through.

Early on in the Egyptian demonstrations, I saw a young woman being pressured by a television journalist to name those she considered leaders of the protests. After repeatedly trying to explain that people were acting on their own, she finally, in exasperation, pointed around at the crowd and said, "Right now it looks like we have half a million leaders." Her words reminded me of those from the group of "Wobblies"—members of the Industrial Workers of the World union—nearly a century before. Asked who their leaders were, they replied, "We've got no leaders—we're all leaders."

To many people the events in Egypt revealed a courage, a solidarity, an activism, and an intelligence that seemed to violate their very sense of what is possible. Many commentators on the scene said things such as "These are not the Egyptians I know" and "This is a new Egypt." At Graterford prison outside Philadelphia, where many of the inmates were glued to the television watching scenes of rebellion in Egypt, a life prisoner named Charles Coley came up to a friend of mine in the hall and summed up a response shared by many around the world: "I just didn't know that people had it in them."

The Egyptian upheaval electrified the entire Middle East. Popular upheavals rocked Bahrain, Morocco, Lebanon, Iraq, Iran, Saudi Arabia, and Syria. Demonstrations in Jordan and Yemen led to the firing and replacement of entire cabinets. Demonstrations in Libya turned into civil war followed by NATO and Arab League military intervention. Comparing them to the upheavals that brought the overthrow of Communist regimes in Poland, Czechoslovakia, and elsewhere in Eastern Europe two decades earlier, commentators began referring to these events as the "Arab Spring."

But the impact of events in the Middle East didn't stop at the boundaries of the region. Students planning anti-government actions in London called for turning Trafalgar Square into a British Tahrir Square; nearly half a million people turned out for the demonstration protesting public spending cuts.[2] As faculty, staff, and fifteen thousand demonstrators backed Puerto Rican students protesting the military occupation of their campus and the repression of freedom of speech and assembly, newscasters compared them to the protestors in Tahrir Square; US Congressman Luis V. Gutierrez said it reflected "a lesson the people of Egypt taught the world last week: Brutal laws and secret meetings and armed enforcers don't extinguish the flame of justice—they are the spark that makes it burn brighter."[3] At a demonstration in Mexico City, Martin Esparza, secretary general of the Mexican Electrical Workers Union, called for a peaceful civilian insurgency, taking its example from the events in Egypt.[4]

The ripples even reached the United States. At the same time as the Egyptian upheaval, a string of right-wing state governors were taking office with the backing of the Tea Party and wealthy energy company executives. In Ohio, Indiana, and many other states they seized on budget crises to pass laws restricting or completely eliminating the right of public employees to be represented by unions.

The epicenter of the struggle was Wisconsin, where newly elected governor Scott Walker introduced legislation to abolish collective bargaining for teachers, social workers, and most other government employees. Students and workers began holding demonstrations in the state capitol rotunda in Madison to protest the new anti-labor laws. First there were hundreds of protesters, then thousands. Eventually more than one hundred thousand people occupied the building, making it the largest demonstration in Wisconsin at least since the Vietnam War.

Wisconsin Republican Congressman Paul Ryan said, "It's like Cairo's moved to Madison."[5] According to a news report, "Many protestors appeared to be taking inspiration from the recent democratic uprisings in Egypt and Tunisia, with some even wearing King Tut hats."[6] Orders for pizza for the demonstrators poured in from around the world—including some from Cairo. And, parodying a famous pop song titled "Walk Like an Egyptian," bumper stickers appeared reading "March Like an Egyptian."

The events in Wisconsin were as unanticipated as those in Egypt. Yet from 1500 BC to today, history shows that nothing is as predictable as unpredictable popular upheavals. How do they happen? What do they mean? Can they help solve the problems people face? Will they instead end badly, leading to domination or disorder? How can we forestall such bad results and instead realize their potential for good?

I've spent a lifetime trying to find answers to these questions. This book tells what I've learned.

INTRODUCTION

ॐ

YOU AND I MAY NOT KNOW EACH OTHER, BUT I SUSPECT THERE ARE SOME PROBLEMS that we share. Perhaps we can do better at solving those problems if we work together.

We live in an era of impending mutual destruction. In 1946, following the first explosion of an atom bomb, Albert Einstein warned, "The unleashed power of the atom has changed everything save our modes of thinking and we thus drift toward unparalleled catastrophe."[1] The rapid acceleration of global warming and other environmental threats in the early twenty-first century—aggravated by ruinous global economic war of all against all—intensified fears for human survival. Sixty years after Einstein's prophesy, the astrophysicist Stephen Hawking warned, "Life on Earth is at the ever-increasing risk of being wiped out by a disaster," such as "sudden global warming" and "nuclear war."[2] Yet the drift Einstein warned of continues unabated. The Doomsday Clock marking the approach of human self-destruction continues to hover close to midnight, now driven not only by the threat of nuclear holocaust but also by human-induced climate change and the unknown unknowns of new technologies.[3]

A quarter of a century ago, when "Save the Whales!" was a popular slogan, a *New Yorker* cartoon showed one whale asking another, "But can they save themselves?" In the early twenty-first century, with the proliferation of weapons of mass destruction and the burgeoning consequences of climate change, experts and ordinary people alike are asking each other whether we humans can save ourselves from the threats we have created.

I doubt there is any way we can save ourselves for long as individuals or as separate social groups. Today, self-preservation depends on common preservation—cooperation in service of our mutual well-being. For any of us to survive, we must preserve the conditions of each other's existence.

Our impending doom is often met with denial or despair. It seems to be driven by forces beyond human control, and there appears little we can do to avert it. Common preservation seems little more than a distant and impossible dream.

This book is the story of a lifelong search for the means of common preservation. It traces my attempt, over the course of half a century, to discover how to understand, and how to nourish, common preservation. It recounts my own experience, but it does so to illuminate how we might be better able to act in common to address the problems we share in common.

As a child I discovered that the world was full of problems that affected my life. In my family's pantry there hung a poster headed "What to Do in the Event of Nuclear Attack," and I became aware at an early age that I and the rest of the world might be destroyed in a nuclear conflagration. Some members of my family were victims of Nazi anti-Semitism and others were subject to anti-Semitism in the United States. Growing up in the McCarthy era I experienced the fear generated by political repression. In the communities in which I lived I discovered, hidden away from public view, the realities of poverty and racial discrimination. I saw that many people around me lived lives of quiet desperation; in order to survive, they were forced to spend most of their waking hours in work they found oppressive, that sickened them physically and mentally, and from which they had little chance of escape. I saw, smelled, and breathed the degradation of the natural environment, and I heard warnings that human beings were threatening the basic environmental conditions on which human life depends.

Initially I felt powerless in the face of these problems. They seemed like a cruel fate that I could do nothing to change. But I gradually realized that, just as I experienced these problems, so did many other people. Maybe if we acted together to deal with them we could make changes that we couldn't make alone.

People are often passive and isolated in the face of problems they can't solve. But at times, sometimes quite unexpectedly, they develop new ways to act in concert to advance shared interests. The emergence of a movement for global economic justice—exemplified by the "Battle of Seattle" that shut down the 1999 global extravaganza of the World Trade Organization (WTO)—provides a widely noted example of such a development. So does the 2011 "Arab Spring." So do the massive strikes, general strikes, and demonstrations in Greece, Poland, Italy, Latvia, Ireland, Britain, Spain, and nearly every other European nation, as well as transnational demonstrations at European Union headquarters in Brussels, protesting layoffs, benefits cuts, rising student fees, and other austerity measures.

The emergence of a multifaceted worldwide movement to protect the earth's climate from global warming represents a new form of concerted action for common preservation. While its extent and success remain to be seen, it has already produced a global day of action with fifty-two hundred rallies from Mt. Everest to the Great Barrier Reef in what CNN called "the most widespread day of political action on the planet."[4]

People turn to new strategies such as these when the problems they face prove difficult to solve either through individual action or through the patterns prescribed by established institutions. Those new strategies often take the form of social movements.

Sometimes people who appear powerless and stymied have used social movements to transform the problems they face—and history and society as well. The US sit-down strikes of the 1930s forced US corporations to recognize and negotiate with the representatives of their employees. The civil disobedience campaigns led by Gandhi won Indians independence from Britain. The civil rights movement of the 1960s gained the abolition of legalized racial segregation in the American South. The Solidarity movement and its general strikes led to the fall of Communism in Poland and helped bring about its demise throughout Eastern Europe and the USSR. The Arab Spring overthrew dictatorships in Tunisia and Egypt and reshaped the power configuration of the Middle East.

For half a century I have been a participant in social movements; for forty years I have been studying and writing about their history and prospects. This book, which I've been working on since the early 1970s, tries to extract from what I've experienced and studied something useful for people trying to solve problems through new common preservations. It takes the form of a personal narrative: the story of my track through the history and experience of such movements. My hope is to produce something that is useful for countering the threat of mutual destruction today.

Common Preservation

While common preservation is as old as or older than our species, it is acquiring a new significance at a time when we are creating the conditions for our own self-extermination, whether through the bang of a nuclear holocaust or the whimper of an expiring ecosphere.

No individual or restricted group can solve such collective problems alone. None of us can count on survival, let alone well-being, for ourselves and those we care about, unless we act together to transform the current patterns of human life. Self-preservation for individuals and groups can now only be ensured through common preservation of our species and its environment as a whole.

I use the phrase common preservation to denote a strategy in which people try to solve their problems by meeting each other's needs rather than exclusively their own. I borrowed the phrase from the seventeenth century English Digger Gerrard Winstanley.

In the midst of the English revolution the impoverished Diggers had formed self-governing work teams, occupied uncultivated lands, and begun producing food for their communities. Winstanley justified this action on the principle of common preservation, the "principle in every one to seek the good of others, as himself."

Winstanley contrasted common preservation to self-preservation, in which those in power "seek their own Preservation, Ease, Honor, Riches, and Freedom in the Earth." Such self-preservation was "the root of the Tree Tyranny, and the Law of Unrighteousness, and all particular Kingly Laws found out by covetous Policy to enslave one brother to another, whereby bondage, tears, sorrows and poverty are brought upon many men." This tyranny is "the cause of all wars and troubles."[5]

Winstanley interpreted common preservation in the religious idiom of his time. But, as he himself asserted, the need for common preservation, and the means for establishing it, don't require religious revelation; they can be found out "by experience." Adam and his family followed the principle of common preservation out of the "the law of necessity": that "the Earth should be planted for the common preservation and peace of his household." Indeed, such necessity was the root of "all particular Laws found out by experience" that provide for common preservation. Today, whatever our differing beliefs, our own experience is teaching us all the necessity for common preservation.

Common preservation is more than coordination, cooperation, or collaboration. Such forms of joint action involve working together, but the result may be to the benefit of some and to the detriment of others. Slaves may cooperate to produce their own fetters; scientists and workers may collaborate to produce the nuclear weapons that threaten to destroy their civilization; corporations may hire workers whose joint labor produces the greenhouse gases that are destroying their biosphere. Common preservation is more than the biological phenomenon of symbiosis, which can take the form of a parasitism that harms one of its partners. Common preservation is not just action in concert, but action in concert for mutual benefit.

Common preservation and self-preservation represent alternative strategies. I don't advocate, or expect, that common preservation will entirely supplant self-preservation—indeed, both in biology and in human society they are often intertwined and even complementary. But when self-preservation generates mutual destruction it is futile and indefensible; it leads to the annihilation rather than the self-preservation of those who pursue it.

Common preservation—often intermingled with more antagonistic relationships—is ubiquitous in human life. From the loving interchanges of parent and child to the international treaties limiting nuclear testing, people use common preservation at many different scales to meet their needs and realize their ends.

Throughout this book I investigate how common preservations come about and why they can make a difference. They often seem to be related to what I call an "ecological shift"—like the shift in worldview from isolated to interdependent organisms introduced by the science of ecology—in which people come to recognize apparently separate, independent entities as part of larger wholes. It often involves the self-organization of people who have been isolated or even antagonistic. And it often overcomes powerlessness by making use of various forms of "people power" based on a refusal to obey those currently in charge.

In an era of mutual destruction, common preservation is not just desirable; it is the condition of our survival.

A Human Preservation Movement?

If common preservation is today the necessary condition for our self-preservation, how do we make it happen? How can we change from a world of mutual destruction to one based on common preservation?

The obstacles to such a transformation are surely sufficient to evoke despair—and sufficient to have until now prevented us from taking the obvious steps to eliminate the threats to our existence. People rarely exercise effective control of their own governments; international institutions are a fragile and often ineffective barrier to actions that threaten survival; superpowers dominate others at will; and corporations pollute the environment and dominate governments with little restraint. Powerful interests oppose effective protections for human survival at local, national, and transnational levels. Different social groups who share an interest in mutual survival are also divided by conflicting interests. People fear that collective action will end up generating disorder and domination.

This book explores the possibility that such obstacles might be overcome through a human preservation movement specifically targeted against the threats to human survival. Such a movement could be powerful because it would represent the most profound common interests of individuals and groups. Addressing the apparently disparate issues of nuclear proliferation, global warming, economic devastation, social injustice, and other threats as part of the broader problem of ensuring human survival could provide a basis for the daunting transformations needed to end such threats. Many of the personal and historical experiences I present in the book were chosen to provide background for how such a movement might arise and how it might do its work.

My Story

In this book I tell what I've learned about creating new common preservations by telling my own story.

Part 1, "Discovering Social Problems," starts the story off with my childhood in the United States in the 1950s. My awareness of social problems was no doubt influenced by the fact that my parents were concerned with peace, racial justice, and other social issues. But it also reflected the real world I saw around me—the black slums I discovered in my pleasant middle-class hometown, for example, and my father's bouts of depression and migraine headaches that we all associated with work-related stress.

In early adolescence I became active first in the then-burgeoning nuclear disarmament movement, then in the civil rights, student, and other movements. Much of my late adolescence was devoted to the radical student movement and the movement against the Vietnam War. Part 2, "Discovering Social Movements," tells what I learned from what are often called the movements of the 1960s.

I found in social movements an alternative to the experience of individual powerlessness in the face of social problems. But I did not feel that the programs and practices of the movements in which I participated were adequate. So I began a still-continuing exploration of the history of social movements and of various ideas about how they do, or should, go about making change.

I spent much of the 1970s and 1980s studying working-class movements. I wrote or cowrote several books including *Strike!, Common Sense for Hard Times, Root & Branch: The Rise of the Workers' Movements,* and *Brass Valley: The Story of Working People's Lives and Struggles in an American Industrial Region.* Part 3, "Discovering Workers Power," tells what I learned from the history of working-class movements.

Starting in the 1980s I became increasingly preoccupied with what is now known as economic globalization and the movements that developed to counter it. I collaborated on three books on the subject: *Global Visions, Global Village or Global Pillage,* and *Globalization from Below.* Part 4, "Discovering Globalization from Below," shows how I used the ways of thinking about common preservation I was developing to grapple with the emerging phenomenon of economic globalization and the countering movements I called globalization from below.

In Part 5, "Human Preservation," I use my experience and study of social movements and social change to sketch what a human survival movement to counter today's threats of mutual destruction might be like, how it might emerge, and what it might try to do.

A brief conclusion sums up what I think this story means.

Many of the materials discussed throughout the book are available on my website, www.jeremybrecher.org.

I am currently completing a companion volume that will provide a fuller conceptualization of how to understand and nourish common preservation. While the application of that method is illustrated throughout *Save the Humans?,* the companion volume will provide an in-depth look at its development, codify it, and show more explicitly how it can be used to interpret and encourage the emergence of common preservation.

* * *

There are few human experiences more satisfying than participating with others who have been divided and oppressed when they break out into action to change their conditions of life. There are few things more exciting than seeing people rise up and liberate themselves from outrageous oppression. There are few things more joyous than overcoming that which divides you from other people and forging new bonds of mutual support. There can be few things as sustaining as a life of participation with others in the effort to make a better world.

I have had the privilege of experiencing all of these. Together they gave rise to another passion, one that has driven and sustained me all of my life. That is a passion to find, improve, and share ways of thinking that people can use to act in concert to improve the world for themselves and each other. While I hope anyone who is curious about social movements and social change will find this book of interest, it is written especially for those who share that passion. For those who hunger and thirst after alternatives to human self-destruction, this book aims to provide food and drink.

PART 1

DISCOVERING SOCIAL PROBLEMS

1

DISCOVERING SOCIAL PROBLEMS

SOCIAL PROBLEMS ARE BY DEFINITION SHARED, BUT EACH OF US APPROACHES SHARED problems from an idiosyncratic personal starting point. As a child I became aware of some of the problems of society through my own and my family's experiences with war, genocide, political repression, racism, environmental degradation, and oppressive labor.

I grew up in a family of educated professionals, first in a pleasant suburb of New York City, then in a rural area in northwestern Connecticut. My parents were writers who often worked together as a team. My father was a very secular Jew; my mother came from old stock Pennsylvania Dutch Calvinists and herself became a Quaker. My father had been a low-level staffer in the New Deal and had the politics of a left New Dealer; my mother was a pacifist and shared the social concerns for which Quakers are known. I had a loving family and a childhood filled with many joys.

But I was also born into a terrible time in history. The years immediately before and after my birth saw the Great Depression, the Second World War, the Holocaust, and Hiroshima.

As I see it now, these years marked the beginning of an era in which the efforts of individuals and groups for a better life were bound to be futile, indeed, likely to accelerate human self-destruction, unless they were part of a broader effort for common preservation. Consciousness of the necessity for common preservation has grown throughout that era, but it has come only fitfully and in fragments and is far from being implemented. Many of the problems I was discovering half a century ago not only remain with us today, but have become more threatening to our individual and common survival.

While I became aware of social problems at a tender age, I had little idea of what to do about them. I experienced the threat of nuclear war, or my father's terrible job-related migraine headaches, as something that affected me as an individual, but that I had no way as an individual to affect.

The story I tell here represents a selection from among the immensely wider range of experiences of my childhood. Were I writing an autobiography, I would tell about my joy in running free in the world of nature, living in the bosom of a tiny community, and being encouraged by my family in all manner of exploration and inquiry. This is instead the story of how I became aware of problems requiring common preservation.

2

KISS YOUR ASS GOODBYE

ਤ

IN THE PANTRY OF MY CHILDHOOD HOME HUNG A POSTER HEADED "WHAT TO DO IN the Event of Nuclear Attack," and that's how I first became aware of "social problems." It was around 1952 and I was probably six. It was the height of the Cold War and we lived near New York City; nuclear war was a palpable threat. I remember my family planning what we would do in the event of nuclear attack: We had friends with a farm in Canada, and my parents said that if we were separated from each other we should all try to reassemble there.

At school in the early 1950s we had air raid drills. Sirens would sound and we would "duck and cover" under our desks. There were plenty of jokes among the kids about our instructions: "In the event of nuclear attack bend over, put your head between your legs, and kiss your ass goodbye."

Such a blasé attitude concealed the fact that my friends and I, like many of our contemporaries, took it for granted that we were likely to die in a nuclear war.[1] I certainly never expected to live beyond twenty or at most thirty if nuclear overkill continued to grow unabated.

In the mid-1950s,[2] *Saturday Review* editor Norman Cousins and others brought a group of victims of Hiroshima to the United States for plastic surgery. They were dubbed the Hiroshima Maidens. Two of them lived with my family one summer. Aka and Toyo's faces and hands were hideously scarred from burns—no, more than scarred; it was as if the flesh had melted and then recongealed. It was difficult for a child to look at or accept, and Aka and Toyo were very shy, but we found the magic to transcend it all—Ping-Pong—and we became pals. The horror of nuclear war was not an abstraction for me, but something I had seen burned into human flesh.

I loved Picasso's painting *Guernica,* but I had no idea what it was about. When I asked my father, he explained that Guernica was a Spanish city that had been bombed by German airplanes during the Spanish Civil War, in the time leading up to World War II, and that the German military had used it as an opportunity to test their air force and bombing techniques.[3] He explained how utterly horrified and outraged people around the world had been at the idea of bombing civilian populations from the air. Then he added that by 1944 the United States was doing the same thing on a massive scale over Dresden and other German cities.[4] It was but a step from that to dropping atom bombs on Hiroshima and Nagasaki.

For me and my contemporaries, the threat of nuclear war was not something imaginary or distant. It was something you heard about on newscasts regarding Washington and Moscow and Bikini, but it was also as close as the family pantry and your desk at school. No doubt my own reaction to it was much influenced by my parents' attitudes, but it was also a response to what I experienced. The threat of nuclear war was part of my reality. It led me to be aware of myself as someone directly affected by what went on in the larger world beyond my own home and community.

Nobody wanted a nuclear war. Yet the forces leading to it seemed inexorable. A few protested, but the Cold War nuclear arms race felt like a self-perpetuating process that was leading to human self-destruction without human intent. Each "side" armed itself out of fear of the other, but each arms buildup only increased the other side's fear and made it act in ways that provoked still more fear. This out-of-control process produced fear but above all, despair. Although human beings set the policies and made the weapons, it was as if they were acting only as the puppets of inhuman forces that no one could control.

3
THIS WAY FOR THE GAS

&.

ONE OF MY EARLIEST MEMORIES IS HEARING MY MOTHER TELL ME THE STORY OF TWO relatives of my father who agreed to kill each other rather than be taken to a concentration camp by the Nazis. The two elderly sisters shot each other as the Nazis were coming to their town to round up the Jews.[1]

My parents were close to my father's cousin Dr. George Brecher and his family, who had only managed to escape from Czechoslovakia as the Nazis marched in. They had fled to London. I was told that during the Blitz their daughter, my cousin, had reacted to the shock of the bombing by regressing to the point where she would only lie curled up in a fetal position.

I also heard about anti-Semitic bigotry closer to home. My father had been an honors student at Swarthmore and went to graduate school at Brown University. After a year or so of study, his senior professor asked him what his plans were. My father replied that he intended to get a PhD and become a professor of philosophy. His professor replied that he could pursue that course if he wished, but there was something he should know first. He then named the only three Jews in the entire United States who had appointments as professors of philosophy. My father dropped out of school that spring, never to return.

When my mother's first husband died in a car crash, she decided to marry my father, who had been her lover in college. Her decision to marry a Jew caused an uproar. Her deceased husband's family hired a lawyer and threatened to challenge her custody of her two children if she went through with the marriage. When she visited the distinguished professor who had been her mentor at Harvard, he advised her not to marry a Jew.

The extermination of six million Jews shaped my consciousness from an early age. I felt personally connected to tragedy and horror. I can still see the piles of bones in the *Life* magazine photos from the concentration camps. And I have never been able to see the world as stable and secure. The notorious horrors of the twentieth century shaped my expectations of what was normal. Millions of

Americans appeared to go into shock over the assassination of John F. Kennedy and a generation later over the attacks on the World Trade Center, but to me these tragedies seemed like part of the normal way of the world.

The Nazis' killing of six million Jews represented the deliberate enactment of evil on an awe-inspiring scale. But it also represented the acquiescence of a seemingly indifferent nation and people to that evil. You could imagine the ease with which apparently mild bigotry like that my parents had been subjected to in the United States could provide an atmosphere that might indulge the greatest of crimes. I sensed that without some kind of conscience or moral compass, apparently innocent people could become complicit in unimaginable crimes.

4

McCARTHYISM

ಎ

IT MUST HAVE BEEN THE EARLY 1950S. I WAS PERHAPS SIX OR EIGHT AND WAS WITH MY mother, who was doing chores in the attic. This particular chore was covering a bright red album of 78 rpm records with a thick adhesive material called contact paper. The album was called *Songs of the Red Army*. I asked her why she was doing it. She told me that at one time the Russians, who had the Red Army, were fighting side by side with the Americans and were regarded as their friends. But right now things were different, and if people saw *Songs of the Red Army* when they came to our house they might get the wrong impression.

When I was a bit older, she told me that after her first husband—a rather conventional Harvard political science professor—died and she remarried, she had their old collection of academic books shipped to her new home near Washington, D.C. When she started to put Karl Marx' *Capital* on the shelf, her new husband, who worked for the Federal Communications Commission, had looked at her in alarm. "You can't put that out there!" "Why not?" "What if an FBI man walked in and saw it?" My mother told me that she had thought at the time, "Oh, my God, I've married a raving paranoid." But the next week, sure enough, an FBI man showed up at the door for a surprise visit.

My parents were never Communists, but they moved in a left-wing milieu where some of their friends and associates were, and where many more were likely targets for charges of "disloyalty" in an era when dissent was often equated with treason. My father regarded it as a principle and a point of pride that he would not cut acquaintances when they came under attack or became dangerous to associate with. My mother believed that we children should be exposed to people who did not share mainstream opinions. I grew up knowing many people who had been victims of the red scare. Clifford Durr, a white Alabama lawyer who had been my father's mentor at the FCC and later known as a hero of the civil rights movement, was red-baited out of one job after another. Ann and Maynard Gertler evacuated the United States to Maynard's native Canada.

The great Central Asian scholar Owen Lattimore coached me in my desperate attempt to pass high school French while describing how he had been taken in and cherished by scholars at the Sorbonne after being hounded out of government and academic positions in the United States. I'd rarely seen my father angrier than when a neighbor refused to shake hands with a visiting Alger Hiss after his release from prison.

I remember everyone gathered around the television—not only in our home but in many others—watching the Army-McCarthy hearings. In the midst of the to-me-incomprehensible proceedings, I remember my mother watching someone refuse to testify against acquaintances and saying, "That's a very brave man." I remember my parents coming home from a community forum arguing with neighbors about whether it was a violation of the right to freedom of association for someone to be compelled by a congressional committee to testify against associates.

We lived very much in an atmosphere of fear. After leaving Washington, my father had gone to work at the United Nations. A congressional committee headed by Senator William Jenner had started investigating "Communist infiltration" of the UN staff, and several associates of my father had been fingered in some way. I was never told the whole story, but I know my parents were waiting for the next shoe to drop. (I learned long after that the parents of my life partner, Jill Cutler, had been under the shadow of the same congressional investigation.) When, for a joke, my brother John listed *The Daily Worker* (which we had never seen) on a school questionnaire as the newspaper that his family read, my parents' conflicting feelings of fear and a desire not to overreact were apparent to me, even though I didn't have a clue what it was all about. Even in high school, I concealed copies of the *Nation* magazine under another publication when I read them in school.

Anti-Communism was part of an amalgam that also included nationalism, patriotism, militarism, religion, and paranoia. The pressures for political and cultural conformity were palpable. Every day in school we recited the Pledge of Allegiance. In school and Boy Scouts we sang patriotic songs with titles like "I Like It Here." (The implied message: If you don't like it here, go back to Russia.) My Scoutmaster explained that they didn't have Boy Scouts in Russia because they didn't believe in God.

Growing up under McCarthyism taught me something of what it is like to be part of a despised and persecuted group. I was aware of society because we were under attack by society. While our lives were never in danger, my parents could easily have lost their livelihood and, had my father been called by the Jenner Committee and refused to testify, he might well have been sent to jail. Political repression and tyranny were not distant evils, but ones that I experienced directly.

Fear was not the only thing I experienced under McCarthyism. I also learned something about what it means to resist pressures for conformity and to remain loyal to one's values, commitments, and associates in the face of public opprobrium. I took pride in being part of a denigrated group and in asserting my identity as part of it.

5

RACE RELATIONS

ò▲

IN THE PLEASANT SUBURB OF LEONIA, NEW JERSEY, JUST ACROSS THE GEORGE Washington Bridge from New York City, Grand Avenue marked the boundary of my childhood neighborhood. Somewhere beyond it lay the great swamps of the Hackensack River—politely referred to as the "salt meadows." One day when I was perhaps eight or nine I decided I was old enough to cross Grand Avenue and see what was on the other side. What I discovered was a neighborhood of run-down housing, barely more than shacks, inhabited by black people. I was frightened, and I raced home and said to my parents, "I didn't know Leonia had slums!"

We moved away soon after that and I never learned anything more about Leonia's slums. But meanwhile I was learning something about "race relations" in another part of New Jersey. My mother's Friends Meeting in the prosperous town of Ridgewood became involved in a small community development project with a group of people known to themselves as "the Mountain People" and to their Mahwah neighbors, derisively, as the "Jackson's Whites."[1]

I remember driving through beautiful woods along a narrow, winding road up into the Ramapo Mountains, past homes surrounded by broken-down cars and small garden patches, until we came to the community center that was being built by an American Friends Service Committee volunteer work camp. I was thrilled because I was just starting to play guitar and some of the Mountain People were real guitarists.

The Mountain People, with mixed colors and physical features, were what historians would call a maroon community. Their ancestors were known to have included waves of Native Americans and African Americans who had withdrawn into the Ramapo Mountains over the centuries. But the local term Jackson's Whites was about as derogatory an attribution of ancestry as one could imagine. According to the local legend, when Hessian mercenaries were encamped on the New York side of the Hudson River during the American Revolution, a sea captain named Jackson contracted to bring a shipload of prostitutes to service

23

them. To do it on the cheap he obtained a shipload of black women from the West Indies. When he arrived with them in New York they were derisively dubbed Jackson's Whites.

The women were placed in a stockade. That winter was so cold the Hudson River froze over. The women escaped the stockade, fled across the ice, and hid in the Ramapos. So the ancestors of the Mountain People were allegedly the runaway prostitutes of mercenaries.

Whatever the mix of fact and slander in this story, the Mountain People were subject to intensive prejudice and discrimination. Only the most menial jobs were open to them. New Jersey supposedly did not allow racial segregation in education, so the children of the Mountain People went to the regular local public schools, but they were "tracked" into separate classes within the purportedly integrated schools.

I lost touch with the Mountain People after we left New Jersey, but the *New York Times* reported a few years ago that they had organized themselves as an Indian tribe and appealed for federal recognition. Challenged on why they were only now claiming to be Indians, one of the elders replied that they had always known that they were Indians, but hid their identity; had they been regarded as Indians, the discrimination and opprobrium they faced would have been even greater.

*   *   *

As news of the civil rights struggles in the South splashed across northern newspapers, an Episcopal bishop asked his parishioners in Connecticut to meet with their neighbors to discuss their role in race relations. In the small towns of northwestern Connecticut, where my family had moved, a committee of respectables was duly formed and its first public meeting announced in the local newspaper.

My parents went to the meeting and came home disturbed. The hope had been that it would be an interracial affair, but only one person came from the Northwest Corner's tiny black (then Negro) communities. While the participants had expected to discuss the terrible things happening in the South, the lone African American attending asked them what they were going to do about discrimination in the Northwest Corner. They were flabbergasted that anyone could even suggest that such a thing existed. He proceeded to lay out the particulars. The one barber in one of the few towns that had a barbershop refused to cut "Negro hair"; local Negroes had to go all the way to the city of Torrington for a haircut. The local bank discriminated racially in its conditions for mortgages. And, while Negroes could play golf at the local country club, they were banned from getting a drink at the country club bar.

The editor of the local newspaper, my parents told me, had said, "I simply don't believe it." Not knowing what else to do, the "interracial committee" agreed to investigate the charges. To their shock they discovered that the local barber did indeed refuse to cut Negro hair; the country club bar did refuse to serve Negroes; and the local bank was at best unhelpful to Negroes seeking a mortgage.

To its credit, the group, which adopted the name Concern, did more than just investigate. Delegations visited the barber, country club, and bank, and all three situations were corrected. Word spread, and soon people from the local black communities not only joined Concern, but took over much of its formal and informal leadership.

These experiences revealed how invisible discrimination and prejudice can be to those who are not subjected to them. They taught me that, whether or not I was aware of it, I could be part of a group that oppressed and discriminated against others.

6

QUIET DESPERATION

ža

WHEN I WAS LITTLE MY FATHER HATED HIS JOB. I REMEMBER HIM COMING HOME FULL of frustration and anger every night. He had migraine headaches that lasted for days; none of us doubted that they were associated with his work. I was too young to understand what the problem was, but I do remember being told, "Edward doesn't like having to work for a boss." He moved to a new job, where he and my mother worked together, but the problem continued.

My parents had always done freelance writing on the side, and finally in the early 1950s, they quit their jobs and became fulltime freelancers. My mother quipped, "We'd rather worry than commute."

Worry they did. They sold about one article a month, and paying the month's bills depended on selling the month's article. My parents actually became reasonably successful, but their financial insecurity remained. The year my father tried to quit smoking their income fell by half. Financial anxieties drove family tensions. My brother Earl, a fine writer, recently wrote a short story based on our family in which the tensions passed over into violence. In reality they didn't, but the edge his story evoked was definitely there.

My parents wrote as a team for the major popular magazines of the era, publications like the *Saturday Evening Post, Collier's, Redbook,* and the *Reader's Digest*. (When asked how they could bear to write for the often loopily reactionary *Digest,* my mother replied, "Think what we keep out!") Every article had to be carefully tailored to the wishes and whims of the editors, with just the right mix of human interest, authoritative information, alarm, and reassurance. Nothing too threatening or controversial, please!

Uncharitably, I saw their work as driven by the commercial forces of the market. It seemed to me that they were pressured to write what their editors wanted, rather than being able to express their own convictions, which I knew were far more radical. (In retrospect my judgment is less harsh: In the context of McCarthyite reaction they managed to infiltrate articles into the mass media

26

on subjects normally excluded—air and water pollution, consumer protection, and even the dangers of nuclear fallout.)

Worse still, I saw the same fate looming for myself. I knew that their situation gave them far more freedom than most people who had to work for a living. I envisioned the basic problem for my future as how to avoid a life of unfreedom—chained to the drudgery of a normal work life. And I saw this as a problem that was shared—even if only dimly recognized—by almost everyone who had to work for a living. I resonated with Thoreau's line, "Most men live lives of quiet desperation."

Similar themes were appearing in the popular social criticism of the day. I found my own thinking congenially expressed in Paul Goodman's *Growing Up Absurd* and Jules Henry's *Culture Against Man,* which portrayed in different ways the conflict between young people's aspirations for personally meaningful, creative, and socially useful work and the constraints imposed on them by a commercially driven economy and culture.

In a book by the psychoanalyst Erich Fromm I came upon the idea of "alienated labor" that he had taken from Karl Marx's early *Economic and Philosophic Manuscripts.*[1] Fromm said that under capitalist production relations, workers were alienated from their own activity because it was not controlled by them but by their bosses. They were alienated from the production process because it was conducted for somebody else's purpose not their own. And they were alienated from each other because their relations were based on the domination of the boss, competition with other workers, and lack of a direct relationship with the consumers who used the products of their labor. The idea of alienated labor made intuitive sense to me as a description of the world I saw around me.

I saw myself connected to this problem both through the experience of my family and through my own likely future. I did not at that time think of the problem in terms of class because it seemed to affect people whose social class positions were very diverse. It appeared to result from an almost inescapable institutional structure that was stonily indifferent to the needs of individuals for self-expression.

7
THE WEB OF LIFE

ᚹ

AT THE AGE OF THREE I FELL IN LOVE WITH THE WOODS. NOT JUST ANY WOODS, but those I visited in a place called Yelping Hill in northwestern Connecticut. That winter when I was sick in the hospital I played that I was in a tree house in Yelping Hill. We started spending summers in Yelping Hill, and when I was seven my parents built me a tree house in a great spreading oak and I thenceforth lived in a tree in the middle of the forest. (Yes, I did visit my family from time to time.)

I remember driving on the highway and hearing my parents mutter imprecations at diesel trucks that poured thick black exhaust into the air. (This was long before environmental laws required emission control devices on trucks and cars.) So far as I know the term environmentalism had not even been invented, but my parents wrote early articles for popular magazines like *Redbook* on air pollution and other issues that would soon be defined as environmental.

Rachel Carson's book *Silent Spring* caused a local sensation when it appeared serially in *The New Yorker*. Towns in our region frequently sprayed DDT from airplanes to fight gypsy moths. Everyone hated the gypsy moths, which defoliated whole forests (including my tree-house tree), but we were also a community of bird lovers who were horrified at the idea that DDT was wiping out the songbirds. Neighborhoods and towns battled over the question: to spray or not to spray?

My father, a science writer and a firm believer in reason and science, considered *Silent Spring* unbalanced. "It reads like a lawyer's brief," he complained.

But *Silent Spring* really used the impact of DDT on songbirds as a metaphor for something more profound. It is hard to realize it now, but at that time ecology was a novelty. The idea expressed in the title of an introductory book on ecology I was given by my mother, *The Web of Life*, conflicted with the common sense of the time that organisms and species were separate entities related to each other only as predators and prey. If mosquitoes treated us as prey, it was only reasonable

28

for us to fight back with DDT. (A neighbor who was by no means a shill for the pesticide corporations, and with whom I went to jail to protest US-backed attacks on Nicaragua thirty years later, wrote a humorous book defending pesticide use called *Bugs or People?*) The idea that such action had to be seen within a set of complex and often hidden interconnections was radical.

That idea was radical in another way too. There was an oft-forgotten tie between the nascent environmental movement and the movement against nuclear weapons.

In 1959, just about the time I was too old to have any baby teeth left, a group called the St. Louis Committee for Nuclear Information put out a call for people all over the United States to send in their babies' teeth (after they had fallen out, presumably) for radiation testing. Their theory was that radioactive isotopes of strontium-90 released by nuclear weapons testing could enter the milk supply and be deposited in children's teeth and bones. Their fears proved all too true: Levels of strontium-90 in American babies' teeth had increased 50-fold in the era of nuclear testing.[1] Soon a newspaper advertisement showing the famous baby doctor Benjamin Spock with a bottle of milk marked with a big X for poison kicked off the mass movement to ban nuclear testing.

I was exposed early to the relationship between environmental protection and economics. Much of our town of Cornwall was covered by zoning that required three to five acres for a building lot. The ostensible purpose was to preserve the rural character of the environment, but the effect, not surprisingly, was to make the price of a building lot unaffordable for all but the well-to-do. It was particularly a source of resentment among those who had grown up in the town and wanted to live there but found building a home financially out of reach. My father was active on town boards at the time and tried to introduce some avant-garde ideas of cluster zoning, but to no avail.

In my youth, environmentalism had an intensely local focus. But in my teens I discovered the work of the "social ecologist" Murray Bookchin, who maintained that industrial society might be disrupting the water cycle, the carbon-oxygen cycle, and the other great natural cycles on which life on earth depends. The result might be a devastating warming of the earth. This was generally regarded as absurd—in fact, it was not even seriously discussed outside of fringe circles. But I took even the possibility as a sign that we had to radically change the way we conducted our life on earth. Today we know that the fossil fuels that drive industrial society are producing global warming and catastrophic climate change.

Ecology's focus on interaction of parts within a whole became an underlying constituent of the way I think. So did the idea of unintended side effects and interaction effects (what economists sometimes call "externalities.") I would discover such an "ecological perspective" expressed in many different forms, ranging from the traditional Chinese idea of the unity of nature embodied in the Tao, to systems theory, to the dialectic. It provided me with a general frame for the many more particular forms of relatedness I was discovering between myself and the wider world.

8

THE START OF A QUEST

ॐ

EXPERIENCES LIKE THOSE RECOUNTED IN PART 1 ARE COMMON. MOST YOUNG PEOPLE discover aspects of their lives that connect them with social problems of one kind or another. Most are part of families and social groups whose historical experience provides them with initial frames for interpreting their relationship to those problems.

We are all born into and enmeshed with history. But becoming aware of those connections is a process. It is part of the exploration of one's world that we all engage in from birth. Learning about the world's problems is part of learning about the world. Like any learning, it can be interfered with and repressed by concealment and social taboo. Or, as in my case, it can be encouraged.

The social problems of which I became aware as a child were diverse. I certainly had no sense of an underlying social or political or economic structure that they might all reflect. At most I perceived them as all revealing that something was wrong with society.

The diversity of these problems reveals the complexity and multiplicity of identity. My developing awareness of each problem reflected a different aspect of who I was. The threat of nuclear annihilation was a shared experience of my generation. My personal relation to the Holocaust and to anti-Semitism resulted from the fact that part of my family was Jewish. My experience of McCarthyism as a personal threat was due to my parents' political views and associations. My experience of race was determined by the fact that under the US caste system I was inescapably defined as a white person. My father's misery at work and my fear of a life of alienated labor resulted from the broad structure of modern economies. My awareness of threats to the environment reflected both my own identification with nature and a growing global consciousness of the environment's importance and vulnerability.

While my concern with all of these problems was rooted in concrete life experiences and conditions, my relation to each of them was different. Nuclear

31

war posed both a threat to my personal existence and a global threat to human life and all that seemed to make it worthwhile. The Holocaust was already history when I was born; its significance for me lay in the potentials for social evil it revealed. McCarthyism represented a direct threat to my family's well-being, but also an atmosphere of fear that encompassed our daily lives. Regarding racial discrimination, by contrast, we were not its object but rather part of the group that was perpetrating it. The miseries and insecurities of the work world were part of my family's daily experience, but caused by an institutional structure that was difficult to escape. The natural environment was something I lived in and cherished; the threats to it were present everywhere, but it often required an environmental perspective and knowledge to perceive them.

I had little clear sense of how these problems were caused. Were they the result of bad people doing bad things? Or were they the result of out-of-control forces that led to bad results that nobody wanted? I had no tools for sorting out the answers.

Although these were social problems, for the most part I experienced them as an individual, not as part of a group that was dealing with them collectively. For a long time after I became aware of these problems I had no idea of acting on them. Indeed, along with social problems I discovered my powerlessness as an individual to do anything about them. The result was often a painful sense of despair. The only choices seemed to be acquiescence in the conditions that prevailed or individual existential revolt. I certainly inclined toward existential revolt, but I also found it inadequate. My despair led me in quest of solutions based on common preservation.

DISCOVERING SOCIAL MOVEMENTS

9

DISCOVERING SOCIAL MOVEMENTS

۞

THE CONDITIONS OF LIFE OFTEN MAKE PEOPLE FEEL POWERLESS. CERTAINLY I FELT powerless in the face of my father's headaches and the threat of nuclear war and the prospect of a lifetime of drudgery.

When many people confront the same problem new possibilities open up. What is impossible for one may be possible for many acting in concert.

Part 2 tells how I became aware of social movements as a means through which people can respond jointly to problems they cannot solve as individuals. I witnessed people, by virtue of their participation in social movements, identify problems, construct new solutions, cross social barriers, form new groups, co-ordinate their activity with other people in new ways, and change the world and their relationship to it. I witnessed the emergence of what I would later come to call common preservation.

I had become an "activist" even before I entered high school in 1959. It was still the Cold War era. The Socialists, the Communists, and the other shattered remnants of the old left appeared doctrinaire, sectarian, and minuscule. The labor movement seemed to be stagnant and largely integrated into corporate America. The embryonic peace and civil rights movements were still small, weak, and isolated. A national peace demonstration was considered a great success if it drew five hundred people.

I continued to be an activist as a student at Reed College in Portland, Oregon, and then as a student at the Institute for Policy Studies (IPS), a think tank that was variously described as the Washington, D.C., outpost of the radical move-ment or as the vanguard of the status quo. I participated one way or another in the cascade of social movements that people now refer to as "the sixties," which didn't really take off until the mid-1960s and only subsided in the mid-1970s.

Growing out of my personal awareness of the threat of nuclear war and my family's social concerns, I made contact with and became active in the peace movement that was just emerging to challenge the nuclear arms race. I became part of the vast hinterland of support that the civil rights movement drew on for its nation-transforming confrontations. I was a devoted activist in the "New Left" Students for a Democratic Society. I witnessed and tried to support the Women's Liberation Movement that grew in the womb of the New Left before becoming a global movement that far transcended those origins. Between 1965 and 1975 I was absorbed by the effort to end the war in Vietnam.

I came to feel that being active, even being an activist, was an essential part of being fully human. I came to see it as natural for people to be active constructors and reconstructors of their world. This view was reinforced by an early reading of the psychoanalyst Ernest Schachtel, who gently but firmly criticized Sigmund Freud for missing the inherently active character of humans from birth and instead seeing humans as simply trying to return to a state of inactivity.[1]

I gradually came to view the propensity to action as more than a capacity of human individuals per se. Rather, the move from passivity to action went hand in hand with the move from individual isolation to social interaction coordinated for common purposes. I was already struggling to understand what I later came to call common preservation. But my initial understanding of common preservation was shaped not by any general ideas about social movements, but by the particular movements in which I participated.

My experience in the movements of the 1960s gave me a sense of the tremendous potential power of concerted action. It also left me with a sense that such power could be abused or frittered away. I came out of the experience with a burning desire to understand where that power comes from and how it can best be used.

10

DOCTOR SPOCK IS WORRIED

ઽ

MY MOTHER'S BROTHER WAS A FLYER WHO DIED IN THE LAST DAYS OF WORLD WAR II. She had responded by becoming a pacifist, something she expressed by becoming a Quaker. Like Tom Paine, I got "a good education from the Quakers." When I asked her about her beliefs, my mother told me she believed in nonviolence as exemplified by Gandhi. I considered myself a pacifist from an early age. (When other schoolboys announced whether they were going to join the army, the air force, or the marines, I said I would join the presumably less militaristic coast guard.)

Our annual Christmas letter to friends and family one year included a poem (written by the jailed Turkish poet Nazim Hikmet and set by Pete Seeger to the haunting melody *The Great Silkie*) about a little girl who had died in Hiroshima. I still remember some of the lines:

> *I come and stand at every door*
> *but none can hear my silent tread;*
> *I knock and yet remain unseen*
> *for I am dead, for I am dead.*
> *I'm only seven, though I died*
> *In Hiroshima long ago.*
> *I'm seven now, as I was then*
> *When children die, they do not grow ...*
> *All that I ask is that for peace*
> *You fight today, you fight today*
> *So that the children of the world*
> *May laugh and dance and sing and play.*[1]

I didn't know then and I don't know today whether I consider them overwhelmingly moving or embarrassingly maudlin or both.

My father subscribed to the *New Statesman*, a British journal of opinion that was more or less comparable to the American journal of opinion *The Nation*, on the grounds that it was important to have a source of news and opinion from outside the United States. I insisted that he read and discuss it with me, and from it I learned about the annual Aldermaston marches in which at first a handful but eventually hundreds of thousands protested nuclear war. Then we read the appeal by Bertrand Russell (always a favorite of my father's anyway) for mass civil disobedience to halt the arms race. We read of the lively debates that followed, the sit-down Lord Russell led in Trafalgar Square, and the resulting mass arrests.

I, too, feared nuclear war and I was in a state of readiness to transform my concern into action. One day a peace march with a few dozen people headed for Washington, D.C., and perhaps inspired by the Aldermaston marches, stopped by at my mother's Friends Meeting in Ridgewood, New Jersey. One cold weekend later that winter, largely at my instigation, my parents and I drove down to the little town of Frederick, Maryland, and joined a protest at Fort Detrick, the home of the US germ warfare program.[2] It was the big national peace demonstration for that year. I think that there were more than four hundred participants.

By the age of eleven I was writing my own anti-nuclear leaflets and printing them on an antique device called a hectograph. They provided information on nuclear overkill and the dangers of radiation. One I remember was headed, "Is This How You'll Die?" I passed them out at school without visible response.

Groton, Connecticut, in the opposite corner of the state from us, was where America's nuclear submarines were built. Militant pacifists, led by the aged and legendary radical minister A. J. Muste, tried to block the launchings with a flotilla of small boats. In New York a coalition of radical pacifists and bohemians, exemplified by the Catholic Workers and Judith Malina of the Living Theater, organized concerted refusals to take cover during official civil defense drills. I thought of joining one of these, but in reality I never even had the courage to refuse to participate in the air raid drills in my own school.

The advocates of peace were subject to unofficial and official harassment and repression. The farm near Groton where Reverend Muste and the submarine-jumpers organized their activities was attacked by the Minutemen, an armed, right-wing vigilante group—what today we might call paramilitaries. On a visit to Washington, D.C., my father took me to observe a congressional hearing in which the world-famous chemist Linus Pauling was threatened with a contempt citation for refusing to disclose the names of young colleagues who had helped circulate peace petitions.

When John F. Kennedy was inaugurated president in 1961, he announced a massive program to build fallout shelters across America. My parents went to a meeting to organize a community forum about it for the little rural towns of northwestern Connecticut. They came home and reported that the psychiatrist for the local child guidance clinic (an admirer of Harry Truman whom I visited in his professional role at a time of family stress and with whom I spent most of the sessions arguing politics) had started the meeting by saying, "Now let's not have a debate about whether or not to build fallout shelters; what we need is to instruct people in how to build them."

After some dialogue, it was nonetheless decided that different viewpoints should indeed be heard. Adam Yarmolinsky, a well-known liberal and Kennedy's point-person for the fallout shelter program, agreed to represent the administration, no doubt seeing it as a great chance to promote his wares. Stewart Meacham, peace education secretary of the American Friends Service Committee, spoke on behalf of peace. Tom Stonier, a professor of physics who had recently issued a study of the effect of a nuclear bomb on New York City, was to present the viewpoint of a scientist.

At the last minute, one of the networks asked to broadcast the forum over nationwide radio, so our little local forum acquired a large national audience. The event turned into a debate between Yarmolinsky and Stonier, who demolished the idea that fallout shelters and other civil defense measures could provide meaningful protection in the event of nuclear attack, even in our rural area a hundred miles from New York City.[3]

The forum had a big impact on local opinion and seemed to have helped discredit the civil defense campaign nationally. Within a few months the Kennedy administration grew reticent about bomb shelters, and our wealthy neighbors who had actually built them began surreptitiously and somewhat shamefacedly converting them into root cellars and swimming pools.

I learned from the experience that sometimes a real public discussion can actually sway public opinion and affect public policy, and that objective, scientific information can sometimes contribute to that effect. (The psychiatrist later told a friend of mine that the political discussions we had in my therapy sessions had contributed to making him less of a warmonger—revealing another though perhaps less efficient way to influence opinion.)

One of the first breaks in the "Cold War consensus" of the 1950s came with the election in 1958 of a half-dozen "peace congressmen." (I knew about them from *I.F. Stone's Weekly,* an independent newsletter that I also insisted my father read with me.) One of them was Colonel Frank Kowalski, a career army officer who had used his credibility as a military man to get away with some peace shenanigans for which any other politician would have been brutally red-baited. My father acceded to my request to take me to hear Colonel Kowalski speak at a nearby city; I was put in touch with his youth coordinator, and soon I was organizing Youth for Kowalski in my high school.

I was a miserable failure as a political organizer. (It didn't help that the instructions from the campaign were appropriate for a personally ambitious budding young politician rather than a premature social activist.) But a bit later a "peace movement political operative" came into the state to organize support for Kowalski. I became his gofer and got my first taste of electoral politics. At the following election Kowalski challenged the rule of Connecticut Democratic boss John Bailey (soon to become chairman of the Democratic National Committee for John F. Kennedy) and was instantly replaced by Bailey's new choice, a dentist named Grabowski whose only announced qualification was his ability to speak Polish. The experience taught me to have a healthy skepticism about how political parties are controlled.

The issue that turned the long-marginalized peace movement into a mass movement was nuclear testing. After studies found radioactive isotopes of strontium-90 in American children's baby teeth, a newly formed National Committee for a Sane Nuclear Policy (soon known simply as SANE) ran full-page newspaper ads headlined, "Dr. Spock Is Worried." A large picture showed the famous pediatrician Dr. Benjamin Spock, whose books were the childrearing bible for tens of millions of Americans, with a bottle of milk labeled X for poison. The ad explained that fallout from nuclear tests was landing on the crops eaten by cows and entering their milk. Children would experience birth defects, radiation poisoning, and cancer from the contaminated milk. The seemingly abstract, remote threat of nuclear war suddenly became a very concrete and immediate threat to the health of Americans' children. Our own government and its nuclear program became the perpetrator of that threat rather than simply our protector against enemy attack.

Thousands responded to SANE's ads, and soon tens of thousands were participating in rallies, marches, and local committees. By 1963 a nuclear test ban treaty became national policy, and a moratorium on nuclear testing, which had been widely excoriated as "unilateral disarmament," was in place.

I was one of those who sent back the coupon attached to the SANE ads; I became a member, wrote letters, went to meetings, and participated in marches. The sudden emergence of the peace movement from the margins to the mainstream was startling. It resulted not from the concerns that had long preoccupied movement activists, but from one that was a side issue for most of them. It was a concern that millions of people, responding to the immediate self-interest of protecting their families from nuclear fallout, found compelling.

Awareness of the dangers of fallout from nuclear testing alerted many people to the broader dangers of nuclear war. Many came to see a halt to nuclear testing and a test ban treaty as just the first steps toward more general disarmament. They moved from a small, concrete concern to a wider shift in worldview. And they learned to question what was said by those in authority.

The peace movement redefined the framework of national and global discourse. As both the United States and the Soviet Union pledged to pursue general and complete disarmament, it almost appeared for a time as if Eisenhower's prophecy—that "people want peace so much" that "one of these days government had better get out of their way and let them have it"—might be coming true. Whatever their real objectives, governments responded to international public opinion by trying to portray themselves as seeking disarmament and peace. (They also tried to manipulate that opinion to their own advantage.) The peace movement had become a power in its own right, able to challenge and affect even the nuclear superpowers.[4]

There was little centralized leadership or organization in which this power was concentrated. The peace movement included a variety of organizations ranging from traditional peace groups and left sects to mass mobilizing campaign organizations like SANE that were little more than coalitions with a list of endorsers and an office that could issue an advertisement or set the date for a rally. Membership and organizational forms were highly fluid. When a few years later a large sector of SANE's New York supporters found the organization reluctant to march against the Vietnam War, they simply organized to do so through an improvised coalition called the Fifth Avenue Peace Parade Committee. The impact on the movement was barely noticeable—the same people kept doing the same things under a different organizational name. People wanted to act, and they treated organizations primarily as vehicles to facilitate their doing so.

The peace movement also illustrates how a movement's fluidity can render it evanescent. As the United States plunged into large-scale war in Indochina, the peace movement's attention—as well as the country's—shifted from nuclear war to Vietnam. US détente with the Soviet Union made the issues of the Cold War seem less pressing. The anti-nuclear movement waned. Then in the mid-1980s Ronald Reagan's nuclear buildup, particularly the development of a nuclear first-strike capacity, generated renewed fears of nuclear war and a revived peace movement in the United States and even more in Europe. It too dissipated as Gorbachev's "new thinking" and then the crumbling of European Communism brought the Cold War as we knew it to an end. But the legacy of that peace movement provided many of the buried roots from which the largest global peace movement in history sprang in 2002 when fifteen million people worldwide demonstrated against the impending US attack on Iraq.

The most important thing I learned from the peace movement was a sense of how, by means of a movement, people transform themselves from isolated, powerless atoms into part of something larger that gives them the power to affect their conditions of life. I saw how self-activating people could become once they felt themselves part of a movement. Whatever the tactics, strategies, organizations, and objectives, movement formation itself might be the most important dimension of change. The experience launched me on a lifetime of participation in and study of social movements and their self-organization.

11

PEACE HOW?

ॐ

A SOCIOLOGIST MIGHT CLASSIFY MUCH OF MY ACTIVITY—AND THE PEACE MOVEMENT'S—as more "expressive" than "functional." Protests and propaganda were largely intended to express our fears, wishes, and hopes. We appealed to other people to share our aspirations, but we rarely had an adequate sense of what changes would realize those aspirations, let alone of a strategy for how our actions could bring those changes about.

For some in the peace movement, protest was really an act of faith. If we spoke out about what we believed and feared, others would somehow awaken from their slumbers, "get it," and—and what? For me protest gradually became insufficient. I wanted some idea of how we were going to bring peace about. I felt a need to underpin my activism with some kind of intellectual understanding.

Even how to define the problem the peace movement was addressing was not self-evident. The peace movement—and I along with it—struggled to orient itself within a multi-layered historical context of which many of us were only vaguely aware.

Nukes made war catastrophic, but did the problem go beyond nukes? No one knows for certain whether our earliest human ancestors engaged in war; but we do know that by the time of the Mesopotamian city-states, armies with specialized military technologies, hierarchical command structure, authoritarian discipline, and claims on social resources battled each other and imposed their rule on neighboring peoples. Imperial conflict between Russia and other countries in Europe dated not from the Cold War but from the Middle Ages. World war between a revolutionary movement–turned–militaristic dictatorship and anti-revolutionary powers seeking to stamp it out and restore their own dominion marked the Napoleonic era. Conflict between Communists and anti-Communists was rampant by the 1870s. Arms races leading to new and threatening military technologies were evident before the First World War. The struggle between Soviet Communism and its enemies went back, notwithstanding occasional truces and alliances-of-convenience, to the Bolshevik Revolution of 1917. What was the origin of the "war problem" and what would solve it?

I was reading. I got the radical pacifist *Liberation Magazine* and the independent but anti-anti-Communist *National Guardian*—no doubt gift subscriptions from friends of my parents who saw me as a likely prospect. I discovered and subscribed to the *Journal of Conflict Resolution,* which published peace research of a highly theoretical character, and I wrote away for early issues of the *New Reasoner* and the *New Left Review,* which reflected the ferment of the emerging British New Left.

For an eighth-grade school project I clipped (with help from the steady scissors of my mother) every newspaper story I could find that showed any positive steps toward peace and pasted them in a scrapbook. I went to the convention of the Student Peace Union. As training to be part of an American Friends Service Committee Student Peace Caravan, I spent a week at a big national peace convocation and summer camp in Cape May, New Jersey, where I got to hear and sit at the feet of David Dellinger and many other leading peace movement spokespeople of the day. The movement was my school.

It's difficult to evoke today how much the issues of the Cold War dominated the discourse of that era. (That difficulty indicates how much paradigms have shifted since the fall of Communism.) The conflict between the United States and the USSR, between NATO and the Warsaw Pact, between "Communism" and "democracy" provided the main interpretive frameworks for both the peace movement and its opponents. Within the peace movement there was debate on what the Cold War was really about. Was it really about ideology—Communism versus democracy, for example? Or was that just a pretext for geopolitical power politics?

Some peace movement activists saw the United States as basically democratic, peace-loving, and good, and they saw Communism as evil and the Soviet Union as aggressive and expansionist. But they argued that using aggressive militarism to oppose Communism was counterproductive. They presented a peace offensive as, in effect, a better strategy against Communism. They believed that their anti-Communism, in addition to being valid in its own right, would help legitimate peace advocacy within the political mainstream.

Others saw such militant anti-Communism as promoting hatred among adversaries, undermining mutual understanding, and impeding peaceful reconciliation. Notwithstanding accusations by red-baiting congressmen, as far as I could see very few peace activists actually supported Communism or the Soviet Union. But a substantial proportion saw the United States as highly aggressive and the Soviets as essentially defensive. For them the basic problem was to block US warmongering. They were criticized by anti-Communists for "reactive politics"—a tendency to make excuses for Communist behavior not from realistic evaluation but from negative reaction to supposed US aggressiveness.

"A plague on both your houses" was the sentiment of the "Third Camp" position. Its advocates, drawn largely from certain tendencies within the minuscule Socialist Party and the Young People's Socialist League (known as the "Yipsels"), argued for a critical stance toward both sides in the Cold War. For reasons I still don't understand, such an approach had only the narrowest support; perhaps that is testimony to the overwhelming polarizing effect of the Cold War itself.

But another way of thinking about the Cold War was catching on: the idea of conflict as a vicious circle. The threat to peace came not from the actions of one or the other party acting on its evil intentions, but rather from their interactions. The result was what we would today call a "cycle of fear" in which the defensive actions of each party provoke fear in the other, which in turn takes defensive actions that provoke still more fear in the other.

In the *Journal of Conflict Resolution* Kenneth Boulding, Anatol Rappaport, and other authors applied game theory and other sophisticated approaches to examine the dynamics of war and peace. There I learned about the Quaker mathematician Lewis F. Richardson and his book *Statistics of Deadly Quarrels*.[1] He constructed mathematical models for what came to be known as "Richardson processes," in which out-of-control interactions led to results that were not intended by any of the participants. Arms races provided a classic example, in which a very simple rule such as "just stockpile one more weapon than your opponent" led to ruinous military escalation.

This approach required a radical shift in paradigm, from analyzing the contestants in isolation to seeing them as part of a larger pattern or system of interaction. The behavior of each could only be understood as part of that interaction. This shift was somewhat akin to that made by the science of ecology, which tried to understand the interactions and interdependencies among organisms and species, rather than studying them in isolation.

This shift to what I would later learn to call a "systems perspective" made it possible to go beyond simply trying to identify who are the good guys and who are the bad guys. The real question couldn't be reduced to who initiated the Cold War or who could or couldn't be trusted. It was necessary to see how the parties involved in the conflict interacted to produce and reproduce that conflict.

From such thinking developed a strategy that came to be known as "unilateral initiatives for peace." The idea was that, regardless of who was responsible for past conflict, one party could take steps to break out of the cycle. Such initiatives did not—as critics charged—imply "unilateral disarmament." They were more like the "confidence-building measures" that have become a staple of today's diplomacy.[2] Their aim was to replace the arms race with a "peace race" in which the direction of interaction would be reversed.

At the start of the Kennedy administration peace organizations took out full-page newspaper ads calling for such unilateral initiatives for peace, in particular a unilateral halt to nuclear testing, which was seen as a prime factor escalating the arms race. Students in Boston organized a peace group called Tocsin which, along with the Student Peace Union and others, called a national student peace demonstration in Washington, D.C., to promote such unilateral initiatives.

The Kennedy administration sent out hot coffee to the student demonstrators in front of the White House, but this was, in fact, not a gesture that reflected the administration's real plans. On coming into office the administration initiated a historic 50 percent increase in military spending and launched a campaign to build fallout shelters—perhaps the measure best calculated to induce the fear that the United States was preparing to engage in nuclear war for real. But in less than three years Kennedy changed direction, declaring a unilateral halt to nuclear testing—rapidly reciprocated by Khrushchev—and starting negotiations for a test ban treaty. This was the starting point for what in the 1970s became Soviet-American détente.

British historian and activist E. P. Thompson, whom I was reading in the *New Left Review,* argued for another kind of unilateral initiative, which won support among the more radical wing of Britain's Campaign for Nuclear Disarmament. His proposal was that Britain should renounce nuclear weapons, withdraw from NATO, and become neutral in the Cold War. This initiative would encourage Eastern Europeans to detach themselves from the Warsaw Pact. The result would be another kind of "peace race," as other countries progressively disengaged from the deadly antagonistic embrace of the superpowers and formed their own neutralist peace bloc.[3]

While this dismantling of the blocs did not receive wide support at the time, Thompson reemerged in the mid-1980s as a leading spokesperson for the European Nuclear Disarmament (END) campaign that for the first time in generations organized a common movement in both Western and Eastern Europe. Since the Soviet Union and Eastern European Communist governments were eager to encourage a peace movement in Western Europe, END was able in effect to establish a protective mantle over Eastern European opposition groups. END helped create the context for the overthrow of Communism in Eastern Europe and for Gorbachev's New Thinking, which ultimately brought about the end of the Cold War. Unfortunately it turned out that ending the Cold War was not tantamount to getting rid of nuclear weapons, let alone getting rid of war.

12

SOCIAL ROOTS OF WAR

ટ..

THE COLD WAR AND THE DANGER OF NUCLEAR HOLOCAUST EXERCISED AN ALMOST hypnotic hold on the minds of peace activists and—when they weren't in denial—on Americans at large. But such a focus left the social roots of war out of the picture. I gradually began to wonder whether including them in the picture might clarify how the war system was perpetuated—and where the potential to change it might lie.

Despite their preoccupation with nuclear weapons and the Cold War, some peace activists recognized some social and economic barriers to peace. They noted, for example, that the culture of war pervaded television, comic books, movies, and virtually every other aspect of popular culture.[1]

Nearly all American boys and many girls had toy guns with which they played—what else?—war. Toy guns were a troublesome issue for Quaker families. My older brother was forbidden to have a toy gun; he wanted one so badly that on a school trip he stole one from a store, then lied that it had been given to him. Both the theft and the lie were so entirely out of character that my parents relented and bought him a toy gun. Their resistance was broken by the time I came along, and I killed and conquered with my Daisy rifle right along with the other neighborhood kids.

Notwithstanding its billboards proclaiming "Peace Is Our Profession," the military itself was also perceived as a source of militarism. When at the age of six I asked my parents why (in contrast to my schoolmates' parents) they were voting against Eisenhower for president, they replied, "We don't want to have a general in the White House." (They later came to believe that Eisenhower had done a better job of restraining the military than his civilian opponent Adlai Stevenson could have done.)

It wasn't just the brass who evoked concern, either. Military veterans formed a large proportion of the counter-demonstrators at peace demonstrations, and veterans organizations, such as the American Legion, provided the most reliable support for belligerent talk and expanded military budgets. (I didn't learn until much later that the American Legion had been set up at the close of World War I in part to rally veterans to oppose strikes and radicalism in the name of patriotic Americanism.)

The Causes of World War III[2] by radical sociologist C. Wright Mills identified political roots for what he characterized as a socially determined drift toward nuclear catastrophe. Mills portrayed American society as increasingly dominated by a "power elite" of top corporate, government, and military leaders, who were not accountable in meaningful ways to anyone except their own bureaucracies. Safe from public control, they were able to follow "balance of terror" policies that he dubbed "crackpot realism."

Mills proposed a political strategy to counter the resulting drift toward war. He called on intellectuals to promulgate programs, not only regarding war and peace, but on a wide range of issues, and to begin constructing publics around them. He saw this as a means to begin to hold elites accountable.

I recall little peace movement discussion of nationalism as a source of militarism or war. Mutual hatred was recognized as a force, but it was generally seen more as a function of "ideology"—Communism and anti-Communism—than of nationality.

There was also little emphasis placed on imperialism as a cause of war—a topic that would be widely discussed a few years later in the context of Vietnam. I rarely if ever heard reference to Lenin's *Imperialism* or Rosa Luxemburg's theoretical alternative. The struggle to dominate the Third World was generally seen as a function of the ideological and geopolitical conflict between the United States and the USSR, not as a desire to control the new post-colonial countries for economic gain.

But the peace movement did identify economic dimensions to American militarism. Most obviously, there was the sectoral economic interest of corporations—and of their workers and unions—who produced for the Pentagon. This included a high proportion of America's largest manufacturing companies and unions. Peace activists loved to quote Eisenhower's warning about the "military-industrial complex."

They also noted a "military Keynesianism" in which expanding military budgets were used to "prime the pump" when national economies faltered. (The preeminent British economist John Maynard Keynes himself had opined that building battleships and sinking them in the middle of the ocean would have the same effect on economic demand as public works projects.)

To relieve such economic dependence on military production, the peace movement urged planning for conversion to a peacetime economy. The first time I remember lobbying was when I hitched a ride to the Connecticut state capitol with our local legislator (a Republican farmer whose wife was a Christian peace activist) to support a bill for economic conversion planning.[3]

The idea that military Keynesianism was actually beneficial for the economy was challenged by maverick Columbia University engineering professor and peace advocate Seymour Melman in his book *Our Depleted Society*.[4] In Melman's view, military production might stimulate hothouse economic growth, but at the same time it was depleting the real resources needed for successful economic development. The diversion of resources to military production was like a ruinous tax on the rest of the economy. Europe and Japan understood this and devoted a far smaller proportion of their economies to the military. For that reason, they had far faster growth in real assets like factories and houses. Their high rate of investment led to higher productivity and a growing challenge to US domination of world markets. (This would prove to be one starting point of the historical process we now call globalization, and one reason the United States eventually became the greatest debtor in the history of the world.)

The idea that military spending might have bad economic effects posed the possibility of a broad social alliance to challenge excessive military spending. Social needs such as education, healthcare, urban infrastructure, and economic development in poor communities were prime victims of the diversion of resources to the military. Why not build a coalition between the peace movement and those adversely affected by military spending? This idea became embodied in proposals for a "Freedom Budget" that would reallocate government spending from the military to domestic needs.

While many social movements, particularly African American ones, were highly receptive to such an approach, it proved very difficult to promote in the national political arena. Even the handful of congressional representatives who were outspoken peace advocates were unwilling to vote for any cuts in military budgets except token ones, lest they be accused of rendering the country defenseless or "not supporting our troops."

My rudimentary exploration of the social roots of war started me looking beneath the obvious surface of events to seek the social structures of power that shape them—and that might be used to change them. It led me to think in terms of common interests and alliances among groups that might at first glance seem to have little in common, such as the peace movement and the civil rights and labor movements. And it began to orient me toward indirect strategies for change that might make use of the potential power of such alliances.

With the fall of the Soviet Union, the Cold War with which the peace movement had been preoccupied was no longer an issue. But the deeper structures of the war system, dating back to the ancient empires of Mesopotamia and now wielding weapons of mass destruction, continue to threaten the future of human life.

13
SOLIDARITY—EVER?

ॐ

I WAS MORE OR LESS BORN INTO THE LABOR MOVEMENT. MY PARENTS WERE UNION members at *Consumer Reports* magazine where they worked. We held family meetings that were referred to as "the grievance committee" and if someone wanted to raise an issue they would announce, "I have a grievance!"

There was a lot of conflict between labor and management at *Consumer Reports,* and finally my parents quit. When I asked why, they said there had been many issues, but the most important was the firing of a secretary who happened also to be the mother of my best friend. I asked why she had been fired. They told me the charges: She brought her own coffee to her desk in a thermos bottle rather than using the coffee provided by the company, and she sometimes wrote down her work hours on slips of paper rather than punching the time clock.

Many years later, after I started writing about labor history, I realized that I had been witness at an early age to an elemental act of labor solidarity. Still later I put two and two together and surmised that the firing of my friend's mother probably had something to do with her sexual orientation—an act of discrimination that only would have intensified my parents' outrage.

My parents had a 78 rpm album of union songs called *Talking Union* sung by the Almanac Singers, a Depression-era group that included Woody Guthrie and Pete Seeger. My mother told me that the Almanac Singers used to go out and sing on union picket lines. (I remember wondering what a picket line was.) I played the songs incessantly and still can remember almost every word. Many of the themes I would later write about were already present in those songs.

From the talking blues "Talking Union" I learned about strikes:

> *Now you know you're underpaid but the boss says you ain't*
> *He speeds up the work till you're about to faint.*
> *You may be down and out, but you ain't beaten*
> *You can pass out a leaflet and call a meeting.*

Talk it over ... speak your mind ... decide to do something about it.
Now suppose they're working you so hard that it's just outrageous
And they're paying you all starvation wages;
You go to the boss and the boss will yell
"Before I raise your pay I'll see you all in Hell!"
Well he's smoking a big cigar, feeling mighty slick
'Cause he thinks he's got your union licked
When he looks out the window and what does he see
But a thousand pickets and they all agree:
He's a bastard ... Slavedriver ... Bet he beats his wife.[1]

(My first book, published in 1972, was titled *Strike!*)

I learned about solidarity from "Solidarity Forever," sung to the stirring tune of "The Battle Hymn of the Republic":

They have taken untold millions that they never toiled to earn
But without our brain and muscle not a single wheel can turn.
We can break their haughty power, gain our freedom when we learn
That the union makes us strong.
In our hands is placed a power greater than their hoarded gold
Greater than the might of armies magnified a thousand-fold.
We can bring to light a new world from the ashes of the old
For the union makes us strong.[2]

(My second book, *Common Sense for Hard Times,* published in 1976, included the phrase "The Power of the Powerless" in its subtitle. The subtitle for my book [coauthored with Tim Costello and Brendan Smith] *Globalization from Below,* published in 2000, is *The Power of Solidarity.*)

As I was growing up there was only a tenuous link between this inspiring, even romantic, idea of workers joining together to fight oppressive bosses and the reality of the American labor movement. I first became aware of this gap in relation to issues of war and peace. Unions in military industries lobbied hand in hand with their employers for weapons programs that would provide contracts for their employers and jobs for their members. Organized labor was a major supporter of expanded military spending and promoter of hawkish foreign policies. As we would later learn, the International Affairs Department of the AFL-CIO (America's principal union federation) cooperated with the CIA in its efforts to overthrow democratically elected governments in Guatemala, Chile, and elsewhere.

Labor's commitment to militarism and nationalism was a barrier to forging a coalition to challenge military spending in the interest of meeting human needs. But I could see no obvious way to change it.

Racism in the labor movement, especially in the trades, provided another barrier to cooperation between labor and other social movements. At a meeting of the Student Peace Union I met a young socialist printer who proudly showed me his card in the radical but nearly defunct Industrial Workers of the World and explained that he did not consider himself a scab even though he was not a member of the official printers' union because the union let its locals exclude black workers. When Hispanic and black workers who had been excluded from national AFL-CIO president George Meany's home plumbers union local were hired by New York City, white union members walked off the job; instead of demanding that the local be opened up to blacks and Hispanics, Meany defended the walkout. "As far as I'm concerned . . . this union won't work with non-union men." If they did, "I'd resign from the union and join some other union."[3]

At Reed College, where I was a student from 1963 to 1965, a few of us tried to help a United Auto Workers (UAW) local president organize small auto industry shops. Left wing trade union officials occasionally showed up at a peace or civil rights meeting or demonstration. But in general I had little contact with unions or even with union members.

Many years later I heard labor historian David Montgomery describe the AFL-CIO in the era of George Meany as a "great snapping turtle" trying to contain the working class within its shell and snapping its jaws at anyone who might cross the border between inside and outside. I experienced the consequences. There was a sort of cultural apartheid that separated working and middle class worlds. That in turn was in part an effect of the political and institutional isolationism enforced by the snapping turtle.

In *The New Men of Power* by C. Wright Mills[4] I found an account of how American labor leaders had acquired significant power, but they had also become allied with the companies whose workers they represented and junior partners within the national "power elite." Unions had become less expressions of workers self-organization than bureaucracies controlled by self-perpetuating political elites.

What this meant in terms of the experience of ordinary working people was a book that was not open to me. But it posed troubling questions for social movements in general. How could a movement that once exemplified struggle against the status quo end up so much its defender? How could a movement dedicated to democracy and solidarity become so bureaucratic and autocratic? How could a movement that had once seen corporate America as its deadly antagonist become a junior partner with management? And how could a movement that once expressed the needs and interests of the dispossessed become in many instances a willing vehicle for their further exclusion?

These questions haunted the social movement activists of the 1960s. Was there anything that could reverse the labor movement's evolution to conservatism and rigidity? Could the same thing happen to our movements too? Was there anything we could do to prevent it?

14
EYES ON THE PRIZE

ﻭ

IN THE MID-1950S, MY FATHER VISITED HIS OLD NEW DEAL MENTOR CLIFFORD DURR to write an article for *Harper's* on some lawsuits he had brought in his hometown of Montgomery, Alabama. When my father got to Montgomery, or so he told the story, Cliff told him to forget the intended article because there was a far more important story in Montgomery: a boycott of city buses by the black community. "Aw, Cliff," my father claimed to have replied, "The magazines I write for have deadlines months ahead of publication, and by the time they published an article, everyone will have forgotten about your little old bus boycott."

No doubt the story was intended to point out how even the self-nominated cognoscenti can be pretty dense when it comes to recognizing historical significance. But it also indicates how limited an impact the Southern civil rights struggle was making in the North, even for those on the left. Even though the Durrs' adolescent daughter Lulah came to stay with us to escape the escalating pressures in Montgomery (Cliff's wife, Virginia, had encouraged Rosa Parks to attend a civil rights training workshop at the Highlander School shortly before she refused to go to the back of the bus and the Durrs had bailed her out when she was arrested for it), I didn't get my first real understanding of the Montgomery bus boycott until I read a comic book about it put out by the Fellowship of Reconciliation.

It was a different story in the spring of 1960 when small groups of black college students began walking into segregated Southern lunch counters, sitting down, and waiting in vain to be served. They became immediate targets of violence—and an electrifying cause célèbre for young people all over the country.

My oldest brother, Earl, a freshman at Oberlin and as far as I knew entirely nonpolitical, phoned home to warn our parents that he had taken part in a demonstration that was going to be broadcast on national television. (Political demonstrations had been almost unknown on college campuses for at least a generation.) At Christmas vacation I met friends of his who had attended a meeting that had brought together the "sit-inners" and their supporters from different cities. Soon we were hearing about the Student Nonviolent Coordinating Committee (SNCC or "Snick") that was spreading the movement through the black colleges of the South. A support group called the Northern Student Movement began picketing Woolworth's stores in Boston and elsewhere in the North demanding that they integrate the lunch counters of their stores in the South.

The impact of the "Snick kids" on my generation was intense. The most obvious reason was their courage, standing up (or rather sitting down) nonviolently in the face of harassment, physical assault, and the ever-present threat of lynching-style mob violence. Their sense of militancy and determination was expressed in songs such as "Ain't Gonna Let Nobody Turn Me 'Round." Their assertion of leadership in the freedom struggle, in spite of their youth, constituted a challenge to adult hypocrisy and cowardice. The directness with which their actions addressed the problem, the way they presented a straightforward moral challenge to the immorality of segregation, made ideological debate and elaborate political justification superfluous.

SNCC rapidly developed a unique collective spirit embodied in their freedom songs and their sense of community. It became ritualized in clothing (sharecropper's overalls) and gestures (an index finger circling in tandem with the emphasis of the sentence). In a sense SNCC constituted an elite, but one whose primary requirements for membership were dedication and self-sacrifice. While what started as a coordinating committee evolved into a staff organization, it remained one that was profoundly hostile to structure and hierarchy. Their commitment to a spirit of inclusion, to the "beloved community," was sung:

> *The only chain that we can stand*
> *is the chain of hand in hand.*[1]

Underlying everything that has come to be referred to as "the sixties" was the spirit of the "Snick kids."

The sit-ins were rapidly followed by the Freedom Rides, organized by the Congress of Racial Equality (CORE), in which integrated groups boarded South-bound busses and refused to leave whites-only seating on the busses and in restaurants along the way. They were met with brutal mob violence—decades later I met Freedom Rider Jim Peck, who was still suffering from the head injuries he received.

When I proposed to raise money for the Freedom Rides in my high school, the principal—well-known locally as a liberal—threatened to throw me out of school. "I know many advocates of civil rights," he told me, "who have no use whatsoever for the Freedom Riders."

Both SNCC and CORE began recruiting northern students for summer projects in the South, and I visited the CORE office in New York when I was sixteen to see if I was old enough to "go South." They didn't discourage me, but I was too cowardly to follow through. A friend and I did drive through the South, visiting the Durrs in Montgomery and the courthouse in Loundes County—"bloody Loundes"—with Bob Zelner, at the time the only white Southern SNCC fieldworker. The notorious local sheriff came up to us somewhat menacingly and asked, "You boys having a good time?"

At Reed College there was a Students for Civil Rights group that functioned as part of the vast hinterland of support for the more direct confrontations of the civil rights movement. We participated in what would now be called a rapid response network to mobilize support for the Southern campaigns, helped with voter registration in Portland's black community, supported a local black political candidate, and hosted John Lewis and other SNCC staffers on their fundraising swings.

While the sit-ins and Freedom Rides challenged the most visible symbols of legal discrimination, they left the edifice of white supremacy intact. No one really knew for sure how to overcome it.

With encouragement and funding from people associated with the Kennedy wing of the Democratic Party, SNCC turned to a strategy of trying to register voters in the rural areas of the deep South. Some SNCC supporters feared that it would end up as a pawn of the Democratic Party.

Some in and around SNCC thought the strategic objective of the movement should be to provoke large-scale federal intervention in the South—a "second Reconstruction." (Something like that actually happened when the 1965 Voting Rights Act sent federal registrars backed by US Marshals into the South to protect the right to vote.) Others questioned this objective, given the close ties between federal agencies like the FBI and the most vicious exemplars of Southern "law enforcement."

There was always tension between SNCC's supporters and the highly publicized campaigns led by Dr. Martin Luther King, Jr. King was regarded by some as pompous and somewhat bumbling—he was sometimes referred to sarcastically as "de Lawd." More seriously, his Southern Christian Leadership Conference (SCLC) was accused of being a top-down operation that moved in on local struggles, taking over control, publicity, and fundraising appeal. Its domination by one charismatic leader contrasted sharply with SNCC's ultra-participatory, anti-hierarchical spirit and ideology.

In retrospect I can see that I had an inadequate understanding of the history and dynamics of the black struggle in the South. Recent historical research has shown the deep roots of the local movements in places like Selma, Albany, and Greensboro, North Carolina; local leaders were able to use King for their own purposes at least as much as he was able to use them for his. Studies of King's oratory have shown how powerfully it drew on and evoked centuries of black struggle of which we were not aware. Nor were we aware of the tremendous pressures that the Justice Department and the FBI were bringing on King and the sub rosa but titanic resistance he was putting up to them. Our perceptions were not necessarily false, but they were lacking the full picture.[2]

Beyond the tensions between SNCC and King's SCLC swarmed other questions of relations between the movement and more established forces like the mainstream civil rights organizations, organized labor, the liberal wing of the Democratic Party, and the Kennedy and Johnson administrations. These tensions came to the forefront at the 1963 March on Washington, when the civil rights leadership, under pressure from the Kennedy administration, tried to cut out parts of SNCC chairman John Lewis's speech that criticized federal complicity in the repression of civil rights activism in the South. They came to a passionate breach when liberal Democrats, led by Vice President Hubert Humphrey and UAW president Walter Reuther, blocked the seating of the SNCC-organized Mississippi Freedom Democratic Party at the 1964 Democratic Convention. These divisions in turn fed into the emerging conflicts over the war in Vietnam.

Meanwhile, civil rights militancy was spreading into the North. But here the issue was not so much legally enforced segregation as economic and social discrimination. Groups like CORE began to disrupt construction sites where blacks were excluded from employment, often with collusion from building trades unions. Martin Luther King, Jr., organized marches for open housing in northern cities. Such campaigns made the movement directly relevant to poor blacks in the North, but also brought it into conflict with much of the white working class.

Passage of the 1964 Civil Rights Act and the 1965 Voting Rights Act marked the end of one phase in the unending struggle of African Americans for equality in America. So did the emergence of the vague but resonant slogan "black power." SNCC renounced nonviolence and asked whites to leave. I heard the last chairman of SNCC, H. Rap Brown, famous for referring to whites as "honkys" and for the slogan, "Violence is as American as cherry pie," electrifying a well-frisked crowd in a Washington, D.C., church in the late 1960s. "We may not be able to make the people on Wall Street or in the government do what we want," I recall him saying, "but that doesn't mean we can't kick a honky up and down Fourteenth Street." I remember thinking that this was not an expression of black power but of black powerlessness.

SNCC, CORE, and the SCLC had all been devoted to the philosophy and strategy of nonviolence. I lacked an understanding of the real dynamics of nonviolent social change—something I didn't get until decades later when I read Gene Sharp's presentation of Gandhi's strategic ideas in *The Politics of Nonviolent Action*.[3] I assumed that nonviolence worked either through an appeal to conscience or through the direct disruption caused by filling lunch counter seats or county jails. And that was indeed how its efficacy was usually portrayed at the time.

But much of the effectiveness of the civil rights campaigns came from a different source. As Sharp points out, any power structure depends on a range of forces that support it; nonviolence works indirectly by undermining those "pillars of support." That was an important part of how the Southern civil rights struggle actually made the changes it did. For example, many Southern businessmen swung from "massive resistance" to encouraging acquiescence in desegregation because they feared the reactions of Northern business to racist violence. The Kennedy administration moved to support civil rights, albeit tepidly, in part from its fear of foreign disapproval of US racism, especially in newly independent African countries courted by the Soviet Union. Democratic Party politicians were highly dependent on large black voting blocs in Northern cities like Detroit and Chicago, but their support was jeopardized when Democrats in the South perpetrated and Democrats in the White House and Congress tolerated highly visible racial oppression. What seemed on the surface a direct confrontation with the evil of segregation in fact drew much of its power from the "indirect strategy" of putting pressure on the forces whose acquiescence made it possible for segregation to persist.

Far from going from triumph to triumph, much of the time the civil rights movement seemed to be going from defeat to defeat. But it practiced a kind of political jujitsu in which a defeat by Bull Connor's fire hoses and police dogs was transformed into a new consciousness of the evils of segregation in the minds of millions of Americans. Call it winning by losing.

The civil rights movement revealed a kind of social change that is neither the result of established democratic procedures nor a revolutionary seizure of power. It certainly did not eliminate racism or black poverty, but it radically changed the terrorist subjugation of blacks in the deep South. It eliminated the legal segregation against which the sit-ins and Freedom Rides were aimed. The right to vote led to the election of local mayors and sheriffs dependent on black votes. There is surely a direct line between the challenge to the status of African Americans by the boycotts and sit-ins of the civil rights movement and the astonishing election of an African American as President of the United States.

The movement also left a legacy whose ripples know no boundary. Catholic protestors in Northern Ireland called their struggle the civil rights movement and modeled it on that of American blacks. Human rights demonstrators from Eastern Europe to the Philippines sing "We Shall Overcome"; in 2004 I heard it sung by Indian activists at the World Social Forum in Mumbai. The movements for women's rights and gay rights extended the principle of nondiscrimination that the civil rights movement had established in American law and culture.

In the months before his assassination, Martin Luther King, Jr., was developing a plan for a Poor People's Campaign that would use an encampment in Washington, D.C., as the base for an ongoing interracial movement to challenge the distribution of power in America. After King's death a "rainbow coalition" of African Americans, Latinos, and poor whites came to Washington by mule train and established a Freedom City in the muddy flats. Without King's charismatic leadership (and fundraising capacity), the movement never took off—an example of the problems that arise when a movement depends on such individual leadership. But I loved to visit the Freedom City encampment, and I've often felt that someday we'd be back.

15

SDS

ঽৡ

At the February 1962 student peace march in Washington, D.C., there were people passing out flyers for an organization I had never heard of, Students for a Democratic Society (SDS). I was familiar with single-issue organizations such as the Student Peace Union and the Congress of Racial Equality. I knew from a greater distance a variety of socialist organizations including the Young People's Socialist League, the Communist Party, the Socialist Workers Party, and the like. But SDS was something different. It was multi-issue, involved with peace, civil rights, and various other concerns, but it didn't address them in the ideological form of the old left. I wrote away to their Peace Research and Education Project and rapidly got involved with their activities.

SDS expressed a rejection of much that I associated with the "Old Left"— whether Communist, Socialist, Trotskyist, or other. While such groups often seemed marked by a sectarian mentality that saw the organization as the source of wisdom and goodness and outsiders as a menacing evil, the SDS kids had an attractive openness to new ideas and new people. In place of ideological hairsplitting and propagation of the correct line they seemed to embody open dialogue and ongoing resynthesis.

SDS had an ancient lineage that was unknown to most of its members, but that I researched with fascination. In 1905 Jack London and Upton Sinclair among others had founded the Intercollegiate Socialist Society. (At one time their largest chapter, I believe, was at the Brooklyn College of Dentistry—perhaps the basis for Leon Trotsky's disparaging quip that the American Socialist Party was "a party of dentists.") When the first generation became too old to pass as student activists, they established a sort of alumni society for themselves, the very moderate socialist League for Industrial Democracy (LID). The LID in turn sponsored a Student League for Industrial Democracy.[1]

In the late 1950s, the LID hired as student organizer a studious, diligent, and visionary young activist named Alan Haber, who changed the archaic-sounding

Student League for Industrial Democracy to Students for a Democratic Society. He haunted organizations from the National Student Association to the University of Michigan political party SLATE in search of progressive student activists to recruit one by one to SDS and, more importantly, to his vision of a New Left.

Sociologist Daniel Bell, then one of America's foremost public intellectuals, wrote a well-known book called *The End of Ideology;* in response SDS distributed a pamphlet called "The End of Ideology as Ideology" with Al Haber's critique and alternative vision. Bell came out of a socialist tradition and still claimed to express it. But he maintained that the basic goals of that tradition had been realized in the liberal democratic state and society as they existed in the United States and Western Europe. Therefore what he called "ideological" challenge to the existing system, based on rejection and replacement of its central features, was not and should not be on the political agenda. Change was still necessary, but only change whose goal was better adjustment of the present system, a process that required the application of technical social knowledge rather than mass political mobilization. *The End of Ideology* reached conclusions eerily similar to those of Francis Fukuyama's *The End of History* four decades later, even though the latter purported to base its conclusions on the recent collapse of Communism. Bell's stifling of even the conceivability of radical change provided a 1950s equivalent to Margaret Thatcher's "There is no alternative."

Haber argued that this view was itself an ideology in the sense that Marx had originally used the word: a set of ideas used to justify a status quo dominated by the interests of a narrow group. In actuality, the world was full of problems—from racial oppression to militarism to poverty to colonialism—that were far from solved, and that required far more than "technical adjustment." New movements were emerging to address these problems. Realizing their goals required a fundamental reorganization of power.

SDS's early vision was articulated in the once-famous *Port Huron Statement,* based on a draft by Tom Hayden.[2] This long manifesto opened not with a general theoretical pronouncement or abstract principle but with an existential situation: "We are people of this generation, bred in at least modest comfort, housed now in universities, looking uncomfortably to the world we inherit." Its starting viewpoint was defined as that of one segment of humanity, not as some intellectual, political, or class elite with a unique overview of the whole. It sought to point out connections among different issues and concerns without deriving those connections from some pre-assumed ideology.

Even more completely forgotten now, but also impressive to me at the time, was the next year's statement, *America and the New Era,* drafted by Richard Flacks shortly before I joined SDS. It identified changes that were bringing about a "new era" beneath the apparent immobility of Cold War stasis and sketched a strategy for social movements to respond. It envisioned an escalating trajectory that might start with very limited demands but would expand to challenge more central features of the system, anticipating what was to become a widespread discussion on the left of "non-reformist reforms." And it saw the potential linking and convergence of such movements as a means to challenge the complicity of liberalism and the Democratic Party in segregation and militarism.

I was dedicated to SDS as an organization in a way I never have been to an organization before or since. I started a chapter at Reed College and, as Northwest Regional Organizer, traveled from Seattle to Spokane, Washington, and Moscow, Idaho, trying to start chapters.

SDS was a school—a demanding one. Al Haber was known to go up to people and ask a challenging question, such as, "What's the relationship between the military budget and civil rights?" You were expected to present a good analytical response. Debates often combined fresh thinking with immediacy of political concern. (I remember contributing from the floor to one debate only to have Doug Ireland, my closest SDS buddy, say "Why did you have to interrupt a great political discussion with that?")

But SDS was also an organization of activists. The "Snick kids" had a huge influence on both its ideas and its style. (It was not unusual to see a speaker in an SDS meeting rotating an index finger for emphasis in the characteristic manner of the SNCC fieldworkers.) The idea of acting directly on a problem, not just studying it or urging politicians to do something about it, was always implicit.

The tension between intellect and activism came out in a pivotal National Council debate between Al Haber and Tom Hayden over the future of SDS's Economic Research and Action Project (ERAP). Al saw the project as a long-term effort to analyze afresh and in detail why the American economic system failed to meet the needs—social and psychological, as well as material—of its people. Tom had coauthored a position paper called "An Interracial Movement of the Poor?" and he argued that ERAP should establish local projects to create such a movement, roughly following the SNCC model of using college students as volunteer organizers. (A number of such projects were indeed initiated, and while few if any proved successful in creating an interracial movement of the poor, they did provide a means by which older SDS activists managed to move beyond the campus and the role of superannuated "student leaders.") Skeptics and Haber supporters characterized it as "ghetto-jumping."

My friend Doug Ireland and I used to call ourselves the youngest of SDS's "Old Guard." We were aligned with yet another position in SDS, referred to jocularly as the Max Faction. Steve Max's father had been a long-time Communist who, along with many others, left the party around the time of the 1956 Hungarian Revolution. Steve was one of the more anti-Communist of SDS's leaders, but he brought to SDS the Communist Party's popular front tradition of working in labor and other mass organizations and in the left wing of the Democratic Party, something that was anathema at that time to people like Tom Hayden. (Tom would later spend decades as a California state legislator and perennial candidate for higher office.) As a campus-based activist, I valued Steve's genuine interest in building student chapters at a time when other SDS elders were more interested in moving beyond the university personally and politically.

Steve propounded the strategy of "political realignment," which he shared with Michael Harrington and other leaders of the League for Industrial Democracy. They argued that American politics was dominated by a "Republican-Dixiecrat Coalition" made up of conservative Republicans from the North and racist Democrats from the South. (Such views were influenced by Southern historian C. Vann Woodward's book *Reunion and Reaction*, which showed how this alliance had been established by a corrupt deal to end Reconstruction and fix the outcome of the 1876 election.)[3] The alliance provided anti-labor, anti–social welfare policies to benefit Republican employers and national complicity in Southern racial domination.

The strategy of realignment was in essence to drive the Dixiecrats out of the Democratic Party. If the Democrats were forced to adopt strong civil rights positions, Dixiecrats would choose to leave the party; blacks organizing to vote in the South could then be protected by the power of Democratic politicians in the national government, thereby undermining the base of Dixiecrat power. Such a strategy would be in the common interest of labor, blacks in both the North and South, and liberals pursuing a welfare state agenda. This analysis taught me how to think about strategy not just in a general, abstract way, but in a concrete historical power configuration. Something like this actually happened in the mid-1960s, albeit with many ambiguities, as a result of the civil rights movement. The backlash against it was thereafter exploited by Nixon's "Southern Strategy."

The Maxites were strange bedfellows for me, illustrating that political alignments can have more to do with social ties that political positions. I valued Steve's ideas because they represented a concrete strategy based on existing social forces rather than ones we hoped to conjure up. But my heart was not in electoral politics. As SDS radicalized, and especially as the Vietnam War escalated, the Max faction became increasingly isolated; by 1965 people were posting signs outside Steve's office saying "Support the War in Vietnam: Register Voters for Johnson."

In the spring of 1965, more interested in politics than school and happier pursuing my own intellectual agenda than one laid out for me, I dropped out of college and became a student at the Institute for Policy Studies, a left-liberal think tank in Washington, D.C. While I continued to participate in some SDS national meetings, like most of the Old Guard I became increasingly alienated from what was happening in the national organization.

Notwithstanding all the debates, the development of SDS after 1963 was shaped by forces that its founders didn't and probably couldn't have anticipated.

The civil rights and black power movement and the Vietnam War turned American campuses into hothouses of radicalism, especially after young people began to feel the heat of the draft. Factors ranging from the coming of age of the baby boom generation to the commercial promotion of themes of revolt led to the emergence of a youth counterculture with overtones of cultural and sometimes political radicalism. Dramatic confrontations at Berkeley, Columbia, and elsewhere gave student revolt a high national profile.

SDS became a vehicle for all these forces. Radicalized students formed SDS chapters, often with little connection to the national organization. Anyone who called themselves SDS was SDS. By the late 1960s there were an estimated fifty to one hundred thousand people who considered themselves SDS members—a growing proportion from working class colleges and high schools. They increasingly acted on their own without direction from the national organization.

The first effect on national SDS was a flood of new members experiencing their first taste of radical politics who found themselves instantly alienated from the political, organizational, and personal style of the existing leaders. As a result there was a breakdown of communication and continuity; national meetings became largely incoherent. Second, a facile leftist rhetoric and a competition to be "more radical than thou" increasingly shaped the life of the organization. Third, national SDS became a target for takeover by a series of left sects, such as the Maoist group Progressive Labor. The national leadership, from which the Old Guard had largely fled, responded by turning itself into a sect, or rather a series of sects, with names such as the Revolutionary Youth Movement I, the Revolutionary Youth Movement II, and, ultimately, the famous Weatherman. Their conflicts led to splits and eventually the dissolution of SDS.

By the time of its demise, SDS was more a parody of the Old Left's rigidity and sectarianism than a realization of the idea of a New Left. But I got a good political education from SDS, and I've tried to continue what it helped to begin.

16

PARTICIPATORY DEMOCRACY

❧

SDS'S BIG IDEA WAS PARTICIPATORY DEMOCRACY, WHICH WAS SUMMED UP IN THE statement that ordinary people should be able to participate in making the decisions that affect their lives. Being for it was easy. But figuring out what it meant was another story.

Participatory democracy was based on the conviction that people could, should, and in fact were capable of shaping their world and that they needed to do so not just through individual but also through collective decision making. Further, the right to participate implied a responsibility to be more than a passive consumer of political results. It called for what older democratic theorists had called "civic virtue," an active taking of responsibility for the social rather than merely the individual realm.

Participatory democracy has sometimes been conflated (even within SDS) with "direct democracy" in which people make decisions themselves, not through representatives—but it's not quite that simple. It did not advocate replacing representative with direct democracy, but it rejected the sham representation that left people without genuine power. Participation in decision making didn't mean that everyone had to attend every meeting; it meant that decision-making processes had to give people effective rather than merely nominal control over the outcome.

In conventional democratic theory, representatives nominated by competing political parties provide the chief means for ordinary citizens to influence the political system. Early SDSers generally advocated some kind of involvement in and reform of the party system—the purpose of the Mississippi Freedom Democratic Party challenge, after all, was to undermine the racist oligarchy by winning fair representation for Mississippi blacks in the national Democratic Party.

But there were problems with conventional electoral politics as the solution to the failings of modern democracy. As C. Wright Mills taught us in *The Power Elite*—and as those with eyes to see could easily confirm—elites based in large modern bureaucracies like corporations, the military, and government agencies controlled the real levers of power. They dominated both their own huge institutions, which lay outside effective democratic control by those they affected, and the ostensibly democratic institutions of government. Even political party leaders functioned only at the middle levels of power, rarely able to sway or control the real power elite. The parties themselves were largely undemocratic institutions, with little means to hold their leaders accountable to the rank and file.

The political system prevailing in North America and Western Europe celebrated itself as democratic. But in fact democratic participation of ordinary people was largely limited to voting for one or another candidate. Such voting merely ratified the system; it provided no way to change it. It supplied a mantle of legitimacy for power that had little genuine democratic accountability. The actual will of the people was not represented, notwithstanding a system that deemed government officials as their virtual representatives.

The absence of active citizenship was celebrated by mainstream political and social scientists: It demonstrated that the people gave their consent to the status quo. The role of the good citizen was to vote, pay taxes, and obey the law. Democracy was to vote for your leaders and then do what they tell you. To oppose this system was allegedly to be anti-democratic.

Such a viewpoint was anathema to participatory democrats. The founding broadside of the British New Left was a book called *Out of Apathy*, and the desire to move from apathy to activism motivated participatory democracy's rejection of virtual representation and passive citizenship. Non-participatory democracy was a kind of alienation in which people act out social roles they have no real power in shaping. Like alienated labor, alienated politics means engaging in activity preprogrammed by others over whom you have no control. Democracy should mean more than performing your social role; it should mean playing a creative part in defining social roles.

Participatory democracy also implied a critique of the theory and practice of both Communism and social democracy—indeed, that critique was a big part of what was "new" about the New Left. Leninist "democratic centralism" was almost the opposite of participatory democracy. The claims of the Communist Party and the Soviet state to represent the people without any effective means for the people to participate in decision making was another fraudulent form of sham representation.

Conventional socialism, as seen in the social democratic parties of Europe, offered far more personal and political liberty than actually existing Communism, but its vision was still far from that of participatory democracy. A famous sociological study of the German Social Democratic Party had shown that from early in its life it had become centralized and bureaucratically controlled, with the membership only passive objects of the party leadership.[1] A nationalization that merely transferred corporations from private ownership to government owner-ship, while leaving social relationships in the workplace and the rest of society unchanged, did little to increase the power of ordinary people to make the deci-sions that affect their lives. I don't recall anyone in SDS ever referring to Rosa Luxemburg's radical democratic critiques of Leninism and reformist socialism, but participatory democracy represented a renewal of some of the same concerns.

In its own organization, SDS sought to combine direct and representative democracy. In principle, SDS was composed of chapters that sent representa-tives to a National Council. But its ultimate governing body was a convention in which all members could—and many hundreds did—participate. There was a tiny national office, but most of the work of the organization was actually con-ducted through projects such as the Peace Research and Education Project and the Economic Research and Action Project, which functioned essentially as self-coordinated activist networks with an occasional paid staffer. There was a strong informal leadership group—what came to be referred to as the Old Guard. But new leaders were easily co-opted onto the National Council, and a new member like Carl Oglesby could arrive at a national convention and leave at the end as president. It was a far cry from either Bolshevik centralism or the active staff and passive membership typical of most issue organizations.

Participatory democracy called for a kind of responsibility, reliability, and self-discipline—of civic virtue—that borders on the puritanical. But a very different, rather antinomian spirit also grew within SDS. It was a celebration of spontane-ity expressed in the SNCC spiritual "You Got to Do When the Spirit Say Do." If activity was un-spontaneous, it might be alienated even though it was being carried out by the same people who had decided to do it. Conversely, if people spontaneously felt like doing something they should do it, even if something else had been democratically decided before. Down with rules, even ones we demo-cratically established ourselves! Such a tendency grew within SDS as a reflection both of a burgeoning youth counterculture urging "be here now" and "do your own thing" and of a growing leftism that viewed the niceties of democratic values and democratic procedure as a sham.

I remember these forces coming together at the SDS national convention in 1965.[2] It was a beautiful sunny day and the never-ending meeting had flowed to an open area outside. SDS had always had a clause in its constitution excluding from membership "advocates or apologists" for "any totalitarian principle." A resolution was made to remove it. The motivation for the change was never clear to me; I was told that it was just to get rid of an old anti-Communist holdover from the past and perhaps to thumb our noses at the LID elders who still firmly be-lieved in such anti-Communist shibboleths. I had no position on the membership clause, but I did believe we stood for something very different from Communism, and I opposed the change without first finding some other way to say so. When the meeting started to vote, I pointed out that the SDS constitution provided that only elected delegates (a small minority of those attending the convention) could vote on a constitutional change, and I said we should have a roll call vote of delegates. I was shouted down; someone yelled, "That will just make it easy for the FBI to know who voted for it." The resolution passed overwhelmingly on a show of hands. Participatory democracy or mob rule: You be the judge.

Even at its best, participatory democracy never produced a worked-out alternative to more conventional political forms. It never developed a clear idea of the process by which a participatory democracy might be established. And it never solved or even fully addressed many problems implicit in the theory, such as how to deal with parties and sects that themselves are hostile to democracy, or what to do when there is irreconcilable division over fundamental issues.

SDS's use of the term "ordinary people" ducked questions of class. Indeed, like much of modern democratic theory, participatory democracy rarely addressed the underlying problem of economic dependence among different social groups. Thomas Jefferson believed that a democratic government could only be based on independent property owners, because those without property were inescapably dependent on and therefore subject to the domination of those who had it. Socialists made a related critique of democracy: Concentrated property will always find a way to dominate the institutions of government, no matter what system of formal democracy may obtain. But this argument also presents a fundamental problem for socialism: If all property is controlled by the state, or even by some kind of system like workers councils or soviets, doesn't that concentration of political power and property make ordinary citizens even more dependent on those who control the unified political and economic power? This relation between economic power and political freedom is a question SDS never got to.

I was always puzzled that the discussion of participatory democracy so rarely focused on the workplace. To me, that was the sphere in which democracy and participation were most blatantly denied. Challenging the alienation of labor in the name of participatory democracy seemed an obvious way to reach out to workers—especially young workers—and include them in the discourse of radical democratization. There was indeed such a dialogue in the British New Left; I had pored over a special issue of the *New Left Review* on "workers control." It's hard to come up with an explanation other than the middle-class perspective of the SDSers. (I remember visiting an SDS leader in his apartment in the midst of the 1967 Newark riot, with police shooting into the windows of the apartment house across the street, and hearing him declare, "There is going to be a revolution in America, and it is going to be made over the opposition of the white working class.")

Despite the limitations of participatory democracy in theory and practice, many subsequent expansions of democracy have reflected its ideals. Some modern environmental laws, for example, provide procedures through which those affected by development decisions can participate in them. Such laws require those wishing to initiate a major project, whether private or governmental, to prepare an environmental impact statement laying out possible hazards to the environment. Environmental and community groups have standing to challenge such statements. In some cases the proponents must even pay for critical research. The public participation under such laws is often far more extensive than in conventional procedures in which government agencies simply hold public hearings and then make what they consider appropriate decisions.

The neighborhood councils and participatory budgets developed by Porto Alegre and other cities in Brazil provide another example. Under this system, a substantial part of the city budget is determined by neighborhood meetings that set priorities for the spending in their communities. This approach is now being imitated in many parts of the world.

The principle that people should be able to participate in making the decisions that affect their lives is extremely radical. It is incompatible with absolute property rights, for example: It implies that when you use your property in ways that affect me, I have a right to a say in how it is used. It is similarly incompatible with absolute national sovereignty: If your nation does things that affect me, I have a right to participate in its decisions even though I am not a citizen. Such implications of participatory democracy are only beginning to be worked out in the era of globalization.[3]

17
WOMEN'S LIBERATION

៛

SDS ESPOUSED AN IDEOLOGY OF RADICAL EQUALITY. BUT CERTAIN DISTURBING phenomena were visible if you didn't avert your eyes. While women always played an important part in SDS leadership, the top leadership roles were taken dispro-portionately by men.[1] When male leaders spoke in a meeting, people listened attentively. But when women spoke, a buzz of whispered side conversations often arose around the room. When there was "shitwork" to be done—running the mimeograph machine or doing the dishes—it often turned out that the guys were busy writing position papers or "out organizing," so the women ended up doing the undesirable tasks. Certain male leaders treated their girlfriends as admiring camp followers who could be counted on to do their shitwork and provide them political support.[2]

For a while, these problems were rarely more than the subject of informal complaining about particularly flagrant abuses, but gradually the discussion became more focused. A group of women in SNCC (some of whom were also active in SDS) circulated a discussion paper about the role of women in the movement.[3] Small groups of women began meeting to discuss it. The last SDS National Council meeting I attended, in December 1965, had the first workshop on "women in the movement," which called for greater "initiative and participa-tion by women" in SDS and a greater understanding of the "woman question" by men in the organization.[4]

Initially SDS women sought to draw movement men into dialogue, but it proved to be tough going. They were often met with the disparaging comment that their concerns were merely personal, lacking the dignity and importance presumably due to the political. To this they developed the rejoinder that "the personal is political." Indeed, their approach exemplified the fundamental SDS idea of connecting private, fragmented discontents with their social sources in order to make them into political issues.

I felt that the inequality of women in SDS—what would soon be dubbed sexism—conflicted with the values that led me to be in the movement in the first place. I felt the same about the leadership style exercised by what came to be known as "male heavies." I also saw challenge to oppression of women as a means to spread the movement to a new constituency. I thought it was a good thing when women at IPS who were associated with SDS formed a women's liberation group. I remember going around as a supporter to labor and other meetings with Marilyn Salzman Webb and other pioneers who were spreading the gospel of women's liberation.

None of this prevented me from acts of insensitivity that still bring a blush of shame. I remember running across a pornographic paperback that purported to be about rebellious women and their liberated sexuality. I thought it was amusing and pinned the cover on the bulletin board at IPS, where I was a student, as a joke. When I mentioned it to a feminist friend she simply said she had seen it and taken it down—but her scornful look was sufficient to ensure I would never do such a thing again.

I was particularly interested in trying to create a way for men to relate positively to the movement. I worked extensively on an essay titled "The Obsolescence of the Male Ego," making the argument that male roles were oppressive to men as well as to women. I circulated it informally around the IPS environment, but I never got much positive response. The movement scene was rapidly polarizing on gender lines. Women were pulling out of SDS and other mixed-gender groups and forming organizations for women exclusively. Many movement men were responding with rage. Women who gave anti-sexist speeches were subjected to heckling and abusive phone calls. The conflict could be very personal: A lot of marriages were breaking up around me.

The great organizational innovation of the women's liberation movement was what came to be known as the consciousness-raising group. This was a group of women, often from the same neighborhood, occupation, or social milieu, who met regularly for the explicit purpose of identifying how gender inequality affected and was manifested in their personal lives. They focused on the realities of everyday life and the actual content of social relationships: who did the dishes and who was listened to at meetings. While these discussion groups largely originated within SDS and its alumnae, they quickly drew in women who were part of a broader left culture, then an even larger group beyond. By the end of the 1960s, women's liberation had completed its parturition and become a separate movement.

The consciousness-raising groups were an expression of participatory democracy and indeed one of the purest. They contributed to the incredibly rapid spread of the women's movement, which soon moved beyond gender issues within the

New Left to those in the broader society. Within a couple of years the women's movement was raising the economic issues of hiring discrimination, the wage gap, and the glass ceiling; questions of the portrayal of women in sexist advertising and the Miss America contest; the role of social rituals, such as men opening doors for women and women making coffee for men in the workplace; domestic violence and rape; the right of women to control their own bodies through access to contraception and abortion; the domestic division of labor and the "double shift" for working women; the roles of men and women in family, home, and childcare; the absence of women in leadership roles in politics; discrimination against women in the military; the need for solidarity among women in their personal lives and worldwide; and other concerns covering every aspect of society.

The growing awareness of the oppression of women opened significant questions for understanding society and social change. The dominant traditions on the left had seen class as the basic division in society and the working class as the basic agent for social change. Could gender oppression somehow be fitted into the mold of class—with the exploitation of women seen as in essence an aspect of capitalism and the liberation of women depending on that of the working class? Or were the labor movement and the male-led left really vehicles to perpetuate the oppression of women? Or were class and gender, perhaps alongside race, categories for understanding society and oppression that could not be reduced to each other but that together provided the necessary framework for analysis and change? I gradually came to believe that the search for the "essential" elements of society and oppression was intellectually misleading and politically counterproductive, but it took a long time before I had even a glimmering of an alternative.

The women's liberation movement has had a huge global impact. It would be difficult today to find a locality or a sphere of life in which gender inequality is not being contested. The challenge to traditional gender roles has also helped fuel a global backlash, often represented by religious fundamentalism and its projection into the political arena. But so far that backlash has rarely returned women to the extent of subordination they experienced before the women's liberation movement.

18

'NAM

ঽ

IN THE SUMMER OF 1961 I TOOK PART IN A YOUTH PEACE CARAVAN SPONSORED BY THE American Friends Service Committee. There was a young woman in my training group who was from Vietnam. I overheard another trainee saying she must be upset because the Vietcong were only 20 miles from Saigon and were shelling the city. I didn't know who the Vietcong were, or where Vietnam was, or that there was a war going on there.

Over the next several years, the United States intervened militarily in third world settings worldwide. The CIA organized the Bay of Pigs invasion of Cuba. US "advisors" picked sides in the civil war in Laos. US troops invaded and occupied the Dominican Republic. These actions replicated such Eisenhower-era interventions as CIA "regime change" in Iran and Guatemala and the landing of US troops in Lebanon. They were not the policies of rightwing, conservative, or Republican politicians, but of Democratic administrations led by John F. Kennedy and Lyndon B. Johnson and staffed and supported by people who called themselves liberals. The polarization that had developed between the New Left and the liberal establishment over civil rights was intensified by these expressions of anti-Communist globalism.

Initially US involvement in Vietnam seemed to be merely one more example of this pattern. But the US intervention in Vietnam grew larger, and larger, and larger, until ultimately it involved more than half a million US troops, more tons of bombs than were dropped on all of Europe during World War II, and the death of fifty thousand Americans and as many as two million Indochinese.

At the end of 1964, not many people had Vietnam at the center of their radar screens, but to SDS it seemed like a good target for raising broader issues about US foreign policy. Anyone could see that, for whatever reasons, the United States was propping up corrupt dictatorships all over the world. When their people rebelled, US military intervention seemed bound to follow.

The US-backed Diem regime in South Vietnam seemed a perfect case in point. After a long debate (I tried futilely to remove the word imperialism from the resolution on the grounds that it would alienate newly active students and that we had never discussed what it meant), SDS decided not to engage in immediate action, but rather to call for a demonstration in Washington the next spring.

Unbeknownst to SDS, the Johnson administration was about to launch a huge expansion of US participation in the war—a policy that came to be known as "escalation." Advisors were redefined as combat soldiers. US planes began bombing Vietnam, first sporadically, then daily. Draft calls escalated in anticipation of what was to be an eight-fold increase in US troops in Vietnam over the coming year. In response to escalation, and without any outside prompting, students on US campuses began organizing meetings and protests about the war.

Except for such scattered protests, public opinion and the Congress supported American policy overwhelmingly. Antiwar demonstrations were forbidden in some places; in others demonstrators were beaten up. When the United States charged that North Vietnamese boats had attacked a US ship in the Gulf of Tonkin (an attack phone taps released long afterward show even Lyndon Johnson believed probably never happened), the Senate passed the Gulf of Tonkin Resolution giving the President a free hand to do anything he chose in Vietnam. The vote was 98–2, with only Senators Wayne Morse and Earnest Gruening opposed.

The first mainstream questioning of US policy came in 1965, after the Johnson administration issued a white paper justifying escalation as a response to a North Vietnamese invasion of South Vietnam. Senator Mike Mansfield held hearings with independent experts on Vietnam who demolished this account. Then teachers and students at the University of Michigan organized an all-night public educational event that they dubbed a "teach-in" after the civil rights sit-ins. They were hoping for five hundred participants; instead three thousand showed up. Within two months teach-ins had been held on more than one hundred campuses, probably the most widespread campus political activity since the 1930s. An estimated thirty-five thousand joined a teach-in at Berkeley.[1]

The spring 1965 SDS Vietnam demonstration, expected at best to double the previous peak for Washington peace demonstrations of about three thousand, instead drew an estimated twenty-five thousand. A lot of people, especially young people, suddenly wanted to act against the war. It was, up to that time, the largest peace march in US history.[2] I was staggered—I had never expected to live to see such a thing.

At that point, SDS was universally recognized as the leader of the antiwar movement. But, astonishingly, it decided to renounce the crown. SDS national leaders had their own agenda, focused on building an interracial movement of the poor or perhaps a revolution. As one leader put it, "Our goal is to build a movement that can stop the seventh war from now." Tens of thousands of students, however, wanted to protest the war, and they often called the groups they formed to do so SDS chapters, even though they had virtually no support or encouragement from SDS as a national organization.

In this vacuum, national antiwar leadership passed to an ever-chaotic, ever-changing ad hoc coordinating body successively known as the Committee to End the War in Vietnam, the National Mobilization Committee, and the New Mobe. There's a saying among Appalachian coal miners: All you have to do is hang a picket sign on a yellow dog and you've got a strike—no miner will pass it to go to work. Fortunately, leading the anti–Vietnam War movement didn't take a lot more than setting a date for the next demonstration and waiting for a few hundred thousand people to show up.

In the early stages of escalation, opposition was almost entirely confined to students. Liberals overwhelmingly supported Lyndon Johnson and the war. Even the established peace movement was wary of the antiwar students, sometimes joining in red-baiting attacks on them. The antiwar movement, which started primarily with small groups on elite campuses, became a mass movement of students in less than two years—no doubt kindled in substantial part by the draft. For several years the movement remained largely isolated on campuses, with little off-campus support. It functioned in a generational ghetto, resulting in slogans such as, "Don't trust anybody over thirty."

Military service—and casualties—were disproportionately concentrated among African Americans in 1965 and 1966, and the next protest to emerge was from within the black community. A SNCC leader, coming out against the war, declared, "No Vietcong ever called me a nigger." Martin Luther King, Jr., began campaigning against the war—to the dismay of liberals, who feared dissention between the civil rights movement and the Johnson administration.

Liberal and middle-class opinion gradually swung against the war. In 1965 it was hard to find a liberal who opposed the war; by 1970 it was hard to find one who had ever supported it.

The AFL-CIO remained a pillar of support for the war to the bitter end—trashing not only the student demonstrators but also war critic and 1972 Democratic presidential candidate George McGovern. But as working class young men began returning from Vietnam and telling their families and communities what was really going on there, as the burdens of paying for the war increasingly fell on working-class shoulders, and as working-class communities began seeing more and more of their young men coming home in body bags, opinion began to shift. By the early 1970s, opinion polls showed that the lower your income, the less likely you were to support the war. This was matched by a rapid expansion of activism at working-class colleges and even high schools.

In 1965, I dropped out of college and started a five-year stint in Washington, D.C. I was based at the Institute for Policy Studies, where I had Arthur Waskow and Marcus Raskin as my mentors. It was a thrilling place to experience what we now think of as the sixties. When I had first registered for the draft at eighteen I had applied for recognition as a conscientious objector, and when my claim was finally accepted on appeal I performed alternative service with the Friends Committee on National Legislation, a Quaker lobby. I wrote antiwar pamphlets, articles, testimony, and speeches for members of Congress. I styled myself a Quaker military expert.

My memory of the Vietnam War era is one of unending pain—a pain that floods back to me even as I write about it decades later. (Yes, it was nothing compared to the pain of those, on all sides, who experienced the war directly.) Every morning for a decade I woke up anticipating news reports on the bombing of villages. Part of my job with the Friends Committee on National Legislation involved regularly calling a colonel at the Pentagon public information service. He would give me the official statistics on American casualties, the number of bombing sorties, and the enemy "body count." Then I would try to get information on topics like civilian casualties, which he always stonewalled. One day the newspapers reported that the Pentagon had admitted accidentally bombing a "friendly" village, and even provided statistics on the casualties. I called the colonel and, after getting the usual statistics, asked him, "How many people have been killed in the accidental bombing of friendly villages?" He replied, "Oh, I'm not going to tell you that—but it was a good try!"

The unending pain led thousands of us to devote our lives to the antiwar movement. But the pain was redoubled because we felt ourselves largely powerless. No matter how strong our arguments, how thoroughly we demolished the indefensible lies told to support the war, how effectively we elaborated alternatives, or how many hundreds of thousands of demonstrators we brought to Washington, the government kept on escalating and escalating. We were told that one powerful antiwar member of Congress, warned that President Johnson might be tapping his phone, replied, "I hope to hell he is—I don't seem to be able to get through to him any other way."

SDS, the student movement, and indeed an entire generation went through a rapid radicalization. "US imperialism," from little more than a Communist epithet, became a palpable reality for many. The struggle against US imperialism increasingly became the frame that defined the antiwar movement's worldview. In that context there was an increasing identification with the Vietnamese Communist resistance to US imperialism and to the struggle of Communist insurgents around the world generally. Che Guevara became an icon and some antiwar demonstrators began carrying Vietcong flags. I remained opposed to Communism as an authoritarian system antithetical to participatory democracy, but such niceties became less and less salient to the movement as a whole.

Meanwhile, we searched desperately for ways to stop the war, or at least to escalate the opposition. From the first draft calls, a small but growing number of young men became draft resisters. Some publicly burned draft cards or refused to show up for induction. Others went underground, many of them eventually making their way to Canada or Sweden. I had little appreciation at that time of the significance of draft resistance. I thought it was too individualistic to develop collective power and too radical to appeal to a mass constituency; even though I was a conscientious objector myself, I thought more in terms of lobbying and electoral politics or mass confrontation. I failed to grasp how such individual moral acts can lead other people to confront their own responsibilities. I also had no idea that, as opposition to the war intensified, what was regarded as treasonous one year might be considered moderate or even patriotic the next.

My blindness is even more striking because I was close to a good example of the power of conscience-based resistance. Marc Raskin at IPS had started talking about the Committee of 121, a group of French intellectuals who had caused a sensation in the 1950s by publicly—and illegally—supporting draftees who refused to serve in Algeria. I rummaged through my old box of *New Left Reviews* and found an English translation of the original statement. It became a model for a *Call to Resist Illegitimate Authority,* which, by endorsing the criminal act of draft resistance, put its signers at risk of prosecution. (The US government eventually prosecuted Marc and other *Call to Resist* supporters, including Dr. Benjamin Spock, Reverend William Sloan Coffin, Jr., and Mitchell Goodman, along with draft resister Michael Ferber, in a highly publicized Boston show trial.) Marc argued that threatening the legitimacy of the government's authority might make US leaders decide the war was not worth the cost. It was an argument that I would make during the Iraq war in a book called *In the Name of Democracy: American War Crimes in Iraq and Beyond,*[3] but that I didn't even understand at the time.

In 1967, I helped set up Vietnam Summer, a campaign designed to break out of the campus ghetto by sending students to canvass door-to-door against the war in the way that students had gone door-to-door to register voters in 1964 for Mississippi Summer. More than twenty thousand students participated nationwide.

By that time, GIs and especially veterans returning from Vietnam were turning against the war. Two fingers held up in a V had recently become established as a peace sign, and I remember the thrill and astonishment I felt the first time I saw uniformed soldiers stationed on rooftops during a big antiwar demonstration in Washington give V signs to the protestors marching below. Activists, often with women in the lead, began opening up "GI coffee houses" near military bases so that alienated soldiers would have some place to come, talk, and learn something about their options. Meanwhile, disgruntled vets organized Vietnam Veterans

Against the War. The unanticipated emergence of antiwar veterans played a crucial role in undermining the sentiment that peace was unpatriotic.

The most visible expressions of the antiwar movement were annual or semi-annual demonstrations. They grew to fifty thousand, a hundred thousand, and eventually uncountable numbers that may have exceeded a million participants. They targeted institutions like the Pentagon and the Watergate complex and often involved day-long street battles with police and military. The strategy underlying these confrontations—expressed in the slogan "bring the war home"—was to create so much domestic disruption that ruling circles would decide to curtail the war to protect their own interests.

As public opinion shifted against the war and the millions who participated in antiwar demonstrations became visible as a potential constituency, politicians began to challenge the war in the electoral arena. First a few movement activists ran as peace candidates, mostly as independents or on third party tickets. In 1967 liberal Senator Eugene McCarthy ran for the Democratic presidential nomination as a somewhat ambiguous peace candidate, followed by the soon-to-be-assassinated Senator Robert Kennedy. But these efforts, and even the capture of the Democratic Party in 1972 for George McGovern, seemed to have little impact on the war.

Ultimately, though with excruciating slowness, the antiwar movement did help bring the war to an end. Growing social tensions did lead those in power to decide the cost of continuing the war was too high. Perhaps the first indication of this came when President Johnson replaced Defense Secretary Robert McNamara with Washington super-lawyer Clark Clifford. Clifford made the rounds of his corporate comrades and advised Johnson to de-escalate the war. As substantial numbers of soldiers began refusing to fight and even began "fragging"—blowing up with fragmentation bombs—officers who ordered them on patrol, the military itself came to fear demoralization of the troops. Above all, the unending stream of body bags led a lot of people to ask the questions—moral and pragmatic—they should have asked at the beginning. As Vietnamese General Vo Nguyen Giap had predicted years before in his brilliant analyses of the strategic situation (excerpted periodically in the *New York Times*), the American people, like the French before them, eventually grew unwilling to carry the burden of the war.

At a meeting decades after the United States withdrew from Vietnam, US military officers taunted one of their Vietnamese counterparts, "You never defeated us militarily." The Vietnamese officer replied, "That is true. It is also irrelevant." It could similarly be said that it is true but irrelevant that the peace movement never forced the government to end the war. In the end, it was the opposition of the American people, expressed both in the antiwar movement and myriad other forms, that brought the war to an end.

The end of the war presented an opportunity that antiwar activists were too divided, too disoriented, and too tired to seize. Militarism and anti-Communism were weak and discredited. Major congressional hearings by the Church Committee exposed decades of military and security agency malfeasance. With little help from the left Congress put significant limits on the FBI, the CIA, the Pentagon, and the imperial presidency.

The antiwar movement left a big legacy, nonetheless. It taught the American people that even for the United States there can be such things as unwise wars and unjust wars. It left a residue of skepticism about patriotism and militarism—what its opponents decried as the "Vietnam syndrome." And it showed that the people can stop a war.

Despite the Vietnam syndrome, since Vietnam the United States has been in wars in Nicaragua, El Salvador, Yugoslavia, Somalia, twice in Afghanistan, Kuwait, Iraq, Libya, and many less visible places. We have yet to build that movement that can "stop the seventh war from now."

19

A REALM OF NEW POSSIBILITIES

࿐

OUT OF MY EXPERIENCES AS AN ACTIVIST I BEGAN TRYING TO CONSTRUCT AN understanding of social movements. I learned that the seemingly romantic idea of isolated, passive people joining together to act in concert was not just a fantasy; I saw it happen over and over again. I learned that when they do they enter a realm of new possibilities. They have a potential power that they lack as individuals. But I also found that it is not always obvious how to realize those possibilities and make use of that power. I learned that movements can create new forms of domination and new, sometimes monstrous, problems.

The movements in which I participated in the 1960s were responses to the threat of nuclear war, the injustice of racism, the stultification of democracy, the oppression of women, and the US war against Vietnam. I concluded that it is when people experience some kind of problem that they are likely to form or join social movements. Without such problems, no amount of brilliant strategy or dedicated organizing is likely to create a movement.

Yet I knew all too well that, even when faced with the most devastating problems, people do not automatically or inevitably organize or join social movements. They may try to ignore or deny the problems—as many did with the threat of nuclear war. They may seek individual solutions, for example, by acquiescing in racial or gender domination in order to keep out of trouble. Or—like apathetic "stay-at-home voters"—they may reject the status quo but simply see no way to challenge it. Such responses reflect the power of existing institutions. They also reflect the extent to which people are separated, isolated, and divided.

As discontents accumulate, however, such acquiescence may become less and less bearable. People may start to articulate their discontent in the milieus in which they live and to discover that others are having similar feelings. I think of my mother in the depths of the Cold War sending out a Christmas letter with a poem about a child who died in Hiroshima.

The accumulation of dissatisfaction can create in individuals a state of readiness—not necessarily conscious—to join a movement. As in religious conversion as analyzed by William James, the elements of a new approach may already be assembled by an individual internally well before they are expressed overtly.[1] Personal experience and cultural traditions may facilitate or impede such responses; in my case, I'm sure that seeing my family's involvement in the community development effort of the Mountain People in Mahwah, New Jersey, contributed to my readiness to respond to social problems by joining in concerted action.

I saw the initial coming together of people to form a social movement take diverse forms. Sometimes it crystallized out of a particular milieu: SNCC and the 1960 student sit-ins emerged from the growing discontent among students at Southern black colleges, for example. Sometimes it arose in response to the behavior of other actors: The movement against the Vietnam War began as a direct response to the military escalation initiated by the Johnson administration.

A movement can also originate as an offshoot of or revolt against an existing group or institution. The National Committee for a Sane Nuclear Policy was largely formed by peace activists from existing organizations to take advantage of the emerging public concern about nuclear testing. SDS represented both a continuation of and a revolt against its parent, the League for Industrial Democracy. The Women's Liberation Movement arose within but also as a protest against SDS and other New Left organizations.

Individuals who are in a state of readiness can rapidly link up with emerging social movements. I found the peace movement in a group of marchers on their way to Washington, D.C.; I found SDS through a leaflet passed out at a demonstration. Thousands joined the peace, student, antiwar, and other movements just by seeing a poster or hearing a conversation and showing up at a demonstration or a meeting. Their own motivation was far more important than anybody's "marketing strategy" in getting them there.

Some of these movements, like the civil rights movement that developed in Southern black colleges and communities, drew on a pre-existing constituency that shared an identity and common traditions. Some, like the women's movement, shared an identity, but not one that was already seen as a basis for protest or collective action. Some, like the peace movement, addressed issues that affect everyone, and those who joined the movement cut across a wide range of classes, cultures, and other categories.

I was perplexed by the complexity of the relation between problems and constituencies. It was easy to understand, for example, why black students in the South protested racism, but large numbers of whites in the North also joined in, some even sacrificing their lives for the cause. The anti–Vietnam War movement likewise included both highly privileged white college students and highly oppressed African Americans. Working-class women were by most standards far more oppressed than middle-class women, yet the Women's Liberation Movement was primarily drawn from the middle class. The protest movements of the 1960s were highly concentrated among young people, though whether this was because they were young, or because they were part of the specific baby boom generation, or for some other reason was not obvious. These movements were largely isolated from people whose lives were shaped by family and job responsibilities. No simple mechanical theory, such as class position causing class struggle, seemed able to explain what groups were likely to become part of social movements.

I was also impressed by the fluidity of social movement participation. Well over one hundred thousand people went through SDS in its short life. Yet in terms of membership, program, strategy, and style it was for practical purposes a new organization every year or two. The impact of social movements was fluid too: The peace movement fluctuated repeatedly between being a negligible force and a power even the superpowers had to reckon with.

Organizationally these movements were often—in fact usually—chaotic. Organizations conflicted and cooperated with each other, split, merged, disappeared, spawned new offshoots, rose and fell, and generally resembled spectral shape-changers. A great deal of activity was actually coordinated by informal self-organized networks that persisted and operated under the aegis of whatever formal organization was currently in favor. I concluded that movements are able to function despite the chaotic character of their formal organizations because their participants' shared activist mentality allows them to coordinate with each other in whatever way seems necessary for the task at hand. They didn't have to be organized by organizations because they were willing and able to organize themselves.

Sociologists such as Max Weber view movements as the product of charismatic leaders. But that was not my experience. The movements that I saw in the 1960s generally had an informal group who served collectively as leaders. Martin Luther King, Jr., was the closest I ever saw to a leader who was followed because of personal charisma. However even King was rarely followed blindly, simply because of who he was. On the contrary his support was based on his articulation of what his followers wanted him to say and do; he was not too revered to be subject to devastating criticism and even derision within the movement, sometimes from the very people who participated in actions that he led.

All of the movements created some kind of dialogue about their nature, goals, and strategy. This was conducted in constant informal discussion, in endless meetings, and to a lesser extent in printed position papers, articles, and books. SDS was the only organization that I participated in that conducted a serious ongoing formulation of comprehensive positions linking means and ends. But often the theory did more harm than good. SDS's kooky and calamitous decision to abandon leadership of the antiwar movement was driven by a theoretical belief that students were a less important force for social change than an imagined interracial movement of the poor to be initiated by student organizing projects in urban ghettos.

Movement development was more often shaped by experimental initiatives that worked and were repeated or that failed and were modified or dropped. Looking back on the Albany, Georgia, civil rights protest movement, SNCC staff member Charles Sherrod recalled, "We didn't know what we were doing. We'd never done it before."[2] At the time the Albany movement did not achieve its aims, but the lessons learned from it led to a series of campaigns that made major changes in race relations in the South. Sometimes the movements least guided by theoretical discourse were the most successful.

I was not satisfied with my understanding of how social movements actually made change. Various paradigms of change jostled each other in these movements and even within the minds of individual participants. Change might come through electoral democracy or through class-based revolution. It might result from changes in values and culture or from threats to the legitimacy of "the system." Some hoped it might simply result from protest itself.

The movements of the 1960s talked a great deal about power, but we didn't have much conception of what it was or where it came from. Then-trendy phrases like Mao's "Power grows from the barrel of a gun" were not much help. Initially there was some attempt to analyze the structures within which power was rooted, such as the alliance of Southern white supremacists and Northern business interests; later "class analysis" of a sort became all the rage, but it usually took a crude form ungrounded in the experience and situation of real people.

I learned that movements might come to a bad end. The experience of Leninism and of American trade unions already provided a warning that social movements could result not in liberation but in bureaucracy and softer or harder forms of domination. In a few short years SDS went from participatory democracy to farcical parodies of Leninist centralism. I wished for, but did not have, a better explanation for such phenomena than bad leaders who simply grew power hungry or "sold out."

I also saw that social movements could lead to new and destructive conflicts and polarizations. A major unintended effect of the radical movements of the sixties was to turn much of the white working class to the right. They became the base for a backlash against women's, black, and antiwar movements that was eagerly exploited in the 1968 presidential campaigns of Alabama governor George Wallace and Richard Nixon—and that provided a base for right-wing domination of US politics for decades to come. My experience with social movements made me acutely concerned that they could lead to new forms of domination and conflict—and led me to seek ways that movements could forestall such results.

All these problems notwithstanding, I saw the movements of the sixties make significant change. The peace movement was largely responsible for the banning of nuclear testing, the establishment of détente, and indirectly for the fall of Communism in Eastern Europe and the end of the Cold War. The civil rights movement ended legally enforced segregation, greatly expanded African American political representation, largely ended the system of lynching-based racial terrorism, and laid the groundwork for the election of an African American as President of the United States. The impact of the women's liberation movement in the United States and worldwide is too vast and varied even to summarize. The movement against the war in Vietnam helped bring the war to a close; its legacy was a "Vietnam syndrome" that provided a significant if inadequate brake on subsequent US interventionism. Each of these movements also left as a legacy a widely diffused knowledge of how to form and conduct social movements. If these movements failed, we should all aspire to such failure.

My experience in the movements of the 1960s left me full of questions and hungry for answers. Participating in and trying to understand and improve social movements became a passion and an ongoing project. I well knew that we had no adequate solutions to war, injustice, and other social problems. I struggled with the questions of agency, strategy, program, and organization. That led me to pursue historical and social research that went beyond the movements with which I was personally involved.

PART 3

DISCOVERING WORKERS' POWER

20

DISCOVERING WORKERS' POWER

❧

BY 1970 I FELT "BETWEEN TWO WORLDS, ONE DYING, THE OTHER POWERLESS TO BE born." Like many others from the New Left I felt that participatory democracy as we had envisioned it was inadequate for a world of rampant imperialism and repression where even representative democracy was little more than a sham.

I felt wholeheartedly that we needed a revolution. But in contrast to many of my contemporaries I continued to reject the various Leninist versions of Communism as authoritarian travesties of liberation. I sought instead to extend participatory democracy into a revolutionary theory. And I sought a way to expand its base from the world of student activism to the majority of the US population.

That quest led me to the working class. I immersed myself in the intellectual traditions of working-class radicalism. I pored over old left-wing journals. I studied Marx and a variety of Marxists. I read Lenin and Mao, but I was repelled by the whole idea of a vanguard party as a "transmission belt" inculcating socialist consciousness in the masses. I discovered an alternative Marxist tradition that included Rosa Luxemburg and such lesser-known figures as Anton Pannekoek and Paul Mattick, who advocated a participatory democracy-like system of workers councils as an alternative to the Leninist idea of a vanguard party creating a revolutionary state.

I also tried to make these ideas relevant in practice. I worked with a small group to put out a homemade radical journal called *Root & Branch* and a book called *Root & Branch: The Rise of the Workers' Movements*. I initiated a Quixotic effort to spread the 1970 wildcat postal strike to other government workers and to push the huge anti–Vietnam War Moratorium in the direction of a general strike.

Alongside such theoretical and activist excursions, I began discovering the actual history of the American working class. I uncovered a rarely told story of mass revolts and upheavals rooted less in formal institutions like unions and political parties than in informal work groups and communities.

I wrote a controversial book called *Strike!* to tell that story, using the ideas I had gleaned from the intellectual traditions of working-class radicalism as my guide. *Strike!* was less a conventional work of labor history than an attempt to address questions about social change that both old and New Left had failed to answer to my satisfaction. In contrast to both mainstream and conventional left-wing approaches, *Strike!* focused on ordinary working people's own activity. It viewed unions and political parties as vehicles they sometimes used, and sometimes circumvented or even opposed, for their own purposes. It tried to find underlying patterns in the periods of what I called "mass strike" and proposed pushing those patterns past their previous limits as a way to create a new society.

In my writings of that time I incorporated as much as I could of what I found valuable both in American labor history and in the intellectual traditions of working-class radicalism. I also incorporated some of the flaws of that tradition— flaws I have been trying ever since to correct without throwing out what is valid and compelling.

Today, I find much of my work from this period marked by a kind of monomania in which everything in the world is reduced to class relations and by a tin ear for complexity. Nonetheless, my study of mass strikes gave me my first rough answers to how people come together in response to shared problems, how by doing so they increase their power to affect their conditions, and how their movements can come to be a new source of oppression. What I learned from studying workers power helped provide a starting point for understanding the broader problems of common preservation.

Mass strikes and popular upheavals are currently challenging the status quo all over the world from Egypt to Spain to Mexico. The United States has seen the most intense class conflict in a quarter of a century. Working people worldwide are finding existing strategies inadequate to protect their livelihoods. Thus the largely forgotten history of mass strikes may have a renewed relevance today.

GREAT UPHEAVALS

 za

IN A REED COLLEGE HISTORY SURVEY COURSE IN 1965 I HEARD A BRIEF MENTION OF some big strikes in late nineteenth-century America. I was intrigued and started looking in the college library for books on labor history. There was a short shelf of them, few less than twenty-five years old. This was before the rise of what came to be known as the new labor history. E. P. Thompson's revelatory and immensely influential *The Making of the English Working Class*[1] had just been published in England, but the news had not yet reached Portland, Oregon. Labor history was a tiny field, preoccupied with an "institutional approach" that took the history of individual trade unions and the evolution of collective bargaining as its primary subject matter.

Then in a secondhand bookstore I picked up *1877: Year of Violence*[2] by Robert V. Bruce. It sported a lurid jacket with a railroad depot ablaze in bright yellow flames. It told a story that amazed me—one that I was amazed I had never heard before. It described what was seen at the time as a violent rebellion in which strikers seized and closed the nation's most important industry, the railroads, and crowds defeated or won over first the police, then the state militias, and in some cases even the federal troops. General strikes brought work to a standstill in a dozen major cities and strikers took over authority in communities across the nation.

On July 16, 1877, after years of depression, the Baltimore and Ohio Railroad cut wages by 10 percent. In the little town of Martinsburg, West Virginia, railroad workers hung around the yards all day, talking. Finally, a crew walked off a cattle train. Other workers refused to replace them, and the crowd announced that no trains would leave Martinsburg until the pay cut was rescinded. The mayor, after conferring with railroad officials, ordered the police to arrest the apparent leaders. They just laughed at him—backed up by an angry crowd. By next day, hundreds gathered to help halt the trains. The governor, after meeting with railroad officials, ordered in the state guard. A striker shot a militiaman and in turn was fatally shot. Workers refused orders to run a train, and the colonel of the guard telegraphed the governor that he was helpless to control the situation.

With this confrontation began the Great Upheaval of 1877, a spontaneous, nationwide, quasi-general strike. The pattern of Martinsburg—a railroad strike in response to a pay cut, an attempt by the companies to run trains with the support of military forces, and the defeat or dissolution of those forces by crowds representing general popular support—became over the course of a week the pattern for the nation.

President Rutherford B. Hayes sent federal troops into Martinsburg to suppress what his secretary of war called an insurrection, but already the movement was outflanking its opponents. A crowd of fifteen thousand thronged the railroad depot in Baltimore, blocking all the trains; the militia killed ten people in the crowd, but the blockade continued. In Pittsburgh, crowds battled the militia until the militiamen disbanded and slunk away. The crowd burned the railroad yards, destroying one hundred locomotives and two thousand railroad cars.

The strike and accompanying crowd action spread to Buffalo, New York; Reading, Pennsylvania; Newark, Ohio; Chicago, Illinois; Marshall, Texas; and many more points nationwide. In several cities, the movement became a general strike. In Columbus, Ohio, for example, a crowd calling "Shut up or burn" successfully called out workers at a rolling mill, pipe works, fire clay works, pot works, and planing mill. In Galveston, Texas, black longshoremen struck and won pay equal to that of whites; other black workers struck for a two-dollar-per-day minimum wage; white workers joined the strike and two dollars became the going wage for Galveston. In St. Louis, Missouri, a shadowy "Executive Committee" organized a general strike, closed down almost all of the city's industry, and authorized strikers to run passenger trains and collect fares under their own authority.

Federal troops were rushed from city to city quelling what the government declared an insurrection. Ultimately, President Hayes noted emphatically in his diary, "The strikers" were "put down by *force*." More than one hundred of them were killed in the process.

I gradually discovered that there had been other periods of what mainstream labor historian Irving Bernstein described as "strikes and social upheavals of extraordinary importance, drama, and violence which ripped the cloak of civilized decorum from society, leaving exposed naked class conflict."[3] I had of course heard about the sit-down strikes and the great industrial union organizing campaigns of the 1930s, though there was actually very little historical writing about them available in the 1960s. I had heard of the "Haymarket riots," but I didn't know that more than half a million workers struck in 1886, many of them in a nationwide general strike for the eight-hour day. I had heard of labor leader and Socialist presidential candidate Eugene Victor Debs, but I didn't know anything about the huge strikes in all basic industries—steel, coal, and railroads—in the mid-1890s. Nor did I know anything about the big strike waves during and after World War I and World War II. And I couldn't find a single book or article dealing with such periods as a general phenomenon, nor a single book or article besides Robert Bruce's dealing with even one such period as a whole.

As I dug further, I began to piece together a picture of repeated, massive, and sometimes violent revolts by American workers. The story included virtually nationwide general strikes, the seizure of vast industrial establishments, nonviolent direct action on a massive scale, guerrilla warfare, and armed battles with artillery and aircraft.

Such actions called up for me a vision of how ordinary people might liberate themselves from those who oppressed them. They showed people who had been divided and apparently powerless coming together for what I would later call common preservation. It showed them confronting and sometimes defeating the greatest powers in the land. Could that story, I wondered, still be relevant?

22

IF THEY CAN DO IT, WHY CAN'T WE?

ða

ALTHOUGH IT WAS NOT WIDELY RECOGNIZED THEN OR SINCE, THE LATE 1960S AND early 1970s was a period of heightened class conflict in the United States that had many elements in common with the mass strikes of the preceding hundred years. Just in 1969 to 1970, for example, Teamsters on a wildcat strike battled national guardsmen throughout the Midwest; an illegal wildcat strike closed the entire US Post Office; and forty-two thousand coal miners closed the West Virginia minefields for twenty-three days in a political strike that forced the state legislature to pass a law to compensate miners with black lung disease.

Labor upheavals were happening in many other countries as well. In 1968, French workers occupied their factories and closed down much of the country for a month; the "hot summer" of 1970 saw militant labor struggles in Italy; and Poland, Czechoslovakia, Britain, and other countries saw mass strikes in the same period. While detailed information and worthwhile analysis were hard to come by in that pre-Internet era, my friends and I followed these developments as best we could; our little homemade journal *Root & Branch* published a study of the French occupations and through friends studying at the University of Pittsburgh I had a chance to meet some of the young Italian militants. These events and discussions influenced the way I viewed American mass strikes and helped persuade me that their history might still be relevant.

The largest of the US strikes of the 1970s was a national wildcat of postal workers. Working with the writer and activist Stanley Aronowitz, I closely followed the strike, wrote about it for *Root & Branch*,[1] and tried to become involved in spreading it.

A government study in 1968 reported "widespread disquiet" among postal workers as a result of "antiquated personnel practices," "appalling working conditions," and "limited career opportunities."[2] The disquiet finally exploded in New York City, where high living costs forced many postal workers onto welfare to supplement incomes eroded by the inflation of the late 1960s. After several small wildcats and "sick-outs," letter carriers voted to strike on May 17, 1970, and set up picket lines around the city's post offices. Twenty-five thousand drivers and clerks honored the picket lines, bringing postal operations to a halt. Within two days the strike had been joined by workers throughout New York, New Jersey, and Connecticut. The strikers organized themselves through informal channels; within two days the New York local reported it had received phone calls from letter carriers in 589 communities saying they would join the strike.

It was a felony for government employees to strike, and the courts quickly issued an injunction against the New York strikers. The head of the national letter carriers union sent a telegram to the head of the New York local threatening to expel the local; the local president then urged members to return to work. Meanwhile the postmaster general made a deal with postal union leaders to "urge their striking workers back to work in return for prompt consideration of their demands." But six thousand workers in Chicago, the postal system's central hub, voted to join the strike. The next day New York postal workers voted to defy their leaders and the back-to-work agreement. "Branding their national union leaders 'rats' and 'creeps' for urging a return to work" the rank and file "roared their refusal to accept the proposed settlement."[3] By March 21, the strike had spread to more than two hundred cities and towns nationwide. Despite pleas from the seven major postal unions, more than two hundred thousand postal workers in fifteen states ultimately joined the wildcat.

Even more alarming to government and union officials, the strike seemed on the verge of spreading to other public employees. The head of one national government union reported he had to intervene personally to prevent several strikes in his locals. Another said his locals throughout the country wanted to strike in support of the postal workers. "The strike definitely could spread throughout the Federal Service." Another top union official said that "tremendous pressure" was being put on the union to authorize strikes, especially in "one of our biggest locals whose primary duty is to supply our war effort in Southeast Asia."

> We have been receiving phone calls from our various local presidents in various agencies throughout the government and throughout the country. They have watched events of the past days and have seen postal workers striking with a degree of impunity, and their question to us is, if they can do it, why can't we?[4]

A handful of radicals in Washington, D.C. (calling ourselves the Ad Hoc Committee of Government Employees to Support the Strike, which most of us were not) passed out a leaflet headlined "If They Did It, Why Can't We?"

The New York postal strikers have suddenly shown how much power government workers have—if they will use it. Now the decision to support and spread the strike is up to you. It is up to you whether you will use the power you have—or lose it.

If the strike is defeated, Congress will act to punish postal workers, and make future action impossible for all government workers, taking away those few rights they now possess. The only way government employees can defend their own interests is to broaden the strike.

Only by using their power can they even protect their own living standards. The proposed 5.7% pay increase for government classified employees is not enough to offset current inflation—especially in a high cost-of-living area like Washington.

Government workers in all areas are poised on the edge of joining the strike. But they will have to do it on their own, the way the postal workers did it in New York—they cannot wait for the unions. The unions have already shown they will not call a strike—they are afraid of government higher-ups.

Talk with people in your work unit. Then send somebody around to sound out others about it. Only by such democratic discussion can government workers decide if they really want to strike—not by waiting for orders from above.[5]

Not surprisingly, our call did not provoke a general strike of government employees. We heard from the grapevine that it was passed out and discussed in a number of government offices, that a few people did in fact walk out (not necessarily as a result of our leaflet), and that a few people were disciplined for one or the other act.

Meanwhile, President Lyndon Johnson declared a national emergency and ordered twenty-five thousand US Army and National Guard troops into New York to break the strike at its most militant point. Echoing the coal miners' adage, "You can't mine coal with bayonets," strikers retorted, "You can't sort mail with bayonets." We heard that many soldiers fraternized with strikers and deliberately created chaos inside post offices to support them.

Though the administration maintained that it would not negotiate until the postal workers returned to work, congressional leaders pledged that they would act immediately on pay increases as soon as the strike was over. A meeting of five hundred local union officials agreed to end the strike but ordered their union president to call a new national strike unless their demands were quickly met. As negotiations began, the New York local constantly threatened to trigger another strike and even called a rump meeting of local leaders from throughout the country to discuss plans for a coordinated slowdown. Congress granted an immediate 6 percent pay increase to all government workers and an additional 8 percent for postal workers.

The 1970 postal wildcat presented a very different picture from the conventional story of unions and strikes, but it fit with many of the patterns I was finding in the history of mass strikes. It emerged unexpectedly. It seemed to be rooted less in the initiative of organizers or pre-anointed leaders than in workers' daily life problems and experience. Workers organized themselves and acted on their own. They reached out to each other across institutional, geographic, and sub-cultural boundaries. They had to confront and resist their own established union leaders. They made use of their ability to halt production to exercise power vis-à-vis their direct employer and even the US government. They had to stand up against government repression, up to and including the US Army. When they did so they acquired the power to change their lives.

My puny efforts to spread the strike were surely ill-conceived, but they grew out of a passionate desire to find a way to expand that power.

23
GENERAL STRIKE AGAINST WAR?

ôà

THE FIRST VIETNAM WAR TEACH-IN AT THE UNIVERSITY OF MICHIGAN IN 1965 HAD originally been conceived as a "moratorium" in which students and teachers would stay away from classes as a protest against the war. The moratorium idea continued to percolate. As opposition to the war grew, antiwar activists proposed a nationwide moratorium. Initially conceived as a general strike against the war, it was watered down to more conventional protests by leaders who, as the *New York Times* put it, "liked the idea of political action but not the threat of a strike." On October 15, 1969, millions of people around the world participated in the first Vietnam Moratorium. A month later an estimated half a million people protested against the war in Washington, D.C., while millions back home participated in local Moratorium activities. Organizers announced plans to make the local Moratorium a regular monthly protest.

I wrote an article for *Liberation Magazine*[1] and promulgated a few fly-ers proposing to move the moratorium movement toward a series of general strikes. I argued that this would give the people some actual power to stop the war, something that other techniques, from draft resistance to electoral opposition to demonstrations, did not seem to provide. (I had support in this effort from prominent antiwar leader Dave Dellinger, who even paid for one of the flyers.)

The *Liberation Magazine* article criticized three tendencies in the antiwar movement. One was the innocent hope that the expression of antiwar sentiment in itself would somehow sway the government to change its course. I noted that a Gallup Poll showed that a bill to withdraw all US troops from Vietnam within a year was supported nearly two-to-one, but that the war went on nonetheless.

The second was to move opposition into the electoral arena, continuing the 1968 Kennedy-McCarthy movement. Such a strategy failed to recognize that the real power over government action didn't lie in electoral bodies, and that peace candidates had repeatedly turned out to be largely opportunistic.

The third was an escalation of confrontation in the streets. Such confrontation didn't offer any way of actually taking control of the country. But "since confrontation can always be interpreted as a deliberate provocation of violence, it plays directly into the hands of the authorities, who through their control of the press can make even a nonviolent confrontation appear a deliberate act of violence." Confrontationists would either try to make future Moratoriums more militant or generate confrontations through separate demonstrations and organizations. "The result will be a tendency toward splitting of the movement, falling off of mass support, new vulnerability to government attack, and no doubt a few concussions."

All these tendencies were rooted in the idea that the real power to stop the war lay in Washington. But it was not the government officials in Washington who did the work and fought the wars. "Rather, it is the people—the same people who support two-to-one the withdrawal of all US troops from Vietnam. If they refuse to work—if they strike—the war must end." To end the war, "the Moratorium must more and more become a general strike against the war. It is here that the real power of the movement lies, not in playing politics or playing with violence."

Throughout the country, workplace committees had sprung up spontaneously to coordinate participation in the Moratorium demonstrations. In New York, for example, Moratorium committees were formed by employees in each of the major newspapers, television stations, and publishing houses; in Boston, by secretaries and lab workers at MIT; in Washington, D.C., by workers in various government agencies. I proposed that war opponents form such workplace organizations wherever they could:

> Set up a Moratorium or strike committee where you work. Coordinate directly with other workplace organizations. Organize teach-ins, educational meetings, and participation in Moratorium-day demonstrations among your co-workers. Move these actions as rapidly as possible toward mass walkouts.

It was not to be. After the second Moratorium, the national leadership of the movement simply shut down its office and told people to focus on local organizing. Soon many of its leaders resurfaced in campaigns for candidates in the 1970 congressional elections. As I had feared, the antiwar movement polarized between electoral and street action.

While my initiative had some plausibility in the hothouse political climate of the day (*Time* headlined its cover story on the Moratorium "Strike against the War") my proposal for a general strike was completely abstract. I had little concept of smaller, more concrete actions that might build in that direction; of intermediate targets where mass pressure might force institutions to withdraw support from the war; or of how to link varied interests to broaden support for such actions. I lacked "feedback loops" that could have allowed my abstract ideas to be corrected by concrete reality and the perspectives of other people. As the chorus of a country song wryly puts it, "Oh, to be sixteen again and know what I know now!"

24

STRIKE!

ॐ

As we agonized over how to end the war in Vietnam, I often talked about the story of mass upheavals I was piecing together from American labor history. Finally one day Marc Raskin at the Institute for Policy Studies told me it was time to stop talking about it and start writing. He got me a book contract with a publishing company being set up by *Rolling Stone* magazine, and I went to work on a book that I originally called *Mass Strike in America* that Straight Arrow Books published under the provocative title *Strike!*

While *Strike!* was ostensibly a work of history and described past events in considerable detail, it was driven by an effort to find underlying historical patterns that might help guide action in the present—a "presentism" that more conventional historians often condemn. Indeed, it was written out of pressing political concerns.

In the struggle against the Vietnam War we had won the public debate, helped persuade the majority of Americans to oppose the war, mobilized millions of people to act, and engaged in massive confrontations with the forces of authority. Yet we didn't seem to have power to stop the war. The mass strikes of the past, whether successful or not, seemed like laboratories of how ordinary people had organized themselves at the grassroots and then used their collective power to contest the power of those who ruled them. I wanted to know what lessons we could learn from them.

Young workers and above all military veterans returning from Vietnam were challenging management authority in American factories. Yet there was more hostility than mutual support between this workplace resistance and the movements opposing the war and making a more general critique of capitalism and imperialism. I wanted to help form a junction between working-class discontent and the New Left, to reduce the elitist anti-worker sentiment that permeated the New Left, and at the same time to help rehabilitate the traditions of working-class radicalism. I saw the history of mass strikes as a medium for all those purposes.

In the late 1960s, the New Left had largely lost its compass. Participatory democracy had been a productive idea, but the dialogue around it in SDS hadn't gone very far. I wanted to extend it to the sphere of production—the workplace. And I wanted to envision a far deeper, indeed revolutionary, social change that would replace existing power centers with forms of popular self-management. But I wanted to find a way that revolutionary social change could empower ordinary working people rather than new elites—including elites spawned by the Leninist organizations to which many New Leftists were then turning. I hoped that the history of mass strikes might illuminate the way.

In the Introduction to an early account of the 1936 to 1937 sit-down strikes in Flint, Michigan, two union leaders observed that there was "an iron curtain between the people and their past" designed to deny "the sense of strength and direction for the future" that history could provide to "the millions of men and women who labor for their living."[1] Since that time, there has been a great expansion of labor history and the histories of other oppressed groups, notably women, African Americans, and other racially defined minorities. But the "iron curtain" separating Americans from the history of their working-class revolts has by no means been lifted. A student who hears about the Great Upheaval and consults the *Encarta Encyclopedia*, for example, will learn no more than that "In the railroad workers' strike of 1877, federal troops had to be used to restore order."[2] *Strike!* aimed to break down that iron curtain.

In 1970 I left Washington, D.C., and went back to my family home in Connecticut to write *Strike!* I was hardly well prepared for the task. I had taken only one brief American history course in college, and I had never even met a real live labor historian until after *Strike!* was completed. Nonetheless, I resolved not to go anywhere—except the stacks of the Yale Library—until it was done.

25

SIT-DOWN

&

I HAD HEARD SINCE CHILDHOOD OF THE GREAT SIT-DOWN STRIKES OF THE 1930S. I
even knew a song about them:

> When they tie a can to a union man
> Sit down! Sit down!
> Sit down, and rest your feet
> Sit down, you've got 'em beat
> Sit down! Sit down![1]

I had always heard the sit-downs described as the action of unions to win recognition from American corporations. But as I began to discover long-forgotten
first-person accounts of the sit-downs from people such as the immigrant worker
and writer Louis Adamic,[2] the Akron *Beacon-Journal* reporter Ruth McKenney,[3] the auto union publicist Henry Kraus,[4] and the *New York Times* labor
journalist A. H. Raskin, a very different picture began to emerge. The actual
origin and history of the sit-down strike wave of the 1930s illustrates how the
story of mass strikes I was uncovering differed from conventional accounts of
American labor. It also illustrates what I was learning from my study of labor
history about what today I would call self-organization and the emergence of
common preservation.

In the early decades of the twentieth century, a huge industrial zone devoted
to autos, auto parts, and tires developed in the American Midwest. Millions of
workers from the American South and around the world poured into cities like
Detroit, Flint, and Cleveland. With the coming of the Great Depression of the
1930s, these workers suffered mass unemployment, job insecurity, and intense
speed-up at work. Workers who had made relatively good wages during the boom
years of the 1920s found themselves working to the point of exhaustion for less
than it took to live on.

Competing with each other for jobs and divided by ethnicity and race, workers seemed to have little choice but to accept the conditions they faced. A worker in the rubber capital of America—Akron, Ohio—wrote plaintively to the local paper, "Only our machines are alive. We must treat them with respect or they turn against us." The previous week a mill had swallowed one worker's hand and part of his arm. "The mills stopped only long enough for us to pull him out, and then they resumed their steady turn." He concluded fatalistically, "We've nothing to look forward to. We're factory hands."[5]

Akron workers did have common problems and to some extent a common identity as rubber workers. They did try to organize unions, but they met severe obstacles. Union activists were often summarily fired. Ethnic and racial conflict blocked cooperation. Above all, unaccountable union leaderships repeatedly threatened to strike, then signed agreements with rubber companies that left intolerable labor conditions unchanged. In the wake of one such agreement, union membership in Akron's Summit County dropped from forty thousand to five thousand.

Then workers in Akron developed a new tactic—halting work and sitting down in the workplace—which they themselves could directly control without need for any outside leaders. When writer Louis Adamic visited Akron in 1936 and asked how the sit-downs had begun, he was told that the first had occurred not in a rubber factory but at a baseball game. During one of the periods of union upsurge, players from two factories refused to play because the umpire was not a union man. They simply sat down on the diamond while the crowd yelled for a union umpire until the non-union umpire was replaced.

Not long after, a dispute developed between a dozen rubber workers and their supervisor. The workers turned off their machines and sat down. Production throughout the highly integrated plant ground to a halt. Other workers wanted to know what had happened. "There was a sit-down at such-and-such a depart-ment." "A sit-down?" "Yeah, a sit-down; don't you know what a sit-down is, you dope? Like what happened at the ball game the other Sunday." In less than an hour, management acceded to the workers demands.

As Adamic wrote, "Sitting by their machines, cauldrons, boilers, and work benches, they talked. Some realized *for the first time* how important they were in the process of rubber production. Twelve men had practically stopped the works. Any dozen or score of them could do it!"[6]

According to Adamic, the sit-downs established connections and broke down barriers in what had been a fragmented mass of workers. "The sit-down is a social affair. Sitting workers talk. They get acquainted." One Goodyear gum-miner told Adamic, "Why, my God, man, during the sit-downs last spring I found out that the guy who works next to me is the same as I am, even if I was born in West Virginia and he is from Poland. His grievances are the same. Why shouldn't we stick?"

Between 1933 and 1936 the sit-down gradually became a tradition in Akron. It became an accepted norm that when one group of workers stopped working, everyone else along the line sat down too. Some sit-downs closed entire factory complexes. Fear of the sit-downs eventually helped pressure rubber company managements to recognize the United Rubber Workers Union.

The Akron sit-downs became the inspiration for similar actions elsewhere. According to the Bureau of Labor Statistics, nearly four hundred thousand US workers engaged in sit-downs in 1937—not counting innumerable "quickies" of less than a day. In Flint, Michigan, a huge sit-down closed much of General Motors and forced it to recognize the United Auto Workers Union. The idea spread like wildfire. Sit-downs occurred not only in factories but also in stores, restaurants, hospitals, government offices, state legislatures, prisons, high schools, and movie theaters. The threat of the sit-down eventually helped persuade bitterly anti-union employers in rubber, steel, auto, and other industries to recognize unions—out of fear of something worse.

Workers continued using sit-downs in auto and other plants even after the unions won recognition. But the unions did everything they could to stop them. A *New York Times* article entitled "Unauthorized Sit-Downs Fought by CIO Unions" reported that "as soon as an unauthorized strike occurs or impends, international officers or representatives of the UAW are rushed to the scene to end or prevent it, get the men back to work and bring about an orderly adjustment of the grievances." Organizers and representatives were informed that they would be dismissed "if they authorize any stoppages of work without the consent of the international officers." "Hot-heads" and "trouble-makers" were "purged." According to the *Times,* the continuing sit-downs were due in part to "dissatisfaction on the part of the workers with the union itself," making them "as willing in some cases to defy their own leaders as their bosses."[7]

A spokesperson explained the CIO's opposition to sit-downs: "The first experience of the CIO with sit-downs was in discouraging them. This was in the Akron rubber industry." CIO representatives cautioned the new unionists against sit-downs on the grounds that "they should use such channels for negotiating grievances as the agreement provided." He added, "When collective bargaining is fully accepted, union recognition accorded and an agreement reached, CIO unionists accept full responsibility for carrying out their side of it in a disciplined fashion, and oppose sit-downs or any other strike action while it is in force." CIO President John L. Lewis was even more blunt: "A CIO contract is adequate protection against sit-downs, lie-downs, or any other kind of strike."[8]

While every mass strike has a different history, they also have a family resemblance. The sit-down strike wave of the 1930s—like the Great Upheaval of 1877—illustrates some of these common patterns. Its roots lay in the conditions, experiences, and traditions of rank-and-file workers. In the course of their daily lives they discovered the conditions and interests they shared. Small struggles and rebellions revealed the power they could develop by acting together. These tended to spread to larger and larger groups of workers. In each case the movement was met by a combination of repression, concession, and cooptation.

When *Strike!* was written, the great American auto, rubber, and steel industries from which the sit-downs emerged were still in place and their workers were still a significant power, organized informally in the workplace and formally in unions, with continuing tension between the two as revealed by the wildcat strikes of the era. Since then, vertically and horizontally integrated national corporations that can be brought to a standstill by factory occupations have been transformed into global corporations that can move their operations all over the world to escape recalcitrant workers; unions have been reduced to a small fraction of the workforce; and informal work groups have been disrupted by the conversion to contingent work. If there are mass strikes in America in the future they will be as different from the sit-downs of the 1930s as the sit-downs were from the Great Upheaval of 1877.

If there are lessons to be learned from these experiences, they are not just about industrial class struggle, but about the wider process of self-organization and social change. The sit-downs still reveal the capacity of people who are disorganized and divided to join together for common preservation. And they still reveal the power of the apparently powerless when they act in concert.

26

INTERPRETING MASS STRIKES

೫

WHAT WAS I TO MAKE OF THE INCREDIBLE STRIKE STORIES I WAS UNCOVERING IN DUSTY history books, moldering newspapers, and tattered archival documents? As I assembled the story of American mass strikes from the bits and pieces I tracked down in the library, I found little in the way of an interpretive tradition to draw on to understand it.

Conventional academic labor history largely ignored mass strikes or treated them as irrational aberrations on the way to orderly collective bargaining. Left historians held a surprisingly similar view, focusing on the organization of unions and political movements more than on what workers themselves were doing. A collection of self-styled New Left historical writings published in 1969 had only one essay dealing with the industrial working class, titled "Urbanization, Migration, and Social Mobility in Late Nineteenth-Century America." It concluded, without the slightest reference to the three great periods of mass strike in late nineteenth-century America, that "what stands out most is the relative absence of collective working-class protest aimed at reshaping capitalist society."[1]

I scratched around for whatever guidance I could find. It was a crucial breakthrough when I discovered Rosa Luxemburg's short book *The Mass Strike, the Political Party and the Trade Unions.* Drawing on the Russian Revolution of 1905 and other class struggles in Europe, Luxemburg developed the concept of the "mass strike." The mass strike, she emphasized, signifies not just a single act but a whole period of class struggle:

> Its use, its effects, its reasons for coming about are in a constant state of flux ... political and economic strikes, united and partial strikes, defensive strikes and combat strikes, general strikes of individual sections of industry and general strikes of entire cities, peaceful wage strikes and street battles, uprisings with barricades—all run together and run along side each other,

get in each other's way, overlap each other; a perpetually moving and changing sea of phenomena.[2]

That sounded a whole lot like what I was discovering.

I found other, largely forgotten traditions from the radical working-class movement that were also of some help. Anton Pannekoek was a Dutch astronomer and Marxist theorist whom Lenin had once celebrated—but subsequently excoriated in a pamphlet called *Left-Wing Communism: An Infantile Disorder.* He had worked with Luxemburg and continued developing similar ideas for decades after her assassination; his book *Workers' Councils*[3] provided many of the ideas I appropriated.

Pannekoek viewed both Leninist and social democratic parties as attempts to replace capitalism with rule by a new elite. He saw trade unions as organizations created by workers to meet their needs; but their role as a means to reach agreement with employers tended to turn them into vehicles for subordinating workers to old or new elites. Workers frequently fought their subordination both to employers and to their own unions through wildcat strikes and other forms of action they controlled themselves.

Pannekoek portrayed the strike committees and other organizations that workers improvise in the course of wildcat strikes as a form of grassroots democratic control that could become the nucleus of a society genuinely governed by rank-and-file workers themselves. He advocated a revolutionary process in which workers, coordinating their action through such organs, would directly take control of production, begin to produce on their own behalf, and disarm and disband the expropriated employers' agents of violence and repression.

Pannekoek's approach drew on the organizations known variously as soviets, factory councils, or workers councils that sprang up in Russia, Germany, Italy, Britain, and elsewhere at the close of World War I. They were composed of representatives of workers from different local factories who periodically sent delegates to wider regional and national councils. They served both to coordinate workers struggles and, in many places where owners and managers had fled or been driven out, took over control of production and civil authority.

In Russia, the power of these councils (soviets) was broken by the Communist Party. In Germany they were made subservient to the government by the Social-Democratic Party. In each case they helped a left party come to power, only to have it suppress their efforts to establish workers control in industry. Yet in Pannekoek's view, such workers councils might in the future provide the starting point for a new form of social organization with no bosses—whether capitalists or government bureaucrats—ruling over the working class.

I had the privilege of long conversations with Paul Mattick, the most important apostle of the workers council tradition in the United States.[4] I collaborated

on *Root & Branch* with his son and political disciple Paul Mattick, Jr. While I
never fully accepted what I considered the Marxist ultra-orthodoxy of "council
communism" (the senior Paul Mattick had once written a book whose title, *The
Inevitability of Communism*,[5] epitomized for me the absurdity of Marxism as a
set of "iron laws"), I applied as much as I could of it to understanding American
labor history.

I drew on whatever other sources I could find. I happened upon the writings
of Martin Glaberman, an auto worker in Detroit and a follower of the Trotskyist
writer C. L. R. James, which provided a complementary view.[6] I discovered an
article called "USA—The Labor Revolt" by longshoreman and labor educator
Stan Weir that put the wildcat strikes and union opposition movements of the
1960s in a similar perspective.[7] I absorbed anarchist theorists like Georges Sorel.

Most of all, I drew on the indigenous traditions of American workers, as represented in movements such as the Knights of Labor and the Industrial Workers
of the World. These traditions viewed the corporate capitalist concentration
of wealth as a subversion of democratic government by a new autocracy. They
rejected wage labor as a fundamental violation of human freedom. They saw
the struggle for the emancipation of labor as a continuation of the struggle to
abolish slavery. And they saw economic cooperation under the control of workers as an alternative both to competition and to domination. In the documents
of the struggles I was studying I found revealing interpretations by participants
of what they were doing and what it meant. My interpretation was most deeply
influenced by them. They inducted me into seeing mass strikes as episodes in
the self-liberation of working people. I found in them a lost historical tradition
for participatory democracy.

As *Strike!* was being written, labor history itself was being revolutionized
by E. P. Thompson, David Montgomery, Herbert Gutman, and others. This
"new labor history" eschewed the institutional preoccupation that had marked
the old labor history in favor of an emphasis on workers' own activity and self-
organization. But most of their work, which would later have a big impact on
me, was not available in time to influence *Strike!* Ironically, the book was more
influenced by traditional labor history and labor economics that viewed conservative American trade unionism as a pragmatic adaptation by privileged "aristocrats
of labor" to their opportunities within American capitalism. I drew heavily on
that older, more conservative interpretation of unionism and collective bargaining, while inverting its celebration of American trade unionism's conservatism
to condemnation.

I also drew on a tradition within American sociology that—starting with Robert
E. Park and E. T. Hiller in the 1920s and continuing through Alvin Gouldner
in the 1960s—analyzed labor struggles as social movements. These sociologists
conducted extensive studies of working-class conditions and strikes. They often

emphasized the role of informal work groups and the importance of what workers themselves thought and did, recognizing that, as a sociological study of the 1919 steel strike put it, "Strike conditions are conditions of mind."[8]

Strike!'s emphasis on periods of mass strike, worker self-organization, and endemic conflict between unions and workers has not found a great deal of resonance among subsequent historians of American labor. It no doubt underemphasized periods of worker quiescence, the role of organizers, and the positive contributions of labor organizations. Yet it would also be a mistake to ignore the reality of those periods of strikes and social upheavals of "extraordinary importance, drama, and violence" which "ripped the cloak of civilized decorum from society, leaving exposed naked class conflict." Understanding what I called the mass strike process can still teach us much both about the actual history of the working class and about the emergence of new common preservations.

27

CLASS AND POWER
THE KEYS TO THE WORKSHOP

ঌ

MY INVOLVEMENT WITH LABOR HISTORY HAD ROOTS IN MY OWN AND MY PEERS' feelings of powerlessness in the face of the war in Vietnam, nuclear holocaust, and our probable future work lives. I wrote in the Introduction to *Strike!:* "The greatest problem we face today is our powerlessness. It underlies every particular problem we face: war, pollution, racism, brutality, injustice, insecurity, and the feeling of being trapped, our lives wasting away, pushed around by forces beyond our control." These problems resulted from the fact that "we do not control the life of our own society. The fundamental problem we face—and the key to solving the more particular problems—is to transform society so that ordinary people control it."[1]

I found in the traditions of the radical labor movement both explanations of such powerlessness and strategies for challenging it. While I now recognize that those traditions frequently reduced complex questions to deceptively simple answers, I believe they can still help illuminate the very different conditions we face today.

Many nineteenth-century American workers saw wage labor as akin to slavery and even referred to it as "wage slavery." They saw the rise of large corporations as creating a new form of tyranny. They envisioned the working-class movement as a freedom struggle that continued the American Revolution's fight against British oppression and the struggle against slavery conducted by the abolitionists and the Union forces in the Civil War.

In this tradition, workers were seen as sharing a common problem: They don't own or control society's means of production, or even the means to produce their own livelihood. Therefore they have little choice but to sell their capacity to work to those who do. The result is that all workers share a subordination to the control of employers, who have the power to make decisions that shape their daily lives.[2] While this perspective is often associated with Karl Marx, it was pervasive in working-class movements before Marx and widely shared by non-Marxist and anti-Marxist workers.

This was not a natural predicament or even a longstanding one. Its origins could be traced historically. They were vividly apparent to machinist Terence Powderly, Grand Master Workman of the Knights of Labor, not a revolutionary or a Marxist, who in 1889 looked back over the changes he had observed in his lifetime:

> With the introduction of machinery, large manufacturing establishments were erected in the cities and towns. Articles that were formerly made by hand, were turned out in large quantities by machinery; prices were lowered, and those who worked by hand found themselves competing with something that could withstand hunger and cold and not suffer in the least. The village blacksmith shop was abandoned, the road-side shoe shop was deserted, the tailor left his bench, and all together these mechanics [workers] turned away from their country homes and wended their way to the cities wherein the large factories had been erected. The gates were unlocked in the morning to allow them to enter, and after their daily task was done the gates were closed after them in the evening.

They no longer carried the keys of the workshop, "for workshop, tools and keys belonged not to them, but to their master."[3]

The enormous expansion of industry after the Civil War had transformed millions of people who had grown up as farmers and self-employed artisans and entrepreneurs into employees, growing armies of whom were concentrated within each of the new corporate empires. Their work was no longer individual and competitive, but group-oriented and cooperative; they no longer directed their own work, but worked under the control of a boss; they no longer possessed the property on which they could work and retain the fruits of their labor, and therefore they could have no livelihood unless someone with property agreed to purchase their labor.

The process of differentiation into "masters" or, as we would say today, employers, and "those who no longer carried the keys of the workshop," or workers, has continued since that time. I learned from Gabriel Kolko's book *Wealth and Power in America* that in 1951 one-fifth of one percent of American "spending units" owned between 65 and 71 percent of all the marketable corporate stock held by individuals.[4] Since then, such concentrated ownership of the means of production has only intensified.[5] It doesn't take a séance with Karl Marx to see that those who lack such wealth are generally going to have to work for those who have it.

These facts went against the grain of the belief that the United States is a classless society. While the United States is often presumed to be a land of individual freedom, most of our society's resources have long been controlled by a few. The rest have no way to make a living except to sell their capacity to work. Most Americans are—by no choice of their own—workers. The basic experience of being a worker—of not having sufficient economic resources to live except by going to work for someone else—shapes most people's daily lives, as well as the life of our society. Individually, workers are powerless and unfree.

Meanwhile, the wealth created by the labor of the many is captured by a tiny minority, primarily through ownership of large corporations that dominate the national and now the global economy. They control the labor of millions of people in the United States and worldwide. The wealth and power of corporations and those who own them is further parlayed into power over the media, the political process, the institutions that shape knowledge and opinion, and ultimately over the government. Workers are thereby rendered relatively powerless, as individuals, even in supposedly democratic societies. Oversimplified as it may be, this critique of the belief that the United States is a classless society remains valid today.

Underlying this approach is the idea that powerlessness grows out of dependence. Others can have power over us when they are able to exclude us from that which we need to survive or pursue our goals. Workers are excluded from control over the large-scale, technologically advanced, integrated means of production that are necessary to make wealth in modern society. Indeed, all except a tiny minority are excluded from that control. This—I thought somewhat simplistically—was a key to understanding the powerlessness my peers and I experienced and observed in so many spheres. I later learned to view class inequality as one example of a broader pattern of differentiation, unequal dependence, and powerlessness not just in class relations, but in many other social relations as well.

28

WORKERS' POWER

ò.

ALTHOUGH THEY RECOGNIZED THE ENORMOUS POWER OF CAPITAL, THE RADICAL working-class traditions I was discovering were uncowed. For, as the labor anthem "Solidarity Forever" put it, "In our hands is placed a power greater than their hoarded gold." Workers as individuals might be powerless, but they are not alone in this condition. They share it with their coworkers and other people who are also workers. When workers see themselves as having interests in common with other workers and in conflict with their employers, they may turn to collective rather than individual strategies for solving their problems. As I studied labor history, I discovered this process recurring in the lives of individuals, the experience of social groups, and the history of the United States and indeed the wider world.

When workers begin to pursue collective strategies, they discover they have far greater power together than they have alone. They are the great majority in any workplace, community, or country. All the functions of their employer—in fact of society—depend on their labor. By withdrawing their labor and by refusing to cooperate with established authorities in other ways, they can bring any workplace, community, or even country to a halt. Mass strikes, like the Great Upheaval of 1877 and the sit-down strikes of the 1930s, revealed the power of workers to virtually stop society, counter the forces of repression, and organize cooperative action on an extended scale.

The same historical process that made workers individually powerless made them collectively powerful—potentially. Paradoxically, employers and other social institutions were dependent on workers *as a group* for everything—including their own power. As I put it in *Strike!:* "Ordinary people—together—have potentially the greatest power of all." It is their activity that makes up society. "If they refuse to work, the country stops. If they take control of their own activity, their own work, they thereby take control of society."[1]

Strike! emphasized that the power thereby created was not the same as the power of employers and other authorities. "Today, power means the power of some people to tell others what to do." But the power created by mass strikes and other worker action was "the power of people directing their own action cooperatively toward common purposes." Ordinary people could only have power over social life "when power as we have known it—power of some people over others—is dissolved completely."[2]

Workers have made use of their potential power in ways ranging from on-the-job resistance to strikes against a single employer to wider forms of solidarity. In *Strike!* I told a story of how, under different conditions, American workers discovered and rediscovered that power.

Participants in mass strikes themselves often believed that the real issue in their struggles was not one or another specific demand but rather the distribution of power, and that this in turn would determine more specific questions of wages, working conditions, and the like. Indeed, the theme reverberates from one mass strike to the next. In the great Southwest Strike of 1886, the workers goal according to historian Ruth Allen was to be recognized by management as "men equally powerful in and responsible for the conduct of the Gould Southwest System" whereas H. M. Hoxie, Gould's top manager on the scene, proclaimed that the time had come "when the question had to be decided whether he should run his own railroad or have the Knights of Labor run it."[3] Half a century later Alfred Sloan, president of General Motors, wrote at the height of the Flint sit-down strike, the "real issue" was, "Will a labor organization run the plants of General Motors" or "will the Management continue to do so?"[4]

From my study of labor history I learned that power that appears unilateral may instead be asymmetrical. Employers exercised power over workers, but workers could acquire counter-power—albeit of a different kind—when they joined together. The need for that power provided a motive for workers to join together to pursue what I would later call common preservation.

THE WORK GROUP
"A GUERRILLA BAND AT WAR WITH MANAGEMENT"

ò·

ONE DAY AROUND 1965 I SAW A CLASSIFIED AD IN *THE NATION* FOR LITERATURE presenting a rank-and-file view of American labor. I wrote away for it and received a packet of pamphlets from a little-known group called Facing Reality, followers of the now-revered but then-obscure Caribbean Marxist writer C. L. R. James. One short pamphlet (unsigned but actually written by Martin Glaberman) published in 1952 titled "Punching Out" had a big impact on me. In straightforward, non-ideological language it described the way workers in the Detroit auto plants organized themselves and used guerrilla resistance tactics to improve their lives on the job. They controlled the pace of work to provide break time for each other; got rid of unpopular foremen by secretly sabotaging production; and turned the shop floor into an informal beauty parlor, restaurant, credit union, and (birthday) party headquarters. "Punching Out" portrayed such actions as an indication that workers' position in production led them to collective action in their own interest that contradicted the logic of capitalism at even the most intimate level. I later found similar views in the writings of rank-and-file longshore activist and labor educator Stan Weir on informal work groups.[1]

My friend and *Root & Branch* collaborator Steve Sapolsky went to Pittsburgh to study labor history with David Montgomery. At that time Montgomery and his students were opening up the whole issue of worker self-organization and resistance on the job and its interaction with scientific management and other employer efforts to control the work process. Little of their research had been published yet. Steve sent me a draft of a paper he was writing on the use of informal on-the-job resistance and some of Montgomery's not-yet-published papers, circulating *samizdat* among his graduate students.

Since workers usually avoid publicizing their tactics for informal resistance on the job, Montgomery and his students were mining the management literature concerned with the horrors of workers "restriction of output." Some had insights that paralleled those of Martin Glaberman and Stan Weir. In a once-famous study of American factories published in 1946, for example, Elton Mayo wrote that in every department he studied, the workers had, whether aware of it or not, "formed themselves into a group with appropriate customs, duties, routines, even rituals" and "management succeeds (or fails) in proportion as it is accepted without reservation by the group as authority and leader."[2]

I adopted the hypothesis that such informal work groups form the venue in which the invisible, underlying process of the mass strike develops. They are milieus within which workers come into opposition to the employer, begin acting on their own, realize their need to support each other, and discover the collective power they develop in doing so. The end product of this process is the rejection of management as "authority and leader," and the transformation of the work group into what one factory worker–turned-sociologist described as a guerrilla band at war with management.[3]

My friend Steve Sapolsky directed me to a 1946 study of Chicago area factories that described how most work groups established a "quota," which the group expected no individual worker to exceed. A new employee was systematically "indoctrinated" by the work group, which looked to the employee "to conform to its system of social ethics." This system was backed by the workers' knowledge that management would use one worker's higher production as a lever to speed them all up. As one worker expressed it, "They begin by asking you to cut the other guy's throat, but what happens is that everybody's throat is cut, including your own."

Workers created time for themselves to talk, read, and do what they referred to as "government work"—using company facilities to manufacture tools to make their own work easier and to make products for themselves and their friends. This required "a system of social controls imposing, upon the individual, responsibility to the group." Essentially what results is an informal secret organization. Workers employ "a social ethic which requires that each individual realize his own goals (social and pecuniary) through cooperation with the work group."[4]

I discovered that such informal groups had developed right along with the emergence of industrial capitalism and had begun constructing their own vision of their situation and prospects. As machinist and Knights of Labor leader Terence Powderly wrote after describing the transformation of independent craftsmen into employees, "Thrown together in this way, in these large hives of industry, men became acquainted with each other, and frequently discussed the question of labor's rights and wrongs."[5] Another worker's autobiography described how, in the small railroad town of Sedalia, Missouri, in the depression of 1884, a group led by a cobbler and a railroad machinist met night after night, discussing the condition of workers and how to change it; from them came the leaders of future strikes in the area.

Eighty-six years later the *Wall Street Journal* noted that, in response to the recession of 1970, there was a "pickup in 'group therapy sessions,' when employees gather around water coolers and elsewhere to moan about layoffs, past or pending. An office worker at the Otis unit in Cleveland says he noticed that such sessions were well attended 'almost every time I went to the men's room.'"[6]

I got my finishing school on informal on-the-job resistance from Tim Costello, a young fuel oil delivery driver who used to show up occasionally at *Root & Branch* meetings in New York. Tim worked an incredible number of hours, often twelve to fourteen a day, six or seven days a week. He was, however, a world-class expert at stealing time—indeed, he regarded it as the fuel oil drivers' principal form of class struggle. He would entertain us with stories of cooperation among drivers to establish their own work rates for the various jobs. Tim and I became friends and writing collaborators for the next forty years.[7]

I began to think of informal work groups as the cellular units of mass strikes. In them took place a process of group formation, a mutual recognition of common interests, and a move from individual to collective strategies. When those transformations, occurring almost invisibly in myriad workplaces and communities, moved across the borders of the work group, the workplace, the locality, and the ethnic, racial, gender, occupational, and other established boundaries, they produced the great upheavals I was calling mass strikes. While mass strikes appeared to be huge, dramatic events, I came to believe that they actually had their roots in the daily life settings of workplaces and communities. As I put it in *Strike!* mass strikes grew out of the daily problems of ordinary people. "What happens when we go to work or school, make a home, shop, try to make a life, may seem at first glance far removed from making history." But "in trying to solve the problems of their daily lives, people sometimes find they must act in ways which also challenge the whole organization of society."[8]

I've subsequently taken informal self-organization by work groups as a pattern for understanding self-organization more generally. The paradoxical result of pursuing individual self-preservation may be that "everybody's throat is cut, including your own." And in such situations, individuals may develop into a group with a social ethic that requires that "each individual realize his own goals" through cooperation with the group. Such a group formation process did not require indoctrination from the outside. It might emerge as a pragmatic response to a situation in which other strategies amounted to people cutting their own throats—and therefore evoking a shift to what I would now call a strategy of common preservation.

30
"WHATEVER HAPPENED TO THE UNIONS?"

৯

"WHAT EVER HAPPENED TO THE UNIONS?" THAT WAS A CONSTANT REFRAIN AMONG liberals and leftists in my youth. Many people I knew had worked to build unions in the 1930s and 1940s, but they found themselves detached and disillusioned by the 1950s and 1960s. I myself had grown up with a romantic image of the rise of industrial unionism in the 1930s as workers joining together to combat their corporate bosses. But I lived with the reality of unions that pursued labor-management cooperation and were in effect junior partners in American capitalism.

Some blamed the workers themselves. They had gotten too fat. But I wanted an answer that was less of a smug self-justification for people who themselves had abandoned the struggle for a better society. The answer I proposed was perhaps *Strike!*'s most controversial aspect.

Periods of mass discontent revealed that workers could coordinate action on a large scale. They started with their own work groups. Action spread from there. Classic labor historian John R. Commons, no friend of mass strikes, described how the 1886 strike wave began with "spontaneous outbreaks of unorganized masses." For example, when a ten-hour day law passed by the Michigan legislature was not enforced, "in response, and with little previous organization, the predominantly Polish and American workers in the lumber and shingle mills struck for an immediate ten-hour day with no reduction in pay. The strikers marched in a body from mill to mill, demanding that the men quit work, and shut down the entire lumber industry."[1]

Coordination could spread far and wide despite the absence of preexisting formal organization. Virtually all unions had been broken in the years leading up to the Great Upheaval, for example, but, as Robert Bruce observed, workers were able to act in concert out of a "sense of unity" that was "not embodied in any centralized plan or leadership, but in the feelings and action of each participant." The editor of the *Labor Standard* pointed out that "there was no concert of action at the start. It spread because the workmen in Pittsburgh felt the same

114

oppression that was felt by the workmen of West Virginia and so with the workmen of Chicago and St. Louis." Bruce recorded that in Newark, Ohio, "no single individual seemed to command" the strikers. "They followed the sense of the meeting, as Quakers might say," on proposals any of them put forward. "Yet they proceeded with notable coherence, as though fused by their common adversity."[2]

When workers wanted to make their relations more permanent, they organized unions. Initially these might simply be vehicles to perpetuate the organization of work groups and their connections. The first unions were just associations of workers in the same trade in a given locality.

Unions could serve simply as the means for linking worker-initiated activity. In the 1894 Pullman boycott, as Eugene Victor Debs, president of the American Railway Union explained, "The committees came from all yards and from all roads to confer with us. The switchmen, for instance, would send a committee to us, and we would authorize that committee to act for that yard or for that road, and that committee would then go to that yard and take charge of the affairs."[3] The informal structure of strike committees allowed the improvised coordination of hundreds of thousands of strikers and supporters over a vast area of the country despite the lack of organized preparations.

However, over time most unions developed a leadership separate from the rank and file. They developed a permanent bureaucracy of organizers, officials, and professionals that could serve as a political machine for the leadership. They in turn developed institutional interests distinct from those of their members. This process had been traced by a wide range of analysts, from radicals such as Sidney and Beatrice Webb and Antonio Gramsci to conservative scholars including the American labor economist E. A. Ross.

I found divisions between union leaders and the rank and file almost ubiquitous in US labor history. As early as the 1880s, labor historian John Commons found that "extreme bitterness toward capital manifested itself in all the actions of the Knights of Labor, and whenever the leaders undertook to hold it within bounds they were generally discarded by their followers, and others who would lead as directed were placed in charge."[4] Indeed, Knights leader Terence Powderly issued a "secret circular" designed to sabotage the burgeoning movement for an eight-hour day.[5] Eighty-five years later we could see the same phenomenon in the 1970 postal wildcat strike: union officials attempting to undermine strikes and other independent action by their own rank and file.

In periods of mass strike, workers often organized unions or used existing unions as vehicles for coordinating their activity and confronting management and government. But they also frequently found existing unions and their leadership unsupportive or even hostile to their actions. In such cases, they either created new unions, created or used other forms of organization, or linked informal work groups outside of official union channels.

The mass strike wave of 1919, which saw major conflict in the steel, railroad, coal, and other industries, as well as the famous Seattle General Strike, illustrated all these tendencies side by side. Where—as in the Seattle General Strike—the rank and file was able to control existing unions, the militancy and class-consciousness of the workers gave union action radical forms. Where—as in steel—unionization had been prevented, establishing unions was the primary objective of strike action. In the two basic industries that had been thoroughly unionized—coal and railroads—the unions tried desperately to head off or kill off rank-and-file strike action, and workers had to organize against their own unions.

In the twentieth century both government and corporations came to see unions as vehicles they could use to control an unruly working class. World War I placed workers in a uniquely powerful position because of the shortage of labor and the imperative for war production. Alexander Bing, wartime labor mediator, wrote that "the workers could, had they seen fit to do so, have taken advantage of the scarcity of labor and the enormous need for commodities, which the war produced, and have demanded radical changes in industry, and it is very difficult to see how such demands could have been successfully resisted."[6] Employers and government turned to the unions to resist such demands. In effect, this policy took the form of a deal in which the major labor federation, the American Federation of Labor (AFL) agreed to combat strikes in return for the guarantee of the right to organize craft unions in substantial parts of American industry. The government also eliminated the AFL's competition by violently repressing its radical rival, the Industrial Workers of the World.

Employers also used unions to establish labor discipline in the workplace. For example, as we saw above, workers in the 1930s had used the sit-down to establish a direct counter-power to management—freedom to set the pace of work, to resist arbitrary orders from foremen, to share work equitably, to determine their share of the product, and the like. They saw unions as a way to guarantee this power. The new CIO unions—like any political organizations trying to win a following—presented themselves as the fulfillment of the workers desires. But to management they described a CIO contract as insurance against strikes and sit-downs. And they subsequently enforced the contract against the workers with discipline, firing, and blacklists.

I've come to see what has happened to the unions as an instance of a broader problem of participants' loss of control over their own organizations. The differentiation of leaders and led, the emergence of unaccountable control of organizations from above, and the reduction of the rank and file's ability to coordinate their own action directly are common patterns not just in labor organizations but in many other social spheres. They form a fundamental—though perhaps not irremediable—problem for democracy.

31

"SPREADING BY CONTAGION"

ớ

CLASS CONFLICT WAS THE RESULT OF A SYSTEM THAT DIFFERENTIATED WORKERS AND employers. The domination of workers by employers was embodied in each workplace, but it was also a feature of society as a whole. So I argued that, while the microcosmic cell units of mass strikes lay in workplaces and their informal work groups, mass strikes were also part of a macrocosmic national and even international system.

Mass strikes were related to the periodic crises—economic, political, or military—that have been features of industrial capitalism since its beginnings. The mass strikes of 1877, 1886, 1894, and the 1930s were associated with worldwide depressions. Those of 1919 and 1946 were part of the reconstruction that followed World Wars I and II. The Vietnam War–era labor upheavals accompanied the global crisis of "stagflation" that marked the end of the relatively steady economic growth after World War II. Such broad crises forced employers to put pressure on workers in a myriad ways, even at the risk of provoking revolt. As Tim Costello pointed out, even when they raise wages, such crises undermine the rhythms of daily life, the patterns of adaptation to which people have become accustomed.[1]

Such pressures generated what I called a "mass strike process" that began with the invisible and unrecorded daily skirmishes of working life in normal times. Clayton Fountain, a Detroit auto worker and later a UAW official, describes one such conflict on a cushion production line at a non-union Briggs auto parts plant in 1929. Working on incentive pay, workers would "work like hell for a couple of weeks, boosting our pay a little each day." Then "Bingo, the timekeeper would come along one morning and tell us that we had another new rate, a penny or two per cushion less than it had been the day before."

One day when this happened,

We got sore and rebelled. After lunch the whistle blew and the line started up, but not a single worker on our conveyor lifted a hand. We all sat around on cushions waiting to see what would happen.

In a few minutes the place was crawling with big-shots. They stormed and raved and threatened, but our gang stood pat.... We didn't belong to a union and we had no conception of organization. There were no leaders chosen by us to deal with the angry bosses; we all pitched into the verbal free-for-all with no epithets barred.

After forty-five minutes, the bosses agreed to reinstate the previous piecework rate. Looking back, I can see that, in a small and disorganized fashion, we tasted the power of the sitdown strike on that far-away day in the Briggs plant in 1929.[2]

At a time of growing discontent, in which invisible, low-intensity conflicts at the workplace level generate a potential basis for solidarity, the action of one group of workers often serves as the inciting example to large numbers of others. Rebellion was often described as "spreading by contagion." The strike and defeat of the militia in Martinsburg, West Virginia, started a chain reaction in the Great Upheaval of 1877; successful sit-downs of rubber workers in Akron set off the sit-down wave of the 1930s; and the illegal strike of New York postal workers ignited a nationwide postal wildcat in 1970 and helped spur a national wave of wildcats. Each exemplary action demonstrated the power workers had because they could stop production. And it showed their willingness and capacity to withstand retaliation, often violent, from employer or government forces, thus infusing other workers with confidence and an appreciation of their ability to stand up for themselves and stick together and the potential power they wielded when they did so.

Labor historian John Commons described what happened when a strike forced railroad magnate Jay Gould to meet and bargain with the Knights of Labor: "Here a labor organization for the first time dealt on an equal footing with the most powerful capitalist in the country. It forced Jay Gould to recognize it as a power equal to himself." The "oppressed laboring masses" finally discovered "a champion which could curb the power of a man stronger even than the government itself." All the pent-up feeling of bitterness and resentment that had accumulated during the two years of depression "now found vent in a rush to organize under the banner of the powerful Knights of Labor."[3] The Knights grew from seventy-one thousand in 1884 to seven hundred thirty thousand in 1886.

The sit-down wave of 1936 to 1937 illustrates the same phenomenon. The sit-down idea spread so rapidly because it dramatized a simple, powerful fact: No social institution can run without the cooperation of those whose activity makes it up. Once people saw others using the sit-down, they realized they could apply it to their own situation. The power of the sit-downs and their rapid spread electrified the country: In March 1937 alone the Department of Labor identified 170 reported industrial sit-downs with 167,210 participants; no doubt a great many more went unrecorded.

Defeats or impending defeats might also lead workers toward wider solidarity and more dramatic tactics. For example, in 1892 the violent suppression of a nationally publicized strike of skilled steelworkers at Andrew Carnegie's works in Homestead, Pennsylvania, by a small army of Pinkerton agents was followed closely by workers throughout the United States. Secretary of the Treasury Charles Foster, campaigning in Ohio, reported "trouble among laboring men." They were "talking about Homestead, about Carnegie being too rich, while they were poor."[4] The Homestead strike revealed to workers throughout the United States their capacity for cooperation and resistance. But its defeat also revealed that even heroic struggles by isolated, local groups of workers could be overcome by the superior force of the corporations. This conclusion contributed to the expanded solidarity that characterized the huge, overlapping strikes two years later in 1894. One railroad worker said the lesson of that year's nationwide multi-industry "sympathetic strike" in support of workers at the Pullman company was to "demonstrate to laboring men that they must get together; that no single organization can win."[5]

As a result of such lessons mass strikes tended to spread to wider and wider circles, cutting across existing lines of cleavage within the working class. In the mass strike of 1886, Commons noted "the obliteration, apparently complete, of all lines that divide the laboring class, whether geographic or trade."[6] In 1894, the great majority of American railroad workers joined a sympathetic strike in support of the workers who were not even railroad workers but merely manufactured Pullman railroad cars. Scores of traditionally hostile groups, once separated by nationality, religion, language, history, and the deliberately invidious policies of employers, joined together with close cooperation in the steel strike and the textile strikes of 1919. Black and white workers in Southern cities such as St. Louis in 1877 and New Orleans in 1892 joined together in general strikes supporting each other's demands. Indeed, *Strike!* argued that "the tendency of mass strikes—never fully realized—is toward joint action of all working people."[7]

Such conflicts also tended to develop into broad class polarizations. What Pullman strike leader Eugene Victor Debs said of that strike could be said of many other such struggles: "The struggle with the Pullman Company has developed into a contest between the producing classes and the money power of the country."[8]

Mass strikes led to counter-mobilizations by employers and their allies. The Great Upheaval was followed by the organization of militias and the building of armories for the suppression of domestic unrest. After the strike wave of 1886, there was a "tidal wave of formation of employers' associations to check the abuses of unionism, even to crush it." Thousands of workers were fired and blacklisted.[9] In 1892, the Pinkertons' detective agency's agents and reserves, used primarily for labor disputes, totaled more than the standing army of the nation. State and federal troops have intervened in labor disputes more than one hundred sixty times.[10] According to historian Leon Wolff, "One searches United States labor history in vain for a single case where the introduction of troops operated to the strikers' advantage." In virtually all such conflicts "the state guard acted, in effect, as a strike-breaking agency."[11]

32
THE CHALLENGE TO AUTHORITY

৵

IN TRYING TO UNDERSTAND THE "PERPETUALLY MOVING AND CHANGING SEA OF phenomena" that characterized mass strikes, I identified three crucial processes: the challenge to authority, the spreading of solidarity, and the growth of worker self-management. Each of them arose repeatedly in periods of mass strike. They represented "emerging properties"—characteristics of the working class that arose out of the mass strike process itself. I believed they could serve as the basis for transforming society.

At the turn of the 1970s we were living in an era of rebellion. Blacks were rebelling against racism; students and young people were protesting the Vietnam War; soldiers were "fragging" their officers; women were revolting against sexism; and workers were challenging their bosses and often their own unions as well. I identified with all of these rebellions, and I was happy to celebrate mass strikes as a heritage of mass rebellion.

Conventional labor economics treats a strike as a vendor's withholding of a commodity from the market to get a better price. Drawing on the tradition of Eugene Victor Debs and the Industrial Workers of the World (IWW), I maintained in *Strike!* that when workers cease to work—strike—it is a kind of revolt. It is, as sociologist Alvin Gouldner put it in his book *Wildcat Strike,* "a refusal to obey those socially prescribed as authorities in that situation, that is, management."[1]

Strike! could have made it clearer that not all strikes are rebellions. Some really are more like a vendor's withdrawal of a commodity from the market to raise its selling price. Once unions are officially recognized by law and management, participation in an authorized strike can be less a revolt against authority than obedience to the union leaders who have become the legally prescribed authorities. But many strikes, especially wildcats and strikes for recognition, are indeed revolts against the established authorities.

Viewing strikes as withdrawals not just of the commodity labor power but of obedience to authority connects them with the general pattern of civil disobedience most often associated with Gandhi. I learned much later that while Rosa Luxemburg was studying the lessons of the 1905 Russian Revolution from the west, Gandhi was studying them from the east. Contrasting the Russian general strike that forced the tsar to grant a limited parliament to previous actions, he wrote, "This time they have found another remedy which, though very simple, is more powerful than rebellion and murder. The Russian workers and all the other servants declared a general strike and stopped all work." He added, "We, too, can resort to the Russian remedy against tyranny." Shortly thereafter Gandhi announced his first campaign of nonviolent resistance.

If authority grows out of the agreement of those subject to it to obey, the withdrawal of that agreement—the refusal to acquiesce—represents a type of social action that violates established authority without necessarily taking the form of insurrectionary violence.[2]

33
SOLIDARITY

ð

As a young child I had listened over and over to a song with this refrain: "Solidarity forever, solidarity forever, solidarity forever, for the union makes us strong." But what is solidarity and where does it come from?

As the powerlessness of workers or indeed any individuals makes their position look less and less tenable, the psychology of "looking out for number one" becomes futile. The need to support others who in turn will support you can become evident, and a spirit of all-for-one and one-for-all can spread in a bond that is at once an intellectual recognition of necessity and an emotional feeling of unity. That bond is summed up in the hallowed labor movement adage, "An injury to one is an injury to all." That bond is worker solidarity.

The reason this sense of solidarity crystallizes so suddenly is the feeling that, as Paul Mattick, Jr., used to put it, "I will only make sacrifices for you when I can sense that you will grasp the need to make sacrifices for me." Such mutuality develops in a thousand miniature experiments taking place in the background of a mass strike—like the railroad blockade in Martinsburg in 1877 and the Briggs work stoppage in Detroit in 1929.

One result of this process is the sense of being part of a class. That is in some ways comparable to the sense of being part of a nation, but, I maintained, its source and result are different from those of nationalism. The common situation of workers is that individually they are powerless, but together they embody the entire productive force of society. Workers' solidarity reflects their discovery of this. It is rooted in the fact that in modern society individuals can gain control of the social forces that determine their lives only by cooperating. Thus "individualism" keeps the individual weak, while solidarity increases the individual's control over her or his life. Once the consciousness of this need for solidarity develops, it becomes impossible to say whether the motive for an act such as joining a sympathetic strike is altruistic or selfish, because the interest of the individual and the collective interest are no longer antagonistic; they have come to be the same. (*Strike!* was less forthright on the ways in which those who shared some interests in common might nonetheless have others that conflicted.)

Worker solidarity is a special case of what I would now call common preservation. It can be undermined, of course, by pursuit of the narrow self-interest that economists refer to as the "free rider problem"—the attempt to share in the benefits of joint action without sharing in its sacrifices. But that is often overcome by a shared understanding that cutting the other guy's throat ends up with everyone cutting their own throat; by the experience of benefit through mutual support; by a process that I would later come to call de-centering, which allows you to see yourself in others' shoes; and by a view of solidarity as a better way to live and act.

34

SELF-MANAGEMENT

ᴥ

I FIRST RAN INTO THE CONCEPT OF SELF-MANAGEMENT IN A SPECIAL ISSUE OF THE *New Left Review* devoted to workers control. I enthusiastically adopted it as the application of participatory democracy to the workplace. At the Institute for Policy Studies I got to know Gerry Hunnius, author of a book on self-management in Yugoslavia, and attended a seminar on self-management in Algeria with the former Algerian Ambassador to the United States Cherif Guellal. I read what I could find on the attempt by factory committees to institute workers control in the early days of the Russian revolution and the workers management of production in Catalonia during the Spanish Civil War.

In most organizations, whatever the formal organizational chart may say, workers exercise a degree of self-management just to get the work done. In workplace conflicts over the speed and organization of production, workers often establish tacit counter-power, take over part of the management function, and coordinate their own activity in their own interest.

In a strike, the normal power of the employer to shape daily life is broken, and workers are put in a position to think, act, and coordinate their actions for themselves. A strike requires workers to manage many activities, including picketing; countering employer and government violence; providing food, health care, and other vital needs of the strikers; coordinating strike activity; reaching out to supporters and the public; providing information; and setting strike strategy. If a strike seriously affects the public, strikers often find it necessary to continue part of their usual work to show their social responsibility and keep public sympathy; for example, railroad strikers have often run passenger and mail trains while blocking freight traffic.

This tendency of strikers to conduct social activities under their own management perhaps reached its height in the Seattle general strike of 1919, when the various striking trades provided the necessary services for an entire city—explaining any violation of the ban on work with signs reading "Exempted by the General

Strike Committee." Indeed, the view of self-management that influenced me most came from the stirring history of the 1919 Seattle General Strike prepared by the General Strike Committee. It described the existing world "of strife and insecurity, of unemployment, and hungry children." It was "not a pleasant world to look upon." The solution? "We see but one way out. In place of two classes, competing for the fruits of industry, there must be, eventually ONLY ONE CLASS sharing fairly the good things of the world. And this can only be done by THE WORKERS LEARNING TO MANAGE."

> When we saw, in our General Strike:
> The milk Wagon Drivers consulting late into the night over the task of supplying milk for the city's babies;
> The Provisions Trades working twenty-four hours out of the twenty-four on the question of feeding 30,000 workers;
> The Barbers planning a chain of co-operative barber shops;
> The Steamfitters opening a profitless grocery store;
> The Labor guards facing, under severe provocation, the task of maintaining order by a new and kinder method;
> When we saw union after union submitting its cherished desires to the will of the General Strike Committee:
> THEN WE REJOICED....
> Some day, when the workers have learned to manage, they will BEGIN MANAGING ...
> And we, the workers of Seattle, have seen, in the midst of our General Strike, vaguely and across the storm, a glimpse of what the fellowship of that new day shall be.[1]

The tendency toward self-management in working-class history is rooted in the reality that, unless people direct their own activities, someone else will direct them—in ways that prevent them from pursuing their own ends. Self-management is the only alternative to disorder or management by somebody else. Self-management can arise out of the immediate needs of a struggle—keeping the workplace closed, feeding strikers, and the like. But I argued that all the actions of a mass strike can be viewed in essence as responses to the fact that when a small minority manage society, they will generally do so in a way that conflicts with the needs of the majority. Mass strikes embody a partial replacement of management by others with workers self-management.

The concept of self-management provides a way to think about how participatory democracy could replace top-down organization of work. Workers activity in strikes illustrates and expands their capacity for self-management. But *Strike!* never addressed how managing a slowdown, or a wildcat strike, or even an insurrection is similar to or different from managing a factory, let alone managing an economy or a society. The normal exclusion of ordinary people from decision making concentrates skill and knowledge in the hands of elites, casting doubt on the adage that "any cook can govern." How social movements can realize self-management, rather than simply installing new managerial elites, remains an unsolved challenge for advocates of basic change in work relations.

35

YOU SAY YOU WANT A REVOLUTION?

৵

IN *STRIKE!* I PORTRAYED THE MASS STRIKE AS A PROCESS IN WHICH WORKING PEOPLE, in order to solve their problems, transformed themselves. It was marked by the three processes that embodied the transformation of the working class itself and the possibility of transforming society: workers challenge to existing authorities, workers development of solidarity with each other, and workers taking charge of their own activities. These were what philosophers of science call emergent properties—ones that are not present at the beginning of a process but develop during the course of the process itself.

I portrayed the transformation of the working class and of society as a revolutionary process in the sense that it had the potential to eliminate the present ruling class. "Because it challenges the real power-holders of our society—the industrial managers—and because carried to its logical conclusion it would have to replace them, the mass strike can be considered in essence a revolutionary process." But this revolutionary process was more than merely a struggle for power between two groups. Out of that struggle develop "the tendencies toward self-management and toward solidarity—qualities which if extended could form the basis of a society different from any now existing." Most people in their work life and community life are "passive—submitting to control from above." They are also "atomized—separated from each other." What I saw in mass strikes was the beginning of "a transformation of people and their relationships from passivity and isolation to collective action."[1]

Drawing heavily on the ideas of Anton Pannekoek, I presented the emergent properties workers developed in class struggles as the basis for a different kind of society. "This unity of individual and collective interest and the feelings of unity it generates are the necessary basis of a society based on cooperation rather than competition." From one perspective, therefore, the mass strike could be seen as "a process in which workers are transformed from competitors to cooperators." Combined with a replacement of managers by self-management, this would result in "a society of free human beings working together to meet their own needs by meeting each other's needs." So the mass strike could be considered "a revolutionary process" whose "outer expression" lies in "contesting the power of the existing authorities" and whose "inner expression" is "the transformation of those who do society's work from passive and isolated individuals to a collective of self-directing cooperators."[2]

I knew, however, that such a transformation was not the only tendency within mass strikes. The need for coordination could and often did create new coordinating centers—unions, parties, or even workers councils—that made use of their position to assert themselves as new authorities over workers and society. When this occurs, "conflict next arises between the agency attempting to assert the new authority and the subjects of that authority."[3] That was seen in the conflicts between workers and the unions and parties that claimed to represent them.

The revolutionary potential expressed in workers councils and workers self-management was nascent in American mass strikes. I pointed out that it had proceeded much further in such other initiatives as the Russian factory committees of 1917, the Italian factory occupations of 1920, and the self-managed Catalan factories during the Spanish Civil War.

While celebrating the initiative workers took and their visions of liberation, *Strike!* also emphasized that the outcome of these revolutionary efforts had often been the establishment of new dominations. Forestalling that result remains a central problem for advocates of social change.

Like many radicals of the time, I took revolution—defined as the replacement of one ruling class by another—as *the* historical model for "real social change." As Karl Marx famously said, "The working class is revolutionary or it is nothing." Today I would see revolutions as only one rather special case of the process of social change. In a 1997 revision of *Strike!* I tried to address the relation of mass strikes and revolution in a more nuanced way. "Most of the time a kind of equilibrium exists among classes." This embodies "a formal or informal class compromise," which most members of the respective classes conform to whether they like it or not. This equilibrium "reflects the unequal power of classes, but rarely a total domination of one over the other." It provides each with "certain guarantees that they consider their entitlement." This balance is often embodied in "rules and institutions ranging from minimum-wage laws to collective bargaining agreements." Periods of mass strike "reflect the disruption of such equilibriums." This may occur because the underlying power relations have shifted or because the aspirations of the parties have changed. Mass strikes "challenge the subordinate position of workers and foreshadow transformations of their position in society."[4]

Mass strikes, I added, also changed the position of workers in society in more immediate ways. The Wagner Act, grievance procedures, seniority systems, and other reforms "are largely the result of the threat of disruption and revolution implicit in the mass strike. Mass strikes have shifted the equilibrium between classes, winning for workers rights and entitlements they were previously denied."[5]

Mass strikes have also forestalled a reverse shift in equilibrium. A railroad engineer observed after the suppression of the Pullman strike in 1894, "If there had never been a strike or a labor organization I am satisfied that every railway employee in the country would be working for one-half what he has been working for of late. Strikes are not generally successful, but they entail a heavy loss on the company and it is to avoid that loss that the company ever meets us at all."[6]

I still believe that it is often necessary to change power relations to solve the problems faced by workers and indeed by any subordinate group. But I doubt that changing power relations can be reduced to a simple dichotomy between revolution and the status quo. The changes we require to solve the global problems of today's era of mutual destruction are in many ways greater than those that have been made by any revolution. I doubt that those changes will look very much like the revolutions of the past. They require something more than, and other than, the replacement of one ruling social group by another. I am sure, however, that they will require—and evoke—the kind of transformation of people and their relationships from passivity and isolation to collective action that mass strikes showed to be possible.

36

BEYOND REDUCTIONISM
MY CRITIQUE OF STRIKE!

೩

IN A LAUDATORY BUT ALSO CRITICAL REVIEW OF *STRIKE!*[1] MY FRIEND STEVE SAPOLSKY wrote that the book "suffers from the utilization of preconceived categories that do not do justice to the complexities of history." Each strike seems to be like every other strike. "There is very little investigation of the goals and aspirations of the strikers, and instead, they seem to be robots, propelled into action with unfailing regularity by the relentless course of history." Parodying Hegel's idea of the "World Spirit," Steve wrote that each strike, instead of "erupting out of particular environments and structured by particular intentions," emerges "courtesy of the Spirit of the Proletariat, kind enough to reveal itself as it makes its way through the world."

Actually, I was developing my own post-publication critique of *Strike!* along similar lines. While I certainly didn't renounce the book, I became increasingly conscious of how much was left out, from race and gender to government and politics, and how much of what was there was squished into "preconceived categories" that had not been adequately adapted to fit workers actual experiences.

Indeed, *Strike!* is marked by a sort of monomania. Everything can ultimately be derived from one relationship: wage labor and capital. This class relationship is not seen as interacting with other realities. Everything not an expression of that core contradiction can be ignored. That which relates to the central contradiction is, as they say, "privileged."

Like so much of the tradition from which it grew, *Strike!* tended to reduce all social conflict to that between workers and employers, ill-attending even to other classes, let alone other kinds of social groups and identities. It often treated other kinds of injustice besides class oppression as secondary and derivative. It viewed institutions like the state or racial discrimination merely as an aspect of class relations.

In 1997 I had the opportunity to revise *Strike!* for a twenty-fifth anniversary edition initiating the South End Press Classics series. I experienced the process as "a collaboration between myself of twenty-five years ago and myself of today."[2] In many ways I liked what my younger collaborator had to say, even if I sometimes had to smile at his brash over-confidence. But I bridled at *Strike!*'s many lurking traces of preconceived categories and its allergy to complexity.

For example, like theorists of many persuasions, I presented "society" as if societies were self-contained wholes; there was little sense of the complexity of social institutions and networks that overlap and cut across each other. Similarly, instead of grasping human beings as complex and multifaceted beings, there was a tendency to view people as acting and interacting simply as expressions of their positions—specifically their class positions—in a particular society.

From the perspective of today's globalizing economies and societies, it is stunning how much *Strike!* takes the primacy of a national framework for granted. Except for a brief acknowledgement that the post–World War I mass strike was part of a worldwide crisis, mass strikes are seen almost exclusively in a national context. The United States was pretty much taken as "a society," capable of being understood in isolation from the rest of the world. This unquestioned national framework and conflation of society with nation was manifested in such statements as, "If [ordinary people] refuse to work, the country stops. If they take control of their own activity, their own work, they thereby take control of society."[3]

Marxist theory often proclaimed the "primacy of production" on the grounds that society was only possible if the things it needed were produced. Somehow this extremely broad idea of production became identified specifically with the economy. I narrowed this privileging of the economy still further, to assume the primacy of the industrial workplace. The work group became my touchstone both for interpreting workers history and for projecting the key locus of future social change.

If the economy determines the rest of society, then it follows that the only kind of social stratification that really matters is class. This privileges the working-class struggle as the most important aspect and motor of social change. The political implications of this approach were invidious, and feminists were beginning to argue that it downplayed the sphere of "social reproduction" and therefore the critical role that women played within it. *Strike!* barely touched on conditions that might give class struggles different meanings for men and women or for members of different racial and ethnic groups, let alone considering struggles that such people might engage in that were not first and foremost expressions of their class situation.

In *Strike!*, class itself is reduced to relatively homogeneous categories of capitalists and workers. There is little consideration of what have come to be known as "contradictory class positions"—for example, women who work in low-paid menial jobs but who are married to capitalist executives; highly skilled manual workers whose pay far exceeds many small business people; or highly educated but low-paid and contingent college teachers. "Workers" are, with few exceptions, equated to blue-collar industrial workers. The "middle class" is noticed primarily as a supporter of workers or capitalists in class struggles or as a group that is being progressively reduced to the conditions of workers. Economic power is portrayed as the possession of those it calls "industrial managers," with little concern about the changing relationship of ownership and management over the history of American capitalism.

Even within the life of the working class, *Strike!* addresses only direct antagonism to employers. The cultural life of working people, their daily life institutions, and their community building are treated as significant only as they bear on large-scale resistance. Even the normal institutionalized class struggle, embodied in unions, collective bargaining, and conventional strikes, is largely ignored. So is all conventional political activity. And the complexities of compound identities and multiple group memberships are not considered. Mass strikes and wildcats are the gold standard to which all other aspects of working-class experience are to be compared—and inevitably to be found wanting.

Indeed, the real gold standard was revolution. Class struggle was significant only insofar as it was potentially revolutionary. All social change was reduced to what it contributed to revolution. Mass strikes were appealing in part because they looked a little like nascent revolutions. While *Strike!* distinguished between a social revolution that changed basic human relationships and a conventional political revolution based on the seizure of state power, I still took for granted the replacement of the rule of one class by another as the criterion for whether or not social change was meaningful.

Because of its emphasis on the workplace, *Strike!* reduced society to domination and struggles against domination. Even issues of great interest to Marx, such as the "anarchy of the market" with its unintended side effects and interaction effects, were largely ignored.

Strike!'s presentation of how unions become dominated by leaders and bureaucrats was likewise conditioned by its narrow focus on class relations. The specific drive to modulate class conflict through union contracts and the paraphernalia of industrial relations was undoubtedly important in this process. But *Strike!* ignored the factors that create similar forms of organizational alienation in institutions ranging from governments and political parties to churches and even social clubs. Labor organizations have no monopoly on the "iron law of oligarchy."

With its narrow emphasis on class, *Strike!* rarely recognized the ways in which people, including workers, are organized on bases other than class. As a result, I saw class formation as exclusively a move from individual to collective strategies. I failed to recognize that many workers are already acting on collective strategies—but collective strategies of other collectivities, such as ethnic and racial groups, occupational groups, religious groups, or nations. Working-class rebellion therefore often involves less a shift from individual to collective strategies than from one collective strategy to another.

Today I see the relation between mass strikes and systemic social change as more problematic than the way it is portrayed in *Strike!* The immediate response to the conditions of everyday life and to the employing class, even for the most proletarianized, is not necessarily adequate for the changes that are needed in society. *Strike!* portrayed a transformation of working people through the process of class struggle, but didn't really measure that change against the kind of transformation necessary to make the social revolution it advocated. *Strike!* demonstrated, in a way I still find compelling, that mass strikes and other worker action in some ways prefigure such a change. But it never adequately assessed what would be necessary to realize that potential. That doesn't necessarily mean that some other group has to "bring consciousness" to the working class. But it does at the least require the mediating and transforming process embodied in social movements.

Some of *Strike!*'s flaws have come to matter more over time. For example, in the early 1970s the economy, class relations, and culture of the United States coincided far more closely with the boundaries of the nation; my tendency to treat the United States as a bounded society whose connections with the rest of the world could be ignored led to only occasional distortions. Three decades later, with the global interpenetration of corporations, labor markets, and cultures— "globalization"—such a tendency would produce colossal howlers.

Similarly, the rise of multiculturalism and widespread recognition of the multiplicity of individual identities has made the assumption that large numbers of people might act simply on their identity as workers even more problematic than it was in the past.[4] And in the 1960s and 1970s, national economies controlled by a handful of huge "oligopolistic" corporations and regulated by powerful national governments made the issues of domination seem far more central and the problems of markets and economic chaos seem far less important than they are today.

Many of these flaws I gradually discovered how to correct in later work. For example, the book I wrote after *Strike!*, *Common Sense for Hard Times*, specifically addressed the differing experiences of black and white and male and female workers. *Brass Valley: The Story of Working People's Lives and Struggles in an American Industrial Region* gave communities equal billing with the workplace. *Building Bridges: The Emerging Grassroots Coalition of Labor and Community* recognized that social actors came from multiple starting points, including but not limited to class-based ones, so that the key to realizing their common interests was their ability to coordinate their action notwithstanding their differences.

One thing I learned from developing my own critique of *Strike!* was not to be afraid to discover and admit my own mistakes. I came to consider such correction a necessary and valuable part of the process by which we learn. To paraphrase Gregory Bateson, there is no trial-and-error learning without error. I have come to consider making errors and correcting them essential for progress for individuals, societies, and social movements.

37

CLASS AND BEYOND

ॐ

MY STUDY OF LABOR HISTORY AND THE TRADITIONS OF WORKING-CLASS RADICALISM provided me with a way, albeit an incomplete and flawed one, of investigating the questions raised by my own experience in social movements. It was incomplete because it addressed people's problems solely from the perspective of their role as workers; but it could be generalized to move beyond that limitation. It was flawed because of its tendency to preconceived categories and oversimplification; but it could be corrected by a greater willingness to criticize my own categories and not to run away from complexity.

Many of the ideas I developed in *Strike!*, stripped of their oversimplification, remain central to my approach to social change. I have extended them beyond their original context and incorporated them in a more general interpretation of common preservation.

For example, I continue to see alienated labor as a ubiquitous form of oppression. But I would now say the same regarding all activity conducted for the benefit and under the control of others. A struggle for self-liberation can be a valid response to all of them.

Class division provides something of a paradigm case for understanding other forms of social stratification. The problems of individuals and groups generally have roots in the way people are socially differentiated and their activities integrated. This applies not only to class and workplace oppression, but also to inequality between women and men and the unrestrained power that allows corporations to dump their waste into the environment without recourse from the victims. In such situations, solving a problem may require not just individual action or established forms of collective action but new patterns of concerted action that change social relationships—new common preservations.

In the course of acting together, people develop new capacities and characteristics—emergent properties. In labor and other social struggles, cooperation and self-direction are essential to success. They therefore tend to emerge in such struggles—or rather people construct them in response to the perceived necessities of the struggle. They also construct new understandings that transcend limited individual and group perspectives and place their experiences in a wider context—manifesting what I later came to call an "ecological shift."

People who are separated can join together. Solidarity is not a given, but it can be created and historically it has been created over and over again. It requires a process in which people abstract from their differences sufficiently to recognize their commonalities—what I would later learn to call "de-centering." It involves the construction of collective identities and the incorporation of collective identity as an aspect of personal identity.

The idea that dependence provides a basis for potential power can be extended beyond workers and beyond the workplace. Any social institution—and society as a whole—depends on the cooperation or at least the acquiescence of those whose activity makes it up or who are in a position to affect it. Therefore apparently powerless people currently excluded from the control of institutions and societies nonetheless may be able to change them. The power of the powerless is captured in sayings such as "You can't mine coal with bayonets" and "What if they had a war and nobody came?"

While people must organize themselves to act effectively, they may also lose control of the organizations they create, whether those are unions or any other kind of organization. Such institutions may even become vehicles for disorganizing or oppressing them. Unless people retain control of their organizations, those organizations may turn against their creators like a Frankenstein's monster.

In the decades since *Strike!* was written, the United States has been in a state of one-sided class war by employers against workers. Both strikes and the labor movement have undergone a dramatic decline. I detailed that decline in the twenty-fifth anniversary edition of *Strike!*, published in 1997. But with the outbreak of mass action in response to the Tea Party agenda of outlawing labor rights, the American class war has once again become two-sided. The occupation of the Wisconsin statehouse by a hundred thousand workers, students, and allies represented the first return volley. It also showed that defense of worker rights and conditions of life is likely to require something more than conventional collective bargaining tactics. Perhaps the story of mass strikes in America will have a future as well as a past.

Worldwide, mass strikes have continued to make history. The mass strikes of the late 1980s in Poland led the way for the fall of Communism throughout Eastern Europe. And mass strikes are proving to be a significant feature of the era of globalization. A single two-year period saw general strikes and other mass labor struggles in countries as diverse as Argentina, Belgium, Brazil, Canada, Columbia, Ecuador, France, Haiti, Italy, South Korea, and Spain. The "Great

Recession" and governmental austerity policies in its aftermath led to mass strikes in Greece, France, Ireland, Spain, Portugal, Britain, and much of the rest of Europe. Recent people-power upheavals in Tunisia, Egypt, and elsewhere in the Middle East involve substantial worker roles and share many characteristics with mass strikes. If workers power is not the answer to every question, it still has a crucial role to play in expanding common preservation.

PART 4

DISCOVERING GLOBALIZATION
FROM BELOW

38
DISCOVERING GLOBALIZATION FROM BELOW

ૐ

WHILE I CONTINUED A CERTAIN AMOUNT OF DIRECT ACTIVISM DURING THE 1970S, I gradually decided that writing was likely to be the most useful and the most personally congenial contribution I could make to the development of social movements. It also allowed me to support myself, after a fashion, in my parents' trade as a freelance writer. (My father quipped, "You're like the coal miner's son who swore he'd never follow his father into the mines, but what else is there to do?") Most of my bread and butter over the next three decades came from public history media projects supported by the Connecticut Humanities Council and broadcast on Connecticut Public Television and Radio.

Meanwhile I continued writing mostly unremunerative books and articles, and eventually web postings, on historical and contemporary social movements. In addition, I conducted autodidactic raiding parties into such unlikely fields as general systems theory, cybernetics, and genetic structuralism—forerunners of what is now often called nonlinear or complexity theory. My purpose was to find alternatives to reductionism that might provide better ways to understand complex interactive processes and systems. I began trying to integrate them with my own historical research and experience in a manuscript called *Common Preservation* that eventually morphed into *Save the Humans?* and the companion volume I am currently completing. In the meantime I tacitly used this developing approach to guide my more concrete work.

In 1980 I was just finishing up a participatory community history project on the workers in the Naugatuck Valley of western Connecticut.[1] Once the thriving center of the American brass industry, by 1980 the "Brass Valley" was becoming an outpost of the rustbelt before our very eyes. As I strove to understand the deindustrialization of the region, one of my collaborators insisted that we had to look at the global economy in order to find the explanation. I initially rejected the idea; we were doing a local history and the global economy would just distract from our real purpose. But I gradually realized that she was right. Local brass companies had become subsidiaries of international copper companies and then of global oil companies. Local brass producers couldn't compete against foreign ones. Workers were being told to accept lower wages or their work would be moved to foreign countries. I had stumbled onto the phenomenon that a decade later would come to be known as "globalization."

I soon began noticing impacts of globalization on social movements at home. Unions were accepting unprecedented concessions because their bargaining power was undermined by the ability and willingness of their employers to shut up shop and move to "offshore" locations abroad. On the other hand, I was hearing about new expressions of cross-border solidarity, for example, unprecedented collaborations between workers in the United States and Mexico.

I gradually realized that I had to understand what this new thing was. But that wasn't easy. Globalization was a process in which a system was being transformed by the actions of many different actors and by the interactions of those actions. To understand it I tried to use the ideas I had generalized from my study of workers power and to combine them with what I had learned from my intellectual raiding parties.

From Ludwig von Bertalanffy's general systems theory I gleaned the now commonplace notion that people can only be understood as part of larger patterns and processes and systems of interaction—that "no man is an island, entire of itself." The boundaries separating individuals, groups, and institutions are not absolute, but rather are semi-permeable and subject to change. Social life is not composed of discrete entities, but of multiple interacting levels of systems and subsystems. Seeing things that way involves an "ecological shift" in which apparently independent entities come to be interpreted as parts of larger wholes. This way of thinking helped me grasp the complex transformation that has come to be known as globalization.

These wholes or systems or patterns are rarely without their problems, however. Indeed, I learned from the genetic structuralism of Jean Piaget to consider their normal state as one of conflict, contradiction, inadequacy, and disequilibrium. In the social realm, some individuals, groups, and institutions may dominate others, leading to oppression, conflict, and instability. Conversely, people's interactions may be disordered, leading to collisions and failures to coordinate to achieve common interests and ward off shared disasters. The result may be unintended side effects and interaction effects that lead to arms races or economic crises or global warming or other results that were willed by no one. This approach helped me understand the forces that were driving globalization.

From Piaget and from the cybernetics of Norbert Weiner I learned to think in terms of action that is guided and problems that are corrected by means of "feedback" loops. People face problems when they experience gaps between their ends and the actions they take to realize them. To overcome these gaps people have to change the way they act so as to counteract or compensate for the gap. Such change may involve new ways to coordinate with others. Those new co-ordinations may result when people reflect on their situations, their ends, their capacities, themselves, and each other, and when they share these reflections with each other. That may require a de-centering in which people mutually internalize each other's patterns of thought and action. It may require that people conduct experiments—and thought experiments—to learn more about their realities and possibilities. I found these processes at work both in globalization and in the parallel to it I called globalization from below.

On the basis of the information or feedback they receive from these experiments, people may develop new patterns, including the formation of new solidarities, new groups, and new common preservations. Such adaptations involve both preservation and change. Indeed, I learned from Piaget to think of preservation and change not as opposites, but rather as mutually complementary. People change in order to preserve that which is important to them. Conversely, people preserve what they care about by changing it and themselves. It is from this process that new common preservations emerge. The emergence of globalization from below illustrates that process.

These ideas helped me think about globalization as a process arising within an out-of-balance global system. I looked for patterns that were produced and reproduced in repeated cycles, indicating stable structures. I tried to discover how such patterns had originated and how they were maintained. I looked for problems with those patterns that led parts of the system or the system as a whole to have trouble reproducing themselves and reaching their goals. I traced variations in those patterns, made both by elites and by social movements, intended to compensate for such gaps, including new forms of coordination and changes in the differentiation and integration of parts and wholes. I looked for unanticipated side effects and interaction effects and their consequences. I saw globalization as transforming the global economy without ever bringing it to a new equilibrium.

This is a developmental approach. It starts from the things people are already doing, the problems they face, and how they might vary their action to achieve their goals. It is also a "cybernetic" approach in that it interprets action as a way to correct or compensate for or equilibrate an undesired situation. This approach aims to provide a non-reductionist way to explain why people have acted as they have in the past. It does not provide a way for predicting the future. But it does provide a way to look at the future and clarify what variations on present action might be plausible—and what their effects might be. It therefore provides a means for constructing possible solutions and evaluating strategies for realizing them.

I eventually collaborated on two books about economic globalization. The first, *Global Village or Global Pillage,* written with Tim Costello, focused on economic globalization itself. The second, *Globalization from Below*, written with Tim and our new writing partner Brendan Smith, focused on the emergence of transnational social movements embodying what we called "globalization from below."

The emergence of a global social movement in response to globalization was hardly more than a hope (and a desperate need) when we finished *Global Village or Global Pillage* in 1994. Five years later, globalization from below was a burgeoning global revolt whose massive Battle of Seattle famously brought the founding 1999 World Trade Organization summit in Seattle to a grinding halt.

39

CONSTRUCTING WHOLES
THE RACE TO THE BOTTOM

જે

MY ATTEMPT TO UNDERSTAND ECONOMIC GLOBALIZATION DATES BACK TO 1980. As my collaborators and I were interviewing, videoing, and writing about the history of brass workers in Connecticut's Naugatuck Valley, the brass industry was collapsing around us. Employers were threatening to shut down local plants and move the work elsewhere—even to foreign countries—unless workers gave radical concessions on wages and working conditions. The local press, the companies, and much of the public regarded the workers as pigheaded, greedy, and stupid because they refused to accept concessions to save their own jobs. Nonetheless workers repeatedly drew a line and went on strike.

The workers had a radically different perspective, indeed a different paradigm, which was certainly not understood by and was perhaps incomprehensible to their critics. It was expressed by a rank-and-file worker we interviewed on the picket line. We asked him why workers decided to strike, even though it might cost them their jobs, rather than accept wage cuts to save their jobs. He replied that if they accept these cuts here, and then other workers accept them at other places, there will just be more and more cuts "and where is labor going to end up at?"[1]

For me, this remark embodies what might be called a holistic or systems approach. Critics of the strike viewed the local situation in isolation: Would Naugatuck Valley brass workers make concessions to save their jobs? But workers like this one saw the issue as part of a larger system and a larger process. They saw the side effects that their own concessions might have and how those might interact with the actions of others, reverberate through the system, and rebound to hurt them. If they allowed their conditions to be driven down it would create pressures for others elsewhere to do the same. And that in turn would rebound to put pressure on them for further cuts.

They also saw the potential for coordinating their actions with others to provide positive rather than negative synergistic effects. By risking their immediate interests—by going on strike to resist concessions—they were protecting other workers from this process. And if other workers did the same, that in turn would protect them. Local media, failing to understand that local workers were part of a larger system, were unable to anticipate the side effects and interaction effects to which competitive wage cutting would lead. And they did not grasp that workers were expressing a long-established and hard-won strategy of common preservation.

This insight, this ecological shift from a self-centered to a systems viewpoint, lies at the heart of the development of solidarity in labor and other social movements. The development of solidarity through a recognition of reciprocal and common interests that I had described in *Strike!* reflects an epistemological as well as a social transformation.

Naugatuck Valley brass workers understood that the effort to force them into competitive wage cutting with workers elsewhere was not just a national but a global phenomenon. A Waterbury brass worker originally from Puerto Rico who worked for a company owned by the multinational oil corporation Arco told us,

> They're investing in Asia, Saudi Arabia; they just built a plant there for twenty million dollars. They've got people working there for a dollar-and-a-half an hour, doing the same work we're doing here. That's what we can call runaway shops. They just get out of Waterbury, leaving the people of Waterbury without hope, without work.[2]

The elements of these workers' approach—reconceiving local economies as part of a larger, indeed, global whole, noting the interactions revealed by such a reconceptualization, and seeking to coordinate efforts to affect those interactions—became guiding ideas as I began to grapple with what would soon come to be known as globalization. The interactive downward spiral described on that Brass Valley picket line I learned to refer to as the "race to the bottom." I used it as an instrument to explore the inner dynamics of globalization.

THE RELATIVITY OF BOUNDARIES
GLOBALIZATION

ða·

MY FATHER WAS AN OLD NEW DEALER AND A KEYNESIAN. HE STRESSED TO ME THAT trade and the international economy were relatively unimportant to the United States. As I began to inquire for myself in the 1960s, the relatively small proportion of the US economy then formed by international trade persuaded me he was right.

As I studied the history of the brass industry in the Naugatuck Valley of western Connecticut for the Brass Workers History Project, I found this view confirmed. In colonial times, the American brass market was dominated by Britain, but by the mid-nineteenth century the Valley's brass companies had driven British competition out of the American market. As far as I could see, since then the Naugatuck Valley brass industry had been primarily part of a national, not an international, economy. There were exceptions, of course: Munitions exports had soared in wartime, the closely related local clock industry was a large exporter, and the copper companies that owned much of the brass industry owned mines in Chile and Mexico. But in general the boundaries of the American brass industry and market corresponded to the boundaries of the nation.

When, as we approached the completion of the Brass Workers History Project in the early 1980s, one of my collaborators, Jan Stackhouse, said, "We have to deal with the international economy and its impact on the brass industry," I was highly resistant. "We're doing a local project about the people who live here, their lives and their experiences," I told her. "Besides, the United States is pretty much a self-contained national economy; the international aspect just isn't that relevant."

I felt passionately that our project should focus on the often-neglected local working-class community. I wanted community members to be able to tell their own stories and to weave those stories together to give a portrait of the changing experience of ordinary working people. I wanted to avoid imposing an external theoretical or ideological view on their experience—to avoid reducing it to something else.

But even while we were documenting its workers history, the Naugatuck Valley brass industry was collapsing. When I tried to understand why, I was forced to acknowledge Jan's point. Many of the causes seemed to lie outside US national boundaries. The resurgent economies of Europe and Japan were taking over much of the American brass market. They had invested heavily in modern equipment while the owners of the old Naugatuck Valley mills had milked their profits and failed to reinvest to modernize them. Foreign labor costs were far lower—in part because Europe and Japan followed social policies that gave workers a stake in future national economic growth. High energy costs were another big part of local companies' competitive disadvantage—a result in part of the global oil crisis centered in the Middle East.

Meanwhile US copper corporations, which had owned many of the Valley's brass mills since the 1920s, had been acquired by global oil giants. A look at the oil corporations' annual reports showed that they treated the world as a single field for investment and that they regarded their Naugatuck Valley brass mills as little more than specks on their balance sheets. The result was to put Naugatuck Valley brass workers directly in competition with foreign workers; they were being told to accept lower wages or their plants would be shut down and their jobs would be moved to foreign countries along with the capital their labor had generated.

It turned out that what I had thought of as a quite strongly bounded national economy was being transformed. Of course national boundaries didn't disappear, but they were becoming far more permeable to economic and other forces. Institutions, notably corporations, that had once largely coincided with national boundaries, increasingly cut across them.

The word globalization had not, so far as I knew, ever been uttered. But we were witnessing the early stages of the globalization process.

Of course there had been globalization in a sense since Columbus sailed the ocean blue, and historians have identified several waves of globalization since then. Nonetheless, through much of the twentieth century national economies were relatively isolated systems. They were strongly bounded. They were intensively integrated internally. Internal actors were much less integrated with the world beyond the national border. Globalization meant that the differentiation between nations decreased and the integration of their economic processes increased. European labor policies and Middle Eastern oil politics and Arco's global investment options came to have far more impact on whether or not workers had jobs in Waterbury. Within a decade production would be so integrated across national borders that observers were referring to it as the "global assembly line."[1]

Grasping this emerging reality required that I go through an ecological shift myself. It meant seeing the global economy as a developing system that was less and less a collection of separate national economies that just traded with each other. I used the idea of systems with relative and changing boundaries to interpret the transformation of relatively isolated national economies into a globalized economic system. In *Global Village or Global Pillage,* Tim and I used the idea of changing relations of wholes and parts, manifested in changing forms of differentiation and coordination, to understand how globalization was changing the lives of people who continued to live in the same—but also a radically altered—geography.

As the globalization process was increasingly recognized, some interpreters began to argue it meant the end of the nation-state and the rise of a borderless world. Their critics belittled the significance of globalization, pointing out that nation-states were obviously still present and that some of them—notably the United States—were more powerful than ever. A systems framework that assumed the relativity of boundaries and the possibility of changing part-whole relations within a system facilitated a more nuanced approach. For such an approach there could be simultaneously an emerging global economic integration via capital mobility and the persistence of the nation-state system—although the process of change could be riven with conflict and might end in catastrophe.

Global Village or Global Pillage argued that the failure to recognize the transformation of boundaries being wrought by globalization led to colossal confusion in debates on public policy. Although by the early 1990s globalization had become a buzzword, public discussion generally continued as if the United States were still a predominantly national economy. The issues raised by globalization were defined as issues of "trade," meaning the export and import of goods and services between countries. The debate was defined as the classic conflict between "free trade" and "protectionism."[2] It often remains so, left, right, and center, even today.

On the ground, globalization transformed the reality to which such concepts were supposed to refer. As corporations become global, goods and services were increasingly produced in global networks of large corporations and their dependent suppliers. The "American" or "Japanese" cars and computers that "US" or "Japanese" companies "trade" were actually produced in dozens of countries by corporate networks that include companies in both the countries that are supposedly "trading" with each other. If a "US" company owned by investors all over the world outsources to producers in Japan, Indonesia, Columbia, and China to make and assemble an athletic shoe, which it then sells in a hundred countries, who is trading with whom? It became illusory to portray national economies as separate units that produce goods and services and then trade them with each other.[3]

Many issues raised by globalization could not even be considered within such a trade framework. Increased trade was indeed one aspect of globalization, but no more so than investment, governance, democracy and self-government, labor and human rights, regulation, environmental protection, and finance. In all these areas, processes that had once been focused within the boundaries of nation-states increasingly cut across them.

41

CONSTRUCTING AN ACCOUNT
PATTERNS, GAPS, ACTIONS, AND EFFECTS

≥∆

FACTORY SHUTDOWN WAS ONLY ONE OF MANY, APPARENTLY UNRELATED, EXPRESSIONS of globalization that gradually became manifest over the course of the 1980s. The rise of the "Eurodollar market," the "recycling of petrodollars," the growth of "off-shore export platforms," the imposition of "structural adjustment," and the propagation of "monetarism" and "supply-side economics" often appeared to be separate and unrelated phenomena. These seemingly peripheral developments gradually interacted in ways that changed virtually every aspect of life and defined globalization as a new global configuration.

As I observed the effects of these changes on the Naugatuck Valley and on the American labor movement, I felt I had to take up my collaborator's challenge— to understand the changes that were occurring in the global economy and their impact on the people and movements with which I was concerned. I used Piaget's idea of a development from an established pattern or structure through disequilibrium to a new pattern with its own elements of disequilibrium to compose an account of globalization.

The first step was to review the previously existing patterns, how they evolved, and how they were reproduced. In this case the relevant pre-established patterns were national economies and national governments. The second step was to identify conflicts and contradictions—gaps that made it difficult for actors and/ or the system as a whole to reproduce themselves and reach their goals. The third step was to examine their efforts to respond. The fourth step was to review the effects of their actions—including unintended side effects and interaction effects. These effects defined the new stage of the system. Then the process could be repeated, reviewing the gaps within the new stage, the efforts taken to address them, the consequences of those efforts, and the new state of the system and the new disequilibriums that resulted.

The pre-globalization economy. The decades following World War II were often referred to as the golden age of modern capitalism. With much of the world's industrial infrastructure destroyed by war, the United States dominated the markets of the world. Countries followed "Keynesian" policies that used government spending to ward off the recessions that had plagued capitalism from its inception. Internationally, the Bretton Woods system helped countries adjust to exchange rate problems without the ruinous deflation and "beggar-your-neighbor" policies that had generated a downward spiral in the Great Depression of the 1930s.

The crisis of the pre-globalization economy. The post-war system experienced an unprecedented period of sustained economic growth from the end of World War II through the 1960s. But in the early 1970s capitalism entered a worldwide crisis. Global economic growth fell to 2.5 percent, half its former rate. Profit rates in the seven richest industrialized countries fell from 17 percent in 1965 to 11 percent in 1980.[1] In 1973, an economically troubled US renounced the Bretton Woods system of fixed exchange rates.

Economists are still debating the causes of this crisis. In part it can be understood as simply one more example of the periodic downward spirals that have marked capitalism from its inception. The return of periodic crises reflected the exhaustion of the Keynesian fix for the traditional problems of capitalism: Government spending reached the point where it was perceived as a threat rather than a support to the profitability of the private economy. The crisis also reflected major changes among national economies as war-devastated Europe and Japan revived, over a hundred former European colonies became politically independent nations, international competition intensified, and the United States lost its dominant position in world markets.

Correcting the gap. Different actors promoted a variety of responses to this crisis. Third world countries initiated a "North-South Dialogue" to forge a New International Economic Order that would encourage constructive economic development through a reform of international trade patterns. The International Monetary Fund created Special Drawing Rights—"paper gold"—to provide a new form of international liquidity. US President Richard Nixon, a conservative Republican, declared himself a Keynesian and cut the link between gold and the US dollar. Representatives of internationalized capital, notably the Trilateral Commission, advocated expanded international economic integration—what became known as globalization. In the last two decades of the twentieth century this was the solution that won out.

Globalization first became apparent less in the realm of government policy than of corporate direct action. Corporations experienced the crisis as an intensification of international competition and a fall in their profits. They began experimenting with strategies to increase their profits by reducing their labor and other costs. These strategies included building and buying their products in low-wage third world countries, transforming their own structures to operate in a highly competitive global economy, and challenging government policies that increased their costs. Only gradually did they succeed in promoting a new system of global governance to support their other strategies.

At the core of the new strategy was capital mobility—the ability to move work and wealth around the world. Corporations increasingly came to view the entire world as a single market in which they bought and sold goods, services, and labor. The growth of offshore production created the basis for a "global assembly line" in which the components of a shirt or car might be made and assembled in a dozen or more different countries.

Capital mobility was not just about production. When *Global Village or Global Pillage* first appeared in 1994, we reported the amazing fact that the foreign exchange market processed $1 trillion per day. Four years later the second edition reported the figure had grown to $1.5 trillion.[2]

Globalization has often been portrayed either as a natural and inevitable process or as a specific political project. I sought an alternative to this unsatisfactory either/or. Globalization was the result of deliberate human action, but it was polycentric action taken in response to a crisis with limited insight into what would actually result. Globalization was not the result of a plot or even a plan. It was the result both of deliberate efforts by various actors to solve their problems and of unintended and unanticipated side effects and interaction effects. It was partially created by the coordinated global action of businesses and their representatives, for example, in promoting the policy agenda of the Trilateral Commission.[3] But it also resulted from the uncoordinated responses of corporations and investors to uncontrolled market forces.

Contradictions in globalization. Globalization produced a global economic system in the strict sense of a system: No element of the global economy can now be understood independently of its interaction with the other elements and the global economy as a whole. But that system is far from a stable and balanced whole. Globalization has instead produced a system that is full of contradictions.

Globalization promotes a destructive competition in which workers, communities, and entire countries are forced to cut labor, social, and environmental costs to attract mobile capital. When many countries each do so, the result is a disastrous race to the bottom in which all seem to get ahead, but in fact all lose. Wages driven down by competition, combined with mass unemployment due to austerity policies, reduces global demand, aggravating economic stagnation and crisis.

The race to the bottom has brought impoverishment, growing inequality, economic volatility, degradation of democracy, and destruction of the environment.[4]

It globalized rather than solved the traditional problems of unregulated market economies.

These problems generated a crisis in globalization. As we wrote in *Globalization from Below*, the new regime "violates the interests of the great majority of the world's people." It "lacks political legitimacy." It is "riven with divisions and conflicting interests." It has the "normal crisis-prone character of capitalist systems" but "few of the compensatory non-market institutions that helped stabilize pre-globalization economies." And it has "few means to control its own tendency to destroy the natural environment on which it—and its species—depend."[5]

Backlash. One of the unintended consequences of globalization has been a vast and diverse worldwide backlash against it. This has taken a variety of forms, ranging from "IMF riots" and other expressions of mass violence to nationwide general strikes against neo-liberal economic policies and from Battle of Seattle–style confrontations with international economic organizations to globally coordinated policy initiatives like the campaign for AIDS drugs for poor countries. Many of these strands began coordinating with each other in a "globalization from below" that has attempted to provide alternative solutions to the world's economic problems.

Beyond globalization. Globalization from Below predicted that globalization in its present form was unsustainable, but that what will come after it is far from determined. "It could be a war of all against all, world domination by a single superpower, a tyrannical alliance of global elites, global ecological catastrophe, or some combination thereof." Human agency—what people choose to do—can play a role in "deciding between these futures and more hopeful ones."[6]

* * *

This story as a whole represents a cycle I have used increasingly to organize my understanding of social change: pattern, action, gap, feedback, revised pattern, new action, new gap, and so on.

This approach provides an alternative to two others that often characterize discussion of globalization. One is that globalization either does not exist or is nothing new, but rather it is just a continuation of the same established processes of imperialism and capitalism. The other is that globalization changed everything, replacing the nation-state system with a new system that makes national borders irrelevant.

This approach recognized that transformation and preservation go hand in hand. Globalization indeed reflected the effort of corporations and their representatives and controllers to preserve and expand their power and profitability. But in their attempt to do so they transformed the entire global economy and its relation to the nation-state system, creating a new set of problems and possibilities for themselves and for the world's people.

This approach also provides an alternative to both the conventional view of globalization as part of the story of inevitable capitalist progress and the Marxist view of globalization as a step on the way to the inevitable collapse of capitalism and the transition to socialism. Unlike deterministic Marxism, this approach doesn't claim to know what the ultimate outcome or telos for any social process will be. It does not situate historical development in a pre-established theory or myth like the transition from capitalism to socialism. But unlike theories that deify the existing organization of society, it does not assume that the status quo is the culmination of social development and that perfection of the present structure is the goal of human history. It does not claim to know "the end of history," but it does not assume that the present embodies it. It portrays a system in crisis with multiple possible outcomes, shapeable at least in part by human choice.

42

DOMINATION

THE RESTRUCTURING OF GLOBAL GOVERNANCE

è&

WHILE GLOBALIZATION WAS PROCEEDING THROUGH MYRIAD DECENTRALIZED initiatives, a deliberate effort to support globalization through public policy was also emerging. Actors like the Trilateral Commission promoted a global agenda, now widely referred to as neoliberalism, whose goal was to ease the way for the mobility of capital. This agenda was developed over time through give-and-take among major global economic actors. Eventually its implementation became an explicit common objective of pro-globalization players all over the world.

This agenda was implemented in a variety of ways. In the case of trade, the General Agreement on Tariffs and Trade (GATT), an institution that was little more than a framework for negotiating trade deals, was replaced by the World Trade Organization, which was based on rules binding on nations, authoritative decision-making procedures, and a bureaucracy empowered to enforce its decisions. A new regional trade structure, the North American Free Trade Agreement (NAFTA), was negotiated for the United States, Mexico, and Canada.

In the case of the World Bank and IMF, existing institutions changed their policies and transformed their missions to pursue new purposes. The IMF abandoned the role of supporting the ability of countries to follow Keynesian policies at a national level. Instead it tried to force countries to drop national control of currencies and open themselves to globalization. Both the IMF and the World Bank took advantage of the indebtedness of poor countries to assert far greater control over their economies, demanding that they accept radical "structural adjustment" policies of privatization, deregulation, and austerity.

The power of the IMF and the World Bank was based on the dependence of poor countries on a steady supply of new loans to keep their economies afloat. This dependence was intensified by the decision of governments and major lenders to base further lending on the acceptance of IMF "conditionalities." Dependence was parlayed into domination.

The growing power of the WTO, NAFTA, IMF, World Bank, and similar international economic institutions provoked debate over the nature of the changes that were occurring. Some portrayed them—with either satisfaction or alarm—as the development of a world government that was superseding national sovereignty. Others argued that the nation-state was unchanged as the core political institution of the modern world.

My emerging approach invited another perspective. Rather than eliminate national governments, this new system of global economic governance adds another institutional layer—one that at times conflicts with national governments and at times has to bow to them. It lacks the police and military organizations for dominion at home and war abroad that have characterized states from their origin. But its ability to impose its rules on its subordinate parts proved effective—at least for a time.[1]

This new system of global governance was formally authorized by the world's governments, but it is not based in any meaningful way on the consent of the governed. It has no effective institutional mechanism to hold it accountable to those its decisions affect. As one unnamed WTO official quoted in the *Financial Times* said, "The WTO is the place where governments collude in private against their domestic pressure groups."[2] Indeed, it is an exquisite example of "extended authority," in which authority ostensibly granted for one purpose is applied to another one—in this case not so much to benefit the holders of governmental authority as the global corporations and investors whose interests they largely reflect.[3] It should not have been surprising that this emerging system of undemocratic power would call forth global opposition.

43

DISORDER
UNINTENDED CONSEQUENCES

ᐓ

WHILE THE NEW STRUCTURE OF GLOBAL GOVERNANCE EMBODIED IN THE WTO, IMF, World Bank, NAFTA, and their kin was a deliberate construction, globalization also involved uncoordinated initiatives among thousands of actors that resulted in unanticipated and often catastrophic side effects and interaction effects.

One obvious example is global financial destabilization. Neoliberal financial deregulation reduced barriers to the international flow of capital. Before the turn of the millennium, $1.5 trillion was flowing across international borders daily in the foreign currency market alone.

These huge flows easily swamped national economies. In 1998, for example, an apparently local crisis in Thailand ricocheted around the globe. In the following two years Malaysia's economy had shrunk by 25 percent, South Korea's by 45 percent, and Thailand's by 50 percent. Indonesia's economy had shrunk by 80 percent; its per capita gross domestic product dropped from $3,500 to less than $750. As former World Bank chief economist Joseph Stiglitz commented, "Capital market liberalization has not only not brought people the prosperity they were promised, but it has also brought these crises, with wages falling 20 or 30 percent, and unemployment going up by a factor of two, three, four or ten."[1]

Another example of unintended and uncontrolled global interaction is the race to the bottom in which different workforces and countries compete to attract capital by providing subsidies and accepting lower wages, social standards, and environmental conditions. Each participant in the race to the bottom intends to improve their own situation by attracting international capital. But the combined result is simply to drive down the conditions of all.

The race to the bottom has had numerous unanticipated side effects in turn. Whole industrial zones in the United States were turned into rust belts as a result of jobs moving to countries such as Mexico and Taiwan. Then the maquiladora zone on the US-Mexico border to which so many of their jobs had moved was decimated by the migration of jobs to China. In 2001 alone, one hundred maquiladoras shut down and two hundred thousand maquila workers lost their jobs.[2] And Taiwan had the steepest drop in gross domestic product in half a century as "tumbling electronics exports slashed companies' profits and accelerated their flight to China, where costs are lower."[3] As labor costs rose in China, jobs there began migrating to Vietnam, Cambodia, and Bangladesh.

Meanwhile, the cumulative effect of producing more and more products with cheaper and cheaper labor has been to create global oversupply and a global lack of effective demand. This was a, if not the, primary cause of the global recession and deflationary crisis of the early twenty-first century. In response, the United States and some other countries began turning to economic nationalist policies designed to increase exports and reduce imports through currency and trade policies—the classic beggar-your-neighbor policies that exacerbated the Great Depression of the 1930s. The result is a global downward spiral in which each country tries to displace the effects of recession onto the others. This was one cause of the Great Recession that began in 2007.

Another unintended effect of globalization has been both local and global environmental degradation. Countries are forced to compete for investment by lowering environmental protections in an ecological race to the bottom. Many countries rewrote their mining codes to encourage investment. Corporations promoted untested technologies, such as pesticides and genetic engineering, in poor countries that lack the democratic controls and environmental protections that might limit them in more developed countries. Desperate poverty led to desperate overharvesting of natural resources. The cumulative effect of uncontrolled competitive economic development accelerated the emission of carbon dioxide leading to global warming.

These results are all consequences of intentional human action. But they are not the result of actions coordinated with the intent of producing such consequences. Rather, they are the unplanned, unintended, and unanticipated side effects and interaction effects of actions undertaken for other purposes.

44

DIFFERENTIATION AND INTEGRATION
THE RESTRUCTURING OF PRODUCTION AND LABOR

ঽ৶

As corporations sought to counteract declining profits through capital mobility, they restructured themselves to operate in the new global economy. Their restructuring became another aspect of the globalization process.

In the era of national economies, most US industries were dominated by a handful of large corporations. These firms pursued a strategy of "vertical" and "horizontal" integration. Through vertical integration they sought to control all phases of production from raw material through final product—described in the slogan of a copper company that I studied for the Brass Workers History Project as "from the mine to the consumer." Through horizontal integration they sought to fill every product niche in the industry market. The large corporation was the very model of what economists called a "hierarchical organization," with decision making organized from the top, a clear chain of command, and an effort to organize the whole as an integrated system of production and distribution.[1]

As corporations oriented less toward the national and more toward the global economy, they began to restructure. Corporations abandoned the quest for vertical and horizontal integration and pursued only those endeavors that they hoped would "maximize stockholder value" in the short run. They replaced the classical organizational hierarchy with what came to be known as a core-ring structure. They "downsized" and concentrated on their core functions and capacities. All other functions were "outsourced" to a surrounding ring of suppliers dispersed around the globe. These suppliers were often captives of or at least dependent on the core corporation, making them formally outside the boundaries of the firm but very much part of the larger system it dominated. Supplier companies in turn became part of transnational supply chains, which developed their own differentiation and integration.

Corporations increasingly formed "strategic alliances" with other corporations, thus making even more ambiguous the boundaries of the firm; such companies still competed with each other, but they also cooperated. As globalization proceeded, international mergers became more and more common. The cumulative result of these changes was what economist Bennett Harrison called "networked production."[2]

The character of these changes was widely debated. Some economists proclaimed the death of the large corporation and the resurgence of small business to a dominant position in the global economy. Others saw only an increase in global concentration.

From a systems perspective, the result was not so paradoxical. If firms are viewed as part of larger systems, and the boundaries of each firm are presumed to be semi-permeable and subject to change, the emergence of "networked production" can produce both a transfer of production to smaller firms and increased dependence of those firms on core corporations. As Bennett Harrison aptly stated, the "decentralization of production" was combined with the "concentration of control."[3] The capitalist economy remains a system of differentiation and integration, but one based on the "dis-integration" of the classical corporation into the pattern of networked production.

These changes transformed the organization of the labor process. Large integrated corporations had large workforces organized as "internal labor markets" in which workers could expect long-term employment. As corporations downsized, they divided their workforces into a small core that remained internal to the firm and a large group that was either laid off or redefined as external to the firm, hired on a contingent basis or through subcontractors. What had been in part a hierarchical relationship became increasingly a market relationship. This represented a "re-commodification of labor" in which workers increasingly lost all rights except the right to sell their labor power and corporations rejected all responsibilities to their workers. To support this development, employers tried to eliminate public policies that mandated job security, work rules, worker representation, healthcare, pensions, and other obligations that required them to treat labor as something more than and other than a commodity.

Globalization was thus producing at least two major changes in class relations. It was transforming the division of labor from a primarily national to a global system. And it was changing the relation of labor to the firm from one involving long-term mutual commitments to one based on short-term market contingencies.

Neither the classic integrated corporation and internal labor market nor the subsequent dis-integrated corporation and the re-commodification of labor can be explained by the general characteristics of capitalism alone. Each of course reflected a desire to increase profits, but that led to very different results due to the strategies adopted by people pursuing their interests in specific historical conditions.

45

RESPONDING TO CHANGE
A NEW LABOR INTERNATIONALISM

ટેર

GLOBALIZATION CREATED NEW PROBLEMS FOR AMERICAN LABOR. STRATEGIES THAT had evolved to provide institutional stability for unions and a rising standard of living for workers grew less and less effective in the face of corporations willing and able to close operations and move them abroad if their demands were not met. The response of organized labor illustrates how, under changing conditions, feedback plus reflection may lead to change in strategies and even in goals.

From World War II until the 1960s, most of organized labor was closely allied with the international political and economic policies of the US government. The AFL-CIO supported and aided Cold War efforts to combat Communism and establish American military and ideological supremacy around the globe. The ALF-CIO was a strong supporter of "free trade." "Foreign competition" seemed little threat to American workers because American industries dominated the markets of a war-devastated world. Military expansion "primed the pump" at home while it secured the global "free market" for American products—to the apparent benefit of those who produced them.

Starting in the 1970s, as international competition undermined US economic hegemony, many unions switched from free trade to protectionism. Faced with massive loss of jobs in auto, steel, garment, and other industries, the labor movement increasingly campaigned for tariffs and other barriers to imports in order to "save American jobs." Decisions by American corporations to relocate production abroad were often characterized as "foreign workers stealing American jobs." Toyota-bashing became a Labor Day attraction and the employees of "foreign competitors" became objects of hate campaigns.

Yet Toyota-bashing proved ineffective as a strategy for saving American jobs and preserving decent wages in the face of globalization. It was, after all, primarily "American" companies that were moving American workers' jobs overseas.

Globalization made economic nationalist strategies less and less credible. Hence pressures increased at every level of the labor movement to develop an alternative.

Organized labor increasingly moved toward demanding reform of the global economy as a whole, symbolized by demands for labor rights and environmental standards in international trade agreements to protect all the world's workers and communities from the race to the bottom. Its official objective became an "upward harmonization" of global standards that would take labor and the environment out of competition. This approach became the centerpiece of organized labor's participation in the 1999 protests dubbed the Battle of Seattle.

This change required an ecological shift in the way the situation of workers in the global economy was conceived. Globalization had to be seen not just as a question of competition between US workers and workers in some other country, but rather an overall change in the differentiation and integration of work worldwide.

A shift to what was implicitly a systems perspective helped open a way to address problems that had seemed insolvable. If workers defined their problem as beating foreign competition, the apparent solution would be to accept lower wages. But then foreign workers would accept still lower wages, leading to a vicious circle of destructive interaction—a race to the bottom. Recognizing the systemic character of the problem made it possible to break out of such self-reinforcing and self-defeating loops. In this case, the recognition of common interests among workers in countering the race to the bottom became the basis for new forms of international solidarity.

In order to resist the race to the bottom some parts of the US labor movement gradually developed new objectives and new alliances. Ford workers in St. Paul visited Ford plants in Mexico and became involved in supporting Ford workers there. Unions in Massachusetts fought the suppression of labor rights in Burma by supporting a statewide boycott of Burmese products and investments. Trade unionists formed alliances with environmentalists and added demands for global environmental sustainability to their demands for international labor rights.

The international positions of US unions remain varied and at times contradictory. The recessions of the early twenty-first century, marked by huge additional losses of industrial jobs and expanded offshoring of high-tech and other white-collar jobs, revived the labor movement's economic nationalism. That only further illustrates the way in which organized labor's approach to the global economy is not something fixed, but rather something shaped by a combination of experience and reflection on it.

DE-CENTERING
GLOBALIZATION FROM BELOW

ès

HOW DO PATTERNS OF COORDINATION CHANGE? I HAD PLENTY OF OPPORTUNITY TO ponder this question as I watched social movements and popular organizations that had been born and bred in the era of national economies confront the realities of globalization. Because I wanted to understand and participate in that process, I had to clarify, test, and correct my developing views about the process of change.

By the late 1970s I saw plants closing and unions decimated in my home state of Connecticut and throughout much of the United States. Globalization was adversely affecting millions of people around the world. The new powers of the IMF and the World Bank were already undermining the well-being and self-government of many third world countries. New trade agreements such as NAFTA and the WTO, then on the drawing boards, threatened to further paralyze democratic self-government. Meanwhile, the unintended effects of globalization, including financial instability and the race to the bottom, were also having devastating effects on people and the environment.

It was hard to see what might counter globalization. There were, it is true, numerous revolts against these early expressions of globalization, such as the IMF riots that broke out in many countries to protest the austerity imposed by structural adjustment policies. But such activities were almost entirely uncoordinated with each other. Their participants had little sense that they might share interests or concerns with others who were in other countries or focused on other issues. Workers were being played off against each other around the world. I wondered if there was any way workers and others in different countries could get together to forestall the race to the bottom.

It was often said that capital was becoming global, but labor was inherently national. I knew that the labor and socialist movements had once articulated an internationalist antiwar rhetoric, but in World War I they had nearly all ended up supporting their own national governments against their national enemies, even though it meant killing "fellow workers." I had read AFL president Samuel Gompers' appalling observation that "one of the most wholesome lessons that the war taught labor" was that "the ties that bind workingmen to the national government are stronger and more intimate than those international ties that unite workingmen of all countries."[1] Much of the US labor movement accepted the common belief that "internationalism" was the opposite of "Americanism." And labor movements all over the world seemed to be closely tied to their national governments and economies.

The kinds of internationalism I was most familiar with had never been too attractive to me, and they seemed largely irrelevant to this situation. Whatever the loyalties of individual Communists might have been, the official internationalism of the Third International seemed little more than a cover for the domination of parties and unions by the Soviet Union and those serving as its agents.[2] The internationalism of the AFL-CIO was an anti-Communist mirror image, complete with subservience to US foreign policy and its own subversion of foreign labor movements through its government-funded International Affairs Department.[3] The official organizations of labor internationalism—the International Confederation of Free Trade Unions and the World Federation of Trade Unions—seemed little more than a pair of bookends upholding the opposing sides of the Cold War. Starting with the Vietnam War, many opponents of US foreign policy had cultivated an internationalism that consisted of little more than defending whatever foreign regimes the United States was attacking, from Ho Chi Minh to Ayatollah Khomeini to Saddam Hussein.

Tim Costello and I began scanning the horizon for anything that might hint at where a new form of cooperation among workers in different countries might come from. The first breakthrough we learned about was in 1988, when twelve hundred workers struck a factory in Juarez, Mexico, owned by a US subsidiary of a Swedish corporation. The workers were gassed, clubbed, arrested, fired, and blacklisted. Unexpectedly, an "expeditionary force" of teamsters, steelworkers, communications, and sheet metal workers from nearby El Paso crossed the Mexican border on the Fourth of July, bringing several thousand pounds of food as a gesture of support for the strikers. The organizer of the Juarez action was the president of the AFL-CIO in El Paso, a city that had lost fourteen thousand jobs to Mexico since 1980. He said, "A lot of people [in the United States] say that Mexican workers are the enemy. But we can't blame [the loss of US jobs] on the workers. We have to blame it on the corporations."[4]

I made a few research phone calls around the country and turned up some other diminutive straws in the wind. Paul Garver, the head of a Chicago local of the Service Employees International Union (SEIU), filled me in on one of them. Labor movement opponents of Reagan administration policies in Central

America had developed direct ties with a militant labor federation in El Salvador that was not aligned with either side in labor's global Cold War. When top SEIU officials demanded that SEIU locals obey the AFL-CIO policy of "shunning" all but the most definitively anti-Communist unions, the activists mobilized at the SEIU convention and forced a resolution condemning US policy and renouncing the shunning doctrine. By the end of the convention a top SEIU official was sporting the activists' button proclaiming "Labor Solidarity Has No Borders."[5]

Joe Uehlein of the AFL-CIO's Industrial Union Department told me how some International Trade Secretariats (the organizations linking unions in the same industries around the world, now known as global union federations) had begun actively organizing strike support among unions in different countries. One of them set up an international computer network to link members in different countries—a technology then so new that we had to explain to our readers what a computer network was. An Amsterdam-based group called Transnationals Information Exchange organized international conferences for rank-and-file workers; one brought together thirty auto workers from Mexico, Spain, Brazil, Belgium, Britain, Germany, Japan, South Africa, and the United States. A coalition of labor and human rights groups had successfully lobbied for a clause in the US Trade Act protecting international labor rights.

I searched libraries and bookstores for research, historical or contemporary, on labor internationalism. I found slim pickings until I saw a brief announcement of a book published in the Netherlands called *The Old Internationalism and the New: A Reader on Labour, New Social Movements and Internationalism*[6] edited by Peter Waterman. Peter, whom I later got to know, had been a Communist and actually worked for the Third International itself, but he had developed a cutting critique of Communist internationalism and all other top-down forms of organization.

Peter's essays on internationalism made two related points that set me on a very different track for thinking about responses to globalization. First, he pointed out that most of the recent international campaigns addressing labor issues were not conducted primarily by labor organizations, but rather by coalitions that might include unions but were likely to have other social movements and civil society groups at their core. He described the campaign to support workers at the Coca-Cola bottling plant in Guatemala City, many of whose leaders had been murdered or disappeared. Church groups had begun an international support campaign. They were joined by Amnesty International, the food workers international trade secretariat, and Coca-Cola workers in Mexico, Sweden, Britain, and elsewhere. After nine years of strikes, occupations, and international campaigns, Coca-Cola was forced to make substantial concessions to its Guatemalan workers. Second, Peter argued that such a new internationalism was less likely to be organized by the official institutions of labor internationalism than by international communications networks that he saw emerging among a wide variety of social movements all over the world.

Tim and I took these ideas very much to heart. In our first article on the emerging labor internationalism, we wrote that, whatever the future of labor internationalism, it is "unlikely to look like the First, Second, or Third Internationals," in which "large national labor movements came together in a centralized world organization" designed to confront world capitalism. It was far more likely to look like "a developing network of transnational links among groups from many kinds of movements and along many axes."[7] Indeed, the new labor internationalism was already marked by "close ties with religious, human rights, women's, development, and other movements," often drawing on their far more developed international networks.[8]

This change of perspective opened my eyes to a series of responses to globalization that were not defined as labor internationalism. For example, in 1986 a group of environment and development NGOs formed a People's Network for Eco Development and began holding protest gatherings at the annual joint meetings of the IMF and the World Bank to coordinate north/south resistance to their policies. By the 1990 meetings, delegations from more than fifty countries were participating. Meanwhile, large, complex international campaigns against the destruction of the Amazon rain forest and India's Narmada Dam were developing. In 1992, nine hundred NGOs from thirty-seven countries threatened to initiate a campaign to cut off World Bank funding unless it halted its support for the Narmada Dam. Apparently they had found the way to the Bank's heart: The next year it cancelled its loan for the project.

In 1986, international trade negotiators began the "Uruguay Round" to establish what eventually became the World Trade Organization. I heard that there was an organizer named Mark Ritchie who was trying to develop a campaign around it. Mark had helped organize family farmers during the farm crisis of the 1970s and had also worked on the boycott against Nestlé's infant formula that was causing thousands of deaths in third world countries. I got in touch with him and learned that a network of advocates for small farmers around the world had been holding counter-meetings at the trade negotiations.

Mark told me, "We learned to reverse the old slogan, 'Think globally, act locally.' We learned you have to act globally to succeed locally—you have to go to Brussels to save your farm in Texas. It was really important for farmers in different parts of the world to see their common circumstances and to develop win/win approaches, rather than being played off against each other."[9]

International opposition came to a head with a huge demonstration at what were supposed to be the final Uruguay Round negotiations in Brussels in December 1990.

So far as I know it was the first really global demonstration, with farmers, environmentalists, and consumer representatives from every continent organized to affect a global process. There were more than 100 farmers from North America, 200 from Japan, and delegations from Korea, Africa, and Latin America. There were a thousand busses from all over Europe, Norway to Greece—more than 30,000 people. The result was that Thursday night, when the United States made its big push for a free trade agreement, South Korea, Japan, and Europe all said no and they decided to adjourn.[10]

Over the ensuing decade, these early shoots were followed by a massive growth of new forms of transnational social movement collaboration. From the campaign against NAFTA to the anti-WTO demonstrations that shut down the World Trade Organization negotiations in Seattle to the formation of the World Social Forum, a new and largely unanticipated global phenomenon emerged.

This huge global groundswell has come to be known, rather misleadingly, as the "anti-globalization movement." Far from being against globalization in general, it is, in the words of Naomi Klein, "the most internationally minded, globally linked movement the world has ever seen."[11] And rather than being a single movement, it is more a global process through which myriad movements and organizations are creating new patterns of coordination and self-organization that I call globalization from below.

Globalization from below illustrates the emergence of new forms of coordination that cross old boundaries. Prior to globalization, popular movements and organizations primarily pursued the interests of particular constituencies within a national framework, national politics, and national economies. Throughout the twentieth century, nationally based social movements placed limits on the downsides of capitalism. Workers and communities won national economic regulation and protections ranging from environmental laws to union representation and from public investment to progressive taxation.

Globalization undermined this adaptation for many movements, as we saw in the previous chapter for the US labor movement. Corporations could outflank the controls governments and organized citizens once placed on them by relocating their facilities around the world. Many groups found that separately they were powerless against the forces of global capital. They began seeking new strategies. They gradually discovered that, in the new global context, they had common enemies and common interests both with other constituencies and with people in other countries. They began to explore new potentials for mutual aid and coordinated action. They began to develop shared representations both of the situation they faced and of their capacity to address it in concert. Thus the coordination patterns of popular organizations and movements were transformed.

This process involved de-centering. People needed to assimilate the ideas and experiences of others and incorporate them into their own thinking. In 1990, for example, garment union economist Ron Blackwell did something previously almost unimaginable: Before preparing testimony on US trade policy, he went to Mexico to talk with Mexican trade unionists and "to see how the world looks from the other side of the border." He noted that such exchanges had become common: "Everybody is talking to everybody."[12]

I had used the idea of de-centering to explore how individuals become part of a social group—for example, how workers develop informal work groups. Globalization revealed the same process on a different scale. In response to globalization, a wide range of established organizations and movements around the world found themselves unexpectedly assimilating and accommodating to each other's views.

At the Seattle demonstrations against the WTO at the end of 1999 I saw how this process had broadened identities and viewpoints beyond previous limits. For example, the US labor movement, as we saw in the previous chapter, went through significant changes in response to globalization.

While conflict between organized labor and the environmental movement had been chronic, the largest Seattle rally was actually cosponsored by the AFL-CIO and the Sierra Club. When a large contingent of environmentalist youth appeared in Seattle wearing turtle costumes, the new alliance found expression in the slogan, "Teamsters and turtles, together at last!"

The US labor movement had often tended to see globalization as an effort by foreign workers to "steal" American jobs. As it moved toward advocating international solidarity to raise labor conditions in poor countries, however, US labor found itself allying with unions in the countries to which US jobs were moving. This too found a symbolic embodiment in the Seattle WTO demonstrations: US trade union leaders brought to the podium and presented as heroes and heroines workers from around the world who were fighting to organize unions over the opposition of their own governments—and often against US corporations backed openly or tacitly by the US government. These changes did not require organized labor to abandon the identity or interests of American workers, but they did require overcoming the limitations of narrow issue and national perspectives, moving beyond limiting traditions, and in some cases giving up long-established antipathies.

Globalization from below illustrates common patterns in the emergence of new social movements. They often first appear in small, scattered pockets among those who are vulnerable, discriminated against, or less subject to control by the dominant institutions. These nascent movements reflect the specific experiences and traditions of the social groups among which they arise. In periods of rapid social change, such movements are likely to develop in many such milieus and to look very different from each other as a result. In the case of globalization from below, for example, mobilizations ranged from French chefs concerned about preservation of local food traditions to Indian farmers concerned about corporate control of seeds to American university students concerned about school clothing made in foreign sweatshops.

The convergence of these disparate groups and their disparate itineraries into globalization from below illustrates a general process of social change characterized by the historical sociologist Michael Mann. It starts with the appearance of new solutions among people in diverse "interstitial locations"; their linking through networks that create subversive "invisible connections"; and their development of shared beliefs that unify them in their diversity. What follows is their emergence as an independent power and their "outflanking" of existing institutions in ways that force a reorganization of the status quo.[13]

This description fits well the emergence of globalization from below. In response to globalization from above, movements emerged all over the world in locations that were marginal to the dominant power centers. They linked up by means of networks that cut across national borders. They began to develop a sense of solidarity, a common belief system, a common program, and forms of joint action. As a result of their new patterns of coordination, they became recognized by the world's governments and corporations as an independent power—and one to be reckoned with.

47
POWER AND DEPENDENCE
THE LILLIPUT STRATEGY

❧

IN JONATHAN SWIFT'S SATIRIC FABLE *GULLIVER'S TRAVELS*, THE TINY LILLIPUTIANS, only a few inches tall, captured the marauding giant Gulliver, many times their height, by tying him down with hundreds of threads. Gulliver could have crushed any Lilliputian under the heel of his boot—but the dense network of threads tied around him left him immobile and powerless. Similarly, facing powerful global forces and institutions, participants in globalization from below made use of the relatively modest sources of power they possessed and combined them with often quite different sources of power available to other participants. We dubbed their emerging approach the "Lilliput strategy."

Strike! had emphasized that workers, though powerless as individuals, were powerful collectively because employers depended on their labor. Strikes turned this dependence into effective power. My emerging approach generalized this idea. Power relations are maintained by the active support of some people and the acquiescence of others. It is the activity of people—going to work, paying taxes, buying products, obeying government officials, staying off private property—that continually re-creates the power of the powerful.

Bertolt Brecht dramatized this truth in his poem "German War Primer":

> *General, your tank is a strong vehicle.*
> *It breaks down a forest and crushes a hundred people.*
> *But it has one fault: it needs a driver.*[1]

Such dependence gives the apparently powerless a potential power over adversaries—but one that can be realized only if they are prepared to join together to withdraw their support and acquiescence from the status quo. Social movements—including the movement against economic globalization—can be understood as the collective withdrawal of such support and acquiescence.

Specific social relations require particular forms of support and therefore of its withdrawal. The World Bank depends on raising funds in the bond market, so critics of the World Bank organized a campaign against purchase of World Bank bonds, modeled on the successful campaign against investment in apartheid South Africa. WTO trade rules prohibit city and state selective purchasing laws—like the Massachusetts ban on purchases from companies that invest in Burma—making such laws a form of withdrawal of consent from the WTO, in effect an act of governmental civil disobedience. (Several foreign governments threatened to bring WTO charges against the Massachusetts Burma law before the US Supreme Court declared it unconstitutional in 2000.)

Just the threat of withdrawal of consent can be an exercise of power. Ruling groups can be led to make concessions if the alternative will ultimately prove costly. The movement for globalization from below demonstrated this repeatedly. As we have seen, the World Bank ended funding for India's Narmada Dam when nine hundred organizations in thirty-seven countries pledged a campaign to defund the Bank unless it canceled its support. And the agricultural biotechnology company Monsanto found that mounting global concern about genetically modified organisms (GMOs) so threatened its interests that it agreed to accept the Cartagena Protocol to the Convention on Biological Diversity allowing them to be regulated.

The threat to established institutions may be a specific and targeted withdrawal of support. For example, the student anti-sweatshop protestors made clear that their campuses would be subject to sit-ins and other forms of disruption until their universities agreed to ban the use of their schools' logos on products made in sweatshops. Or, to take a very different example, in the midst of the Battle of Seattle President Bill Clinton, faced with loss of electoral support from the labor movement, endorsed the use of sanctions to enforce international labor rights.

The threat may, alternatively, be a more general social breakdown, often expressed as fear of "social unrest." For example, in 1999 under heavy pressure from the World Bank, the Bolivian government sold off the public water system of its third largest city, Cochabamba, to a subsidiary of the San Francisco–based Bechtel Corporation, which promptly doubled the price of water for people's homes. Early in 2000 the people of Cochabamba rebelled, shutting down the city with general strikes and blockades. The government declared a state of siege and a young protester was shot and killed.

Word spread from the remote Bolivian highlands all over the world via the Internet, partly through the efforts of my friend Jim Schulz, a young American working there in an orphanage who had extensive experience as an organizer back home. Hundreds of e-mail messages poured into Bechtel headquarters from all over the world demanding that it leave Cochabamba. A Cochabamba protest leader was smuggled out of hiding to Washington, D.C., where I heard him address an international rally against the IMF and the World Bank. In the midst of local and global protests, the Bolivian government, which had said that Bechtel must not leave, suddenly reversed itself and signed an accord that included all the demands of the protestors. There is little doubt that it did so out of fear of social unrest. (One of the leaders of the protest, an indigenous coca farmer named Evo Morales, was elected president of Bolivia in 2005 and sponsored the International People's Summit on Climate Change in Cochabamba in 2010.)

The slogan "fix it or nix it," which the anti-globalization movement often applied to the WTO, IMF, and World Bank, also embodied a threat. It implied that the movement would block the globalization process unless it conformed to appropriate global norms. And in fact the global movement did block significant elements of the globalization program; in 1998, for example, a massive multinational campaign by civil society groups permanently killed the Organisation for Economic Co-operation and Development's (OECD) proposed Multilateral Agreement on Investment (MAI).

While the media focused on global extravaganzas like the Battle of Seattle, these were only the tip of the globalization-from-below iceberg. The Lilliput strategy primarily involved the utilization of dependences by people acting at the grassroots, as the following examples illustrate.

When the Japanese-owned Bridgestone/Firestone (B/F) demanded twelve-hour shifts and a 30 percent wage cut for new workers in its American factories, workers struck. B/F fired them all and replaced them with twenty-three hundred strikebreakers. American workers appealed to B/F workers worldwide for help. Unions around the world organized Days of Outrage protests against B/F. In Argentina a two-hour general assembly of all workers at the gates of the B/F plant halted production while two thousand workers heard B/F workers from the United States describe the company's conduct. In Brazil, B/F workers staged one-hour work stoppages, then "worked like turtles"—the Brazilian phrase for a slowdown. Unions in Belgium, France, Italy, and Spain met with local Bridgestone management to demand a settlement. American B/F workers went to Japan and met with Japanese unions, many of whom called for the immediate reinstatement of US workers. Five hundred Japanese unionists marched through the streets of Tokyo, supporting B/F workers from the United States. In the midst of this worldwide campaign, B/F unexpectedly agreed to rehire its locked-out American workers.

When South Africa tried to pass a law allowing it to disregard drug patents in health emergencies, the Clinton administration lobbied hard against it and put South Africa on a watch-list that is the first step toward trade sanctions. In response, according to a *New York Times* account, the Philadelphia branch of ACT UP, the AIDS direct action group, decided "to take up South Africa's cause and start heckling Vice President Al Gore, who was in the midst of his primary campaign for the presidency." The banners saying that "Mr. Gore was letting Africans die to please American pharmaceutical companies" left his campaign "chagrined." After media and campaign staff looked into the matter, the administration did an about-face and "accepted African governments' circumvention of AIDS drug patents."[2]

For AIDS activists this was only one victory in a long campaign. Writer Esther Kaplan describes a packed meeting in a stultifying room in a former church in North Philadelphia, "an area of falling-down porches and abandoned storefronts," for a group that might be expected to find the global economy a rather remote concern—recovering drug addicts. John Bell of ACT UP/Philadelphia, a former war veteran with AIDS, was recruiting for a "Stop Global AIDS" march. He began, "Hi. My name is John, and I'm an addict and an alcoholic." According to Kaplan, "as he went on to talk about his gratitude for his lifesaving med[icine]s, it seemed only natural that he'd invite the 100 or so assembled to stand up for HIVers worldwide who don't have access to the same meds." A few weeks later, twelve packed buses from Philadelphia rolled up in front of the United Nations in New York, turning the march into "an energetic African-American protest rally." According to Bell, they were "making the connections between local and global in terms of health care and AIDS. We have been preparing people to be not only US citizens, but citizens of the world."[3]

An international coalition that included Doctors Without Borders and religious networks around the world generated thousands of letters to drug companies and the US government demanding they stop trying to use patent laws to keep people from getting AIDS drugs in poor countries. There were some results. An April 2001 article in the *Christian Science Monitor* headlined "Drug Firms Yield to Cry of the Poor" reported that "39 international pharmaceutical companies unconditionally withdrew a lawsuit against the South African government aimed at barring the country from importing cheap anti-AIDS drugs."[4] And in June 2001, the *Financial Times* reported that the US government "dropped its complaint against Brazil's patent law at the World Trade Organization, dealing a fresh blow to the leading global pharmaceutical companies' business in the developing world."[5]

Before the November 2001 meetings of the WTO in Doha, Qatar, AIDS activists, NGO representatives, and third world officials met and drew up a declaration stating that nothing in the WTO rules covering patents could prevent governments from safeguarding public health. Daniel Berman of Doctors Without Borders reported the results from Doha:

> Since Seattle there has been a seismic shift. Two years ago many developing
> countries felt they were powerless against the will of the wealthy countries

and their drug companies. Here in Doha more than 80 countries came together and negotiated in mass. It was this solidarity that led to a strong affirmation that TRIPS [Trade Related Intellectual Property Rights] "can and should be interpreted in a manner to protect public health." In practical terms, this means that countries are not at the mercy of multinationals when they practice price gouging.[6]

All these examples of the Lilliput strategy involve utilizing one or another form of dependence. The Bolivian government backed down on privatizing Cochabamba's water because it seemed to be the only way to end the disruption of the life of the country—and perhaps because Bechtel itself wanted to escape the huge damage to its image that the global protests were causing. Bridgestone/Firestone rehired its fired American workers largely because it feared the disruption of its labor relations in Japan and in subsidiaries all over the world and the emergence of coordination among its workers worldwide. Vice President Al Gore feared that loss of support among African Americans on the issue of AIDS drugs for Africa might lose him the Democratic nomination for president. Pharmaceutical companies feared that if they were too visible in their gouging of poor AIDS victims it might cause a backlash against them that would lead to more regulation of their lucrative markets in the developed countries. Such action constituted neither revolution nor conventional within-the-system and by-the-rules reform. Rather it constituted a utilization of dependence to bring about a change in the balance of power.

A movement's ability to prevail in such conflicts depends primarily on drawing together sufficient forces to impose negative consequences on opponents and on dividing and undermining opponents' support. This is what the theorist of nonviolent struggle Gene Sharp calls an "indirect strategy."[7] It reflects the idea of achieving a goal by counteracting the forces that prevent its realization.

The idea of the Lilliput strategy was a description of what globalization from below activists were actually doing. But it was also a way of representing a pattern that could be used in thought experiments about future action.

SOLVING PROBLEMS
CONSTRUCTING ALTERNATIVES
TO ECONOMIC GLOBALIZATION

ۏ

SOCIAL MOVEMENTS OFTEN FIND IT EASIER TO SAY WHAT THEY ARE AGAINST THAN what they propose. It is difficult to get beyond extremely general objectives such as peace, freedom, and justice. Alternatives to what exists may be conceived in terms of an ideal world in which such general objectives have been realized. But such utopias, while they may stimulate the imagination and motivate action, often have little connection to what currently exists. That makes it hard to see how they can actually be realized. They are often utopian in the sense of being based purely on what we might want the world to be, without taking into account what it currently is.

My emerging approach provided a means for formulating alternatives to what exists that are based on transformations of current patterns and on actions that make use of capacities that people already possess. This approach starts with the current situation and its problems. It asks what changes would be necessary to correct those problems. This approach is based on the cybernetic idea of counteracting or compensating for deviations from goals.

The next step is to ask what changes in existing patterns of action and coordination would be necessary to produce those corrections. This is, in effect, a thought experiment: "What if . . . ?" "What would be necessary . . . ?" We can try to imagine actions that are variations of what people already are capable of doing that would close the gap between what exists and what is desired.

As I began trying to understand globalization, I discovered that it involved both problems of domination and problems of disorder. As we saw in the chapter on "Domination: The Restructuring of Global Governance," the IMF, World Bank, WTO, and their regional equivalents imposed new forms of authority that had little or no accountability to those they affected. Their actions might result in the destruction of a community by a dam, or the doubling of the cost of water for a home through privatization, or the shutting of a region's farms or factories due to economic policies imposed on a national government.

But as we saw in the chapter "Disorder: Unintended Consequences," not all the problems of globalization result from such domination. Many result from uncoordinated side effects and interaction effects that were intended by no one. The race to the bottom is not anyone's intent; it is the result of myriad decisions taken simply to maximize profit. The same goes for global warming and the environmental contamination of the maquiladora region on Mexico's border with the United States.

Correction of both domination and disorder requires coordinated action by those affected and their allies. Both require that opponents make use of dependencies in order to force change. But the type of change that would solve the two kinds of problems is somewhat different.

In the case of domination, the solution is essentially to set limits on the capacity of actors to perform unacceptable actions. Such limits may be very specific: Critics of the World Bank and IMF have drawn up detailed lists of actions they should be prohibited from performing. Or such limits may involve general reductions in capacity, such as proposals for major reductions in the World Bank's budget. Or they may involve the ultimate limit on an institution—abolition.

Such restrictions raise the often difficult question, What will happen to the functions that are being restricted? There are several possibilities.

The functions can be moved to another institution. Some critics of the IMF, for example, propose that it be abolished and replaced by a new UN agency.

The functions can be decentralized. For example, Walden Bello proposed that the functions of the IMF, World Bank, and WTO be devolved to a network of regional organizations and specialized agencies dealing with topics such as health and the environment.[1]

The functions can remain in the present organization but be subject to new forms of accountability. These may be from below. For example, there are various proposals to give local communities affected by World Bank loans a veto power over them. The new accountability may also be to a higher authority. Some have proposed that the IMF and the World Bank be made subject to a revitalized UN Economic and Social Council.

Alternatively, the functions can simply be abandoned. The Bush administration proposed, for example, that the "rescue operations" of the IMF be severely curtailed. If countries became insolvent, the problem would simply be left to them and their creditors to resolve. Of course, the predictable result would either be even more catastrophic global financial crises or greatly restricted lending to countries that are poor credit risks. Some anti-globalization activists, notably David Korten, argue that the latter would be a desirable result, forcing a return to national self-sufficiency;[2] others see it as leading only to new forms of disorder and impoverishment.

In the case of disorder, solutions are likely to be rather different. They require the construction of new patterns of coordination where uncontrolled interaction reigns. Such new patterns of coordination require new practices, norms, rules, laws, and/or institutions. Formulating generally acceptable proposals for these has been much more difficult for the critics of globalization. However, without such new patterns of coordination, the result of change is likely to be nothing but more disorder.

A case in point is the race to the bottom. Abolishing the IMF, World Bank, and WTO would do little to reverse it. Competition would still drive corporations to search the world for cheap production sites and to press governments and workers for cheap labor, lax environmental protections, and subsidies. Solutions to problems of disorder must transform not just the actions of particular actors, but also destructive patterns of interaction.

In trying to figure out how to address the global race to the bottom, Tim and I (who by this time were sometimes being referred to as the "race-to-the-bottom guys") looked for a historical precedent. We started by considering the earlier race to the bottom that was once a common dynamic within national economies. Local workforces competed by accepting lower wages and sub-national governments competed by reducing public interest regulations, just as national workforces and governments do in the face of global competition today. In the late 1920s, for example, the garment industry ran away from high-wage, highly regulated, unionized New York City to low-wage, union-free towns in surrounding areas in states with little industrial regulation, notably my home state of Connecticut. (I learned about this process when I interviewed some of the garment workers who, as teenage girls half a century before, had organized the first unions in the companies that had run away to New Haven.)

In many industrial countries, the internal race to the bottom was successfully countered starting in the 1940s by a series of measures fought for by workers and their allies. Unions bargained for uniform wages in each industry. This removed wages as a factor in competition among companies. It also protected workers from having to accept wage cuts to keep their jobs from moving to lower wage locations. National laws setting minimum wages, maximum hours, and other labor standards established a floor under labor conditions. National policies used public employment and fiscal and monetary stimulus to promote full employment, thereby giving all workers more leverage at the bargaining table. To realize these conditions, workers fought for the basic democratic rights to speak, assemble, organize, bargain collectively, and participate in the political process.

We looked for parallel strategies for the global economy. An obvious starting point was labor organization. International labor cooperation, international solidarity support for workers struggles, and protection of labor rights worldwide formed a significant aspect of globalization from below. These were not only important for the sake of the workers supported, but also as critical means for reversing the race to the bottom.

While there was no global equivalent to national law, there were many possible means for setting minimum standards that could put a floor under labor conditions. The European Union's "social dimension" provided minimum standards for job security, occupational safety, unemployment compensation, union representation, and social security benefits. The Just and Sustainable Trade and Development Initiative, proposed by unions and social movement organizations in Mexico, Canada, and the United States as an alternative to NAFTA, described in detail a continental development treaty that would establish rights and standards for North America. The Maquiladora Coalition established a code of conduct for corporations in the US-Mexican border region. Such codes might start by being enforced by public pressure, but could ultimately be made enforceable by national laws, international institutions, and agreements among governments. (A similar process saw the labor standards fought for by civil society groups like the Women's Trade Union League in the 1920s embodied in US law in the 1930s.)

Proposals for a global equivalent to national full employment policies had to recognize that there were no global equivalents to national budgets, treasuries, or central banks. A starting point might be the elimination of policies of the World Bank, IMF, G-8, and US Treasury Department that prevent most countries from pursuing full employment by requiring that they run their economies to maximize exports to service their debts. (Some of these policies have indeed been modified in reaction to the Great Recession.) Increasing the buying power of the world's poor and working people via unionization and minimum labor standards would increase demand for worthwhile forms of economic development.

Some form of "global Keynesianism" could counteract global cycles of boom and bust. For example, the IMF once created Special Drawing Rights—"paper gold"—to support international liquidity. We advocated consideration of this tool—something that was in fact adopted on a massive scale in 2009 in response to the Great Recession. In the 1990s, the UN Development Program proposed a new global central bank "to create a common currency, to maintain price and exchange-rate stability, to channel global surpluses and deficits, to equalize international access to credit—and to provide the liquidity and credits poor nations need."[3]

Achieving such changes would require a global process of democratization. Global institutions like the World Bank, IMF, and WTO would have to be replaced or radically democratized. Global corporations would have to be brought under democratic control. The global economy would have to be reshaped to encourage rather than undermine democratic government at all levels. National and local governments would have to be recaptured from the global corporations. Participatory democracy would have to be pursued at a global scale.

Far from being mutually exclusive choices, these various changes could be combined. For example, the IMF and the World Bank could be put under a higher UN authority; many of their functions could be devolved to regional organizations and specialized agencies; and local communities could be given veto power over actions that affect them. Labor organizations could be organized locally and nationally but coordinate globally through global bargaining councils. Minimum labor rights and standards could be set by global institutions like the UN's International Labor Organization but monitored and enforced by local and national governments and by organized workers and communities themselves. A global central bank could operate primarily by coordinating national central banks and channeling resources to local development efforts. Such a multilevel program reflects my emerging approach: Social life is made up not of sovereign entities but of multiple interacting levels that can be subject to multilevel reorganization.

49

GLOBALIZATION AND ITS CRISIS

᠌᠌᠌᠌᠌᠌᠌᠌

IN THE YEARS FOLLOWING THE PUBLICATION OF *GLOBALIZATION FROM BELOW*, globalization from above entered a deepening crisis. The race to the bottom proceeded apace, with jobs that had once flooded into Mexico and Thailand migrating again to China and then to still lower-wage Vietnam and Bangladesh. Global economic growth slowed by some measures to the lowest level since the 1930s. Many countries, notably the United States, abandoned the pursuit of global economic rules and moved instead to blatant beggar-your-neighbor economic nationalism.

In the Introduction to *Globalization from Below*, we indicated that globalization in its present form was "unsustainable." We suggested that the possibilities for what might come after it included "world domination by a single superpower."[1] The administration of President George W. Bush indeed tried to implement this solution to the problems and contradictions of globalization. Bush's "National Security Strategy" document laid out the intention. It asserted that there is "a single sustainable model for national success: freedom, democracy, and free enterprise." And it threatened that the United States "will not hesitate to act alone, if necessary, to exercise our right of self-defense by acting preemptively" and by "convincing or compelling states" to "accept" their "responsibilities."[2] Globalization, once touted as the manifestation of advancing freedom, turned out to be big with the child of global repression.

Meanwhile, globalization from below, or the anti-globalization movement, burgeoned. The Seattle demonstrations that closed down the WTO were replicated at elite international gatherings all over the world. The World Social Forum became a venue for dialogue, networking, and coordination among social movements from all over the world. Lilliputian linking of grassroots struggles reached a scale we had never even imagined a few years before.

The Bush administration's global juggernaut provided a significant challenge for globalization from below. As the US attack on Iraq loomed, the same networks and organizations that had protested corporate-led globalization rapidly mobilized to oppose it.[3] The result was the largest global wave of protest demonstrations in history. In their wake, the *New York Times* wrote, "The fracturing of the Western alliance over Iraq and the huge antiwar demonstrations around the world this weekend are reminders that there may still be two superpowers on the planet: the U.S. and world opinion."[4]

The Great Recession that began in 2007 represented the worst global economic crisis since the Great Depression of the 1930s. It demonstrated that globalization had produced not a new order, but a new disequilibrium. Yet after a brief flurry of international conferences ostensibly determined to fix the broken system, national and global policy turned to an even more intense centralization of global wealth and power. A new wave of popular protests, from African food riots to European anti-austerity protests to the poverty-fed "Arab Spring" spread across the world. Their impact, and whether they can join together in a new round of globalization from below, remains to be seen.

Perhaps the most common criticism of *Globalization from Below,* expressed in a variety of ways, is that it did not link the movement against globalization with a broader project of social change.[5] Indeed, as we wrote in the book's conclusion, "Ultimately, the problem is not to 'solve' globalization. The problem is to develop social practices that can address the evolving challenges of life on Earth. We envision globalization from below melding into a more general movement for social change."[6]

Globalization from below provides crucial lessons for how common preservation can "address the evolving challenges of life on Earth" by means of a movement for human preservation.

HUMAN PRESERVATION

50

HUMAN PRESERVATION

ዾ

At the outset of this book I said I thought you and I might have some problems in common and that we might do better at solving them if we worked together. Now let me say what I think those problems are and what we might do about them.

By pursuing our own individual, group, and institutional self-preservation, we are creating the very dynamics that are threatening to destroy the world and its people. It is as if each of us, by pursuing our own self-interest, is led by an invisible hand to mutual destruction. Whether in the universal destruction of nuclear holocaust and climate change, or in less universal but still catastrophic forms such as conventional war, economic crisis, toxic pollution, resource depletion, and species extinction, we see the pursuit of self-interest leading to mutual self-annihilation.

Yet we have also seen new strategies of common preservation emerging to overcome mutual destruction at every level from the local to the global. In fact, since the beginning of the nuclear era we have been witnessing the emergence, albeit unnamed and without an explicit identity as such, of a movement for human preservation. What else are the anti-nuclear movement, the climate-protection movement, and movements that challenge other threats to human survival?

The threat of mutual destruction gives everyone an interest in resisting mutual destruction. It creates a global common interest that includes, to varying degrees, all individuals, groups, institutions, and nations, as well as the world as a whole. That of course doesn't abolish other, conflicting interests. But it does establish a new and overriding one. The problem for us as human individuals and groups is to act on those common interests to transform states, markets, corporations, and other powerful institutions so that they no longer threaten our survival and well-being.

The most likely way I can think of to accomplish that end is to create a global peoples' movement to halt mutual destruction and lay the groundwork for human preservation. We need to impose what is necessary for human survival on corporations, nations, and the economic and nation-state systems of which they are part. And the only way I know to do that is to do it from below by means of self-organization and people power.

The anti-nuclear, climate protection, and many other movements are already engaged in trying to halt particular aspects of our mutual destruction. But they generally do so in their own silos, not recognizing that eliminating the various threats to human survival requires pretty much the same restructuring of power. As a result, they appear to be simply one or another competing "issue group," rather than the vehicle for all of us to use to ensure our common survival.

We need to recognize that these movements are all part of a nascent movement for human preservation. We need to recognize what they have in common. And we need to weave them together into a combined force that can make the changes necessary to save the humans.

I described in Part 4 how, when Tim Costello and I wrote *Global Village or Global Pillage* in 1994, economic globalization presented huge problems to people all over the world, but there were only minimal and scattered responses. We used those prefigurative actions, our analysis of the problem, what we knew about the history of social movements, and many of the ways of thinking about change presented in this book to project a movement of globalization from below. In Part 5 I am trying to do something similar for the movement for human preservation.

As we have seen throughout this book, the initial reaction to a threat or problem is often to disregard or deny it. That is often followed by despair that anything can be done about it. Such despair is often encouraged by those whom effective solutions might threaten. But when despairing people realize that many others share their predicament, their understandings, and their feelings, they may turn to collective action to solve their problems.

I am not predicting that a human preservation movement will coalesce, still less that it will succeed. I'm only saying that it may provide our best hope of survival. Maybe we are already doomed to mutual destruction. But we won't know till we have tried to prevent it.

The problems we face today are unprecedented. They will take the creative action of millions of people to solve. Part 5 asks what we can learn from the history of past shifts to common preservation that we can use for that purpose.

MUTUAL (BUT HOPEFULLY NOT YET ASSURED) DESTRUCTION

ॐ

HUMAN BEINGS HAVE ENGAGED IN MASS MUTUAL DESTRUCTION FOR MUCH OF OUR history. But only with the development of the atom bomb at the end of World War II did the self-annihilation of the human species become technologically possible. The awareness of that possibility has begun to penetrate our consciousness, but has barely begun to change the way we act and organize ourselves. The "drift toward unparalleled catastrophe" that Einstein warned of continues.

Over the succeeding decades, additional impacts of human activity have come to be recognized as threats to the human future. In 1977, political scientist Charles Lindblom wrote, "Relentlessly accumulating evidence suggests that human life on the planet is headed for a catastrophe. Indeed, several disasters are possible, and if we avert one, we will be caught by another." He enumerates population growth, resource shortage, and global warming. "All this assumes that a nuclear catastrophe does not spare us the long anguish of degeneration."[1]

In 1992, the writer and scientist Jared Diamond wrote, "Until our own generation, no one had grounds to worry whether the next human generation would survive or enjoy a planet worth living on. Ours is the first generation to be confronted with these questions about its children's future." Two clouds hanging over us raise these concerns: "nuclear holocaust" and "environmental holocaust." These risks "constitute the two really pressing questions facing the human race today."[2]

Today the dramatic manifestation of the consequences of global warming in melting ice caps, vanishing islands, devastating storms, and disappearing species is rapidly putting the question of human survival front and center on national and global agendas. Indeed, global warming represents in particularly pure form the dilemmas of human self-annihilation. It cannot be escaped by anyone; even the wealthiest in the long run confront the same doom. No one group or nation—no matter how wealthy or how heavily armed—can protect itself except through cooperation with others. Protection requires radical changes in the way our species lives. These realities—characteristic of all the environmental and military threats to human existence—are being brought out most unambiguously by climate change. While people around the world have stood aghast at the effects of global warming, effective response by either political or economic institutions has barely begun.

From the detonation of the first atom bomb, there was a worldwide impulse to make significant changes in human social organization. Some nuclear scientists and government officials called for international control of atomic energy. The ban-the-bomb movement proclaimed "co-existence or no existence." By the late 1980s the threat of climate change led most governments to back—at least in principle—a binding international treaty that would compel a radical transformation of the world's economy to a low-carbon basis.

Despite apparent recognition of the problems, these doomsday threats to human survival have not yet produced significant changes in the way we organize our life on earth, let alone changes adequate to ensure the survival of our species. Indeed, nations continue to build and stockpile new weapons of mass destruction while individuals and corporations alike pour more and more greenhouse gasses and other destructive pollutants into the environment.

While technology provides the means for our growing capacity to destroy ourselves, our failure to control its use results not from that technology but from our established social patterns. We seem to be locked into ways of acting and organizing ourselves that, instead of solving our problems, keep making them worse and worse. We seem unable to act to meet the most obvious and urgent common interest in our species' survival. There is no shortage of proposals for controlling nuclear weapons, global warming, and threatening new technologies, but we seem to systematically block ourselves from implementing them. The failure to solve these problems often leads not to action but to paralysis. So we despair of reversing the drift toward doom.

All of us have the dubious honor of participating in the strategies of self-preservation that are leading to mutual destruction. But the most important contributors are the political and economic institutions that wield the greatest power for shaping—or destroying—the future.

Governments, corporations, and other powerful institutions evolved at a time when competitive self-preservation often worked at least for some, not an era in which it leads to the destruction of all. They have grown and prospered by pursuing the short-term interests of their citizens and stockholders (or often just a small, dominant elite among them) in competition with the citizens and stockholders of other countries and companies. Nations are adapted to conquest, plunder, and the defense against them. Corporations are adapted to maximizing short-term profits, externalizing costs, denying any interests but those of their stockholders, and smiting those who might oppose their decisions.

Neither nations nor corporations are designed or structured to provide for either the long-term interests or the common interests of the world's people. And their time horizon is determined not by the lifetimes of our children and grandchildren but by the next election cycle or quarterly report. To their leaders, sustainability means getting through the next couple of years without loss of elections or profits.

Sometimes the destructive effects of competitive self-preservation take the form of domination, which produces inequality, injustice, and tyranny, and a resistance to them that is a necessary corrective but can itself lead to destructive outcomes. Sometimes they take the form of disorder, which results at best in an inability to coordinate our activity to realize our common purposes, and at worst in intractable conflict, uncontrolled interaction effects, and a war of all against all. Sometimes the destructive effects of competitive self-preservation combine both domination and disorder.

The dynamic of mutual destruction is not limited to the doomsday threats of nuclear weapons and climate change. There are other problems that may not in themselves threaten the future of our entire species, but that do threaten the survival and well-being of hundreds of millions of people, as well as exacerbating nuclear, climate, and other more universal threats. They include, for example, the crisis of the global economy in the era of globalization; the many forms of environmental destruction such as poisoning of water, land, and air, depletion of natural resources, and extinction of species; the devastation of war, conquest, military occupation, and domination by violence; the prevalence of oppression and tyranny; the deprivation of human rights; and the degradation of food, water, and other natural resources.

We are threatened not only by the problems that have already arisen, but by the "unknown unknowns" that hover unforeseen in the future. These are the emerging technologies, social forces, and environmental conditions that may be creating new forms of destruction either deliberately, or as unintended side effects of deliberate actions, or even as the result of unforeseen interactions among unintended side effects. Such unknown unknowns are a threat to all of us, and taking precautions against them is part of our common interest in human survival. Instead, we encourage such threats by our failure to cooperate to control them.

Nuclear weapons and global warming were once unknown unknowns that could have been warded off in a global regime that forbade implementation of innovations until they were proven safe. We don't know what unknown unknowns may already be gestating future threats because we have not created a global system to make sure that new technologies, social practices, and interaction effects are known and evaluated before they are put into place. Because special interests hope to gain from innovations, they prevent the very precautions that could protect the future of the earth and its people against those unknown unknowns.

In each of these cases of mutual destruction there is a common human interest in addressing and solving the problem. But there are also a multitude of special interests who perceive the solutions to those problems as a potential threat to them.

You and I are living in a time in which mutual destruction is possible but not yet inevitable. We still have a choice between mutual destruction or common preservation.

52

DOOM AND GLOOM

෫෨

"IN THE EVENT OF NUCLEAR ATTACK BEND OVER, PUT YOUR HEAD BETWEEN YOUR LEGS, and kiss your ass goodbye." The blasé attitude reflected in this quip concealed the fact that my peers and I expected to die in a nuclear war if Cold War nuclear conflict wasn't somehow forestalled.

A recent late-night television show joke expressed a similarly blasé attitude about the threat of global warming: "According to a new UN report, the global warming outlook is much worse than originally predicted. Which is pretty bad when they originally predicted it would destroy the planet."[1]

Despair seems a natural, even appropriate, response to such a reality. It is genuinely difficult to know how else to relate to threats to the existence of our species we appear powerless to halt.

Before we think practically about what to do about those threats, therefore, it can help to think about our own responses. Is despair warranted, and if so is it the only appropriate response? Is it already too late to do anything? If a situation is hopeless, isn't psychological denial appropriate—if we can't do anything about it, shouldn't we just ignore it and get on with the rest of our lives as best we can? Is the threat of doom likely to spur us to action? Or is it more likely to make us feel helpless and turn us to apathy? Can despair be a bridge to something else?

We have good scientific reasons to expect that, without any help from us, the human race will sooner or later become extinct and eventually our planet will freeze or burn up or shatter into bits. And we have good reason to think that nothing we can do will avert such a fate.

But self-inflicted, man-made annihilation is different. It cannot be regarded as something human beings are inherently powerless to avert. What we genuinely experience is that we are powerless to avert it *as individuals*. But collectively we could reverse the drift toward doom in a day—if we agreed to do so—simply by halting those activities that are leading to it. The powerlessness we experience is not the result of our destructive capacity, but of our apparent inability to keep ourselves from using that capacity to destroy ourselves.

These social roots of doom are part of a common pattern that we can observe repeatedly in history. People live their lives and pursue their goals by means of strategies that have been developed over time. But sometimes they discover their established strategies aren't working. No matter how hard they try, their problems remain intractable. The natural result is despair.

If many people are living the same experience, an entire social group may be permeated with despair. They can express that despair to each other in many ways—for example, in mordant jokes about nuclear and climate catastrophe.

But the awareness that other people are experiencing the same despair changes the context in which it is experienced. It opens up new possibilities. Perhaps the problems that we despair of solving as individuals can be addressed through some kind of collective action. When people begin to explore that possibility, the result may be a social movement.

The sense of despair in the face of individual powerlessness can be the soil from which new forms of collective action emerge. It is a manifestation of the recognition that our current patterns can't solve our problems. So our sense of powerlessness in the face of today's impending doom can lead not only to despair, but also to a sharing of despair, which can open the way for us to try new social strategies.

Something like this happened during the early years of the nuclear arms race. Awareness of the futility of current strategies, such as pursuing peace and security through nuclear superiority and civil defense, was initially expressed in the hopelessness of "kiss your ass goodbye." But from that awareness emerged the worldwide ban-the-bomb movement for nuclear disarmament and against nuclear testing. As recent historical research has established, that movement both influenced and intimidated world leaders. It played a significant role in bringing about a nuclear test ban treaty, US-Soviet détente, and arms control agreements that reduced the likelihood of nuclear holocaust for a generation.[2]

As each of us looks out over a landscape marked by wars, climate disruption, pollution, starvation, thirst, desertification, and extinction, not to mention unknown new threats that are being allowed to gestate uncontrolled, each of us has ample reason to despair. But we can do so knowing that such despair, shared, is the seedbed from which new forms of common preservation emerge.

53

AN ECOLOGICAL SHIFT

૨૦

GENERALLY UNDERLYING THE EMERGENCE OF NEW COMMON PRESERVATIONS IS WHAT I have called an "ecological shift." An ecological shift consists in seeing that apparently independent elements are parts of larger wholes, that "No man is an island, entire of itself; every man is a piece of the continent, a part of the main." People are part of larger patterns and processes and systems of interaction. The boundaries separating individuals, groups, and institutions are not absolute, but rather are semi-permeable and subject to change.

The ecological shift was represented in the most literal way by the rise of the environmental movement. Before the rise of an ecological consciousness, people generally thought, If insects hurt or annoy us, why shouldn't we use pesticides to wipe them out? Ecological consciousness instead saw nature not as independent entities related as "bugs versus people" but a vast web of interacting elements of which we and bugs are part. DDT, while it is wiping out the bugs, is also wiping out the songbirds and perhaps poisoning our children as well. This deep change in the way people thought about the world led to a deep change in what the public considered acceptable and eventually to environmental laws protecting the water, air, and land.

But the ecological shift is not just about the natural environment. As we saw in Parts 3 and 4, the shift from a self-centered to a holistic or systems viewpoint underlies the emergence of solidarity at every level from the work group to the global economy. We learned of workers who thought they could get ahead by pursuing their own self-interest, only to discover that the competition among workers was used against them. They responded by forming their work groups into a "guerrilla band" with its own norms and rules of conduct for the protection of all. We saw unions and other organizations emerge to protect common interests of those who worked in the same company, craft, or industry. We saw broader movements develop in response to problems faced by workers as a whole. We saw disparate movements worldwide converge in a globalization from below.

All these embodied a solidarity rooted in the recognition of reciprocal and common interests.

Emblematic of the ecological shift for me were the brass workers I knew in Waterbury, Connecticut, who struck to forestall competitive wage cutting—"whipsawing"—among different groups of workers in different locations. They understood that the demands of their employers were being made within a larger system. They knew that if they made concessions the result might be an interactive race to the bottom that could rebound to hurt them. And they saw the potential for coordinating their action with others to prevent that result.

The nuclear disarmament movement reflected a similar shift. From a starting point of "their weapons threaten us," the idea of building more weapons than "them" appeared a natural solution. But gradually more and more people went through an ecological shift in which they came to grasp the process as a whole. They came to recognize that each defensive action by one side was interpreted as a threat by the other side, producing an arms race that was ruinous to all. They grasped the futility of the arms race and recognized that the greatest threat came from the process as a whole rather than from their putative antagonist. The result was a withdrawal of support for the arms race and a popular demand for arms limitation and disarmament, expressed both by worldwide public opinion and by the worldwide peace movement.

Such an ecological shift is critical for moving from mutual destruction to common preservation today. For example, the breakdown of the climate negotiations at Copenhagen in 2010 was primarily the result of each nation trying to realize its competitive economic advantage in the allocation of greenhouse gas reductions, while trying to force their costs onto others. The result was a stalemate in which the common interest in halting global warming was completely trashed. Underlying a practical solution in such cases there needs to be a shift to seeing the common problem as primary and a willingness to pursue separate interests within the framework of a solution to that common problem.

A similar pattern applies to the approach of corporations to climate change. Some corporations have actually supported climate-protection measures because they expect to gain from them themselves. This obviously includes the renewable energy and environmental protection industries, which hope to profit from the transition to a green economy. It also includes insurance companies who are worried that the costs of environmental destruction might fall on them, financial interests that hope to profit from a carbon market, and a handful of others. But far greater economic interests—including almost the entire energy sector and most industries dependent on it—have used every trick in the book to try to undermine climate-protection measures. In both cases, corporations have pursued private interests, albeit with very different results. However, in both cases the common human interest in protecting the climate has played little role.

The danger of nuclear proliferation provides a similar case. The nuclear non-proliferation treaty was a classic embodiment of common preservation. Almost all nations without nuclear weapons agreed that they would not try to develop them. In exchange nations with nuclear weapons agreed to move ahead on eliminating their own. The result would be a nuclear-free world far safer for all. However, over the course of the forty years since the agreement went into effect, the nuclear countries have not proceeded to eliminate their nuclear arsenals. Instead they threatened and sometimes even launched wars against countries they accused of planning to build nuclear weapons. Meanwhile, some nations like North Korea and Israel went on developing nukes undeterred. A successful program to eliminate the scourge of nuclear weapons would require an ecological shift from seeing the power of one country as a means to threaten and dictate to another to one that sees mutual arms reduction as the road to greater security for all.

A similar shift is required for the global economy. Corporations have promoted an unregulated global economy—often referred to as neoliberalism or globalization—so they can go anywhere and do anything they like unimpeded. They have not recognized that their pursuit of their individual advantage, combined with similar actions by others, can have catastrophic consequences all around. It can lead to ruinous races to the bottom; catastrophic "external" side effects and interaction effects; unplanned chaos; staggering inequality; collapsing economic demand; and a failure to mobilize resources to meet long-term human needs. Nation-states vacillate between promoting this kind of unregulated globalization and pursuing their own competitive economic nationalism. Solutions to the world's economic problems require instead an ecological shift to a perspective in which the common interests of the world's people provide the framework in which individuals, enterprises, and countries pursue their more limited self-interests.

Solving the climate conundrum requires an ecological shift from a national or corporate perspective to a common human perspective. So do solving nuclear proliferation and global economic crisis. However neither the states nor the corporations are likely to spontaneously undergo such a conversion on their own. The starting point for such a shift is much more likely to be the world's people, who will have to impose that perspective on powerful special interests.

54

SELF-ORGANIZATION FOR
COMMON PRESERVATION

❧

I REMEMBER MY YOUNGER SELF WITH MY PRIMITIVE HECTOGRAPH, WRITING AND printing my own peace leaflets and handing them out to my fellow eighth grad-ers. Nobody told me to do it. But I believed I had to share what I knew and felt with them. Common preservation starts from people reaching out to each other, calling out to each other about their fears, hopes, and despairs.

This is where social movements start and how they grow. The hallmarks of a social movement are the handwritten picket sign, the basement meeting, and the street rally, joined today by the social networking message. In the women's liberation movement it was the formation of consciousness-raising groups. In the lead-up to the Battle of Seattle it was the formation of affinity groups, the mutual outreach of labor and environmental organizations, and the visits of union members to community meetings throughout the Seattle area. In Egypt it was the exchange of messages on a Facebook page followed by the street meetings in Cairo neighborhoods.

Such movement formation presumes that the other is not purely other; that whatever your differences, you share some things, be they background, present situation, future prospects, problems, needs, or interests. Remember the Akron gum-miner who told Louis Adamic: "Why, my God, man, during the sit-downs last spring I found out that the guy who works next to me is the same as I am, even if I was born in West Virginia and he is from Poland. His grievances are the same. Why shouldn't we stick?"

Common preservation grows out of the recognition that the other is someone whose cooperation you need for your own good. It is that realization of the need for each other's help that can lead to a strategy of pursuing your own good by pursuing the good of the other. The shift to a strategy of mutual aid grows from the recognition of mutual need.

Common preservation requires not just reaching out to others but also responding to them. It involves moving from monologue to dialogue. It involves taking in each other's perspectives and modifying one's own in ways that allow action in common. It requires taking other people's concerns into account—addressing the things that might make them not want to join with you and mutually modifying your goals and perspectives so you can act together for the common good. This is the process I have referred to as de-centering.

While the emergence of common preservation involves cognitive processes like the ecological shift and social processes like de-centering, it is most often realized in action. It is through action that people discover they can act as a group and affect the world and the problems they face. The possibility of solving their problems through such concerted action is the potential reward that can make the trials and tribulations of changing strategies and becoming dependent on others worthwhile.

These processes can occur at very different scales, from the local to the global. Indeed, it is the interaction of different scales that leads to the sudden crystallization and unexpected "spreading like wildfire" manifested by social movements. The changes people have gone through in their own micro-milieus and the connections they have made beyond them create the conditions in which events—whether the firing of a worker, the flooding of a small Pacific island, or the self-immolation of an impoverished fruit seller—can touch off the same response among dispersed and seemingly disparate individuals and groups. Conversely, the emerging possibility of connecting and cooperating on a wider scale promises to make a strategy of common preservation more powerful and effective and therefore more worth pursuing.

This underlying process is necessary to support a change to common preservation today. It begins with communicating our concerns to each other in those milieus of which we are a part. Today, such milieus include not only local networks, workplaces, and communities, but people linked in all kinds of other ways by social media. This is what I did with my hectograph. This is the veiled substrate of common preservation.

In recent decades such self-organization has often been extended and formalized into what have been called "advocacy networks." Advocacy networks have been defined as "forms of organization characterized by voluntary, reciprocal and horizontal patterns of communication and exchange."[1] They can include NGOs, local social movements, foundations, media, religious congregations and denominations, trade unions, consumer organizations, intellectuals, parts of regional and international inter-governmental organizations, and parts of the executive and parliamentary branches of governments.

Advocacy networks provide a venue through which members can communicate, exchange information, learn from each others' experiences, and inform each other of plans and intentions. They can also themselves serve as vehicles for initiating actions. Such networks can help establish a common frame, help select objectives, help initiate and coordinate campaigns, help members support each other's efforts, and help establish and maintain alliances.

The network form allows cooperation among people and organizations that have different agendas other than their area of common concern. Network participants can be highly diverse and may disagree on many matters, as long as they accept the network's defining frame of the issues that it addresses. Individuals can participate in them directly, whether or not they are formally affiliated through organizations. Segments of organizations can participate in them, and in the actions they launch, while other segments remain apart. For example, the environmental committee of a congregation or the health and safety committee of a union could participate without needing more than a generalized blessing of its parent organization.

The network form resists co-optation, since member groups can simply withdraw and re-converge if "sell-out" or other abuse occurs at the top. It reduces fear of losing control of an organization because it allows constant recycling of power to the base.

Today many if not most global movements take the form of global advocacy networks. For example, the international campaign to ban land mines was initiated by a diverse assortment of war veterans, handicap activists, human rights organizations, and health workers, all concerned from their disparate perspectives about the impact of land mines on civilians around the world. From their initiative developed a global network operating in ninety countries and including international NGOs, religious denominations, local veterans groups, legislators, and even the governments of a number of smaller countries. The network allowed them to define objectives, present a common frame to the public, and coordinate their actions.[2]

Self-organization can be made a deliberate objective and an intentional practice. For example, my collaborators Tim Costello, Brendan Smith, and I organized what we called a "bridge-building organization" called Global Labor Strategies.[3] It aimed "to contribute to building global labor solidarity through research, analysis, strategic thinking and network building around labor and employment issues." It built transnational linkages among labor organizations and their allies around issues including global warming, immigration, and the rights of Chinese workers.

Such networks are likely to be the principal means through which people self-organize for human preservation.

55

A HUMAN PRESERVATION MOVEMENT?

෫

WHILE COMMON PRESERVATION IS A UNIVERSAL ASPECT OF HUMAN LIFE, IT CAN AND often has led not to universal common preservation but to conflict and domination among groups and institutions. Today, common preservation for restricted groups can lead to collective suicide.

Common preservation made universal could be called human preservation. Human preservation does not require the implausible utopia of a world without conflict. What it does require is a reduction in domination and disorder sufficient to put human life on a secure footing—to ensure human survival. Perhaps a means to that end could be a movement specifically pursuing human survival.

A human survival or human preservation movement would aim to counter threats to human survival and put human existence on a safe, sustainable basis. Addressing the apparently disparate issues of nuclear proliferation, climate catastrophe, unknown unknowns, and other threats as part of the broader problem of ensuring human survival could provide a new basis for collective action to make the changes necessary to end such threats.

Like the anti-nuclear movement, a human preservation movement might not have a single organization, ideology, or even name. The anti-nuclear movement was not a single, monolithic global structure but rather a fluid, ever-changing convergence of organizations and actions. Different individuals and groups were constantly influencing each other, often across enormous geographical, social, and political barriers. What they had was a shared project guided by common objectives and a common interpretive frame.

A human preservation movement might emerge both from grassroots popular self-organization and from a convergence of movements that already are fighting aspects of mutual destruction, such as the movements for climate protection, nuclear disarmament, global economic justice, and democratization. A human preservation movement could incorporate many of their particular goals. Conversely, movements pursuing more specific ends could incorporate the common goal of human preservation in their own programs. These varied elements would not need to submerge their own identities and objectives in order to recognize themselves and each other as part of a common movement and join into a force that can impose the necessary changes on society.

A human preservation movement may seem like an extravagant, implausible, even ridiculous idea. But we have already witnessed at least two powerful global movements addressing two of the great threats to human survival in the era of mutual destruction. Both the anti-nuclear and the climate-protection movements defined global threats and mobilized millions of people worldwide to combat the policies and institutions that perpetrated them.

At first glance, human self-destruction may appear to be a collection of separate problems: Global warming results from excessive carbon emissions; death of the seas from pollution and overfishing; nuclear proliferation from destructive weapons in untrustworthy hands.

But there are good reasons to treat these apparently disparate issues within a common interpretive frame. All are produced by uncontrolled power centers and their interactions. All need the same kind of interconnected changes in the organization of social power for their solution. Treating them as one problem may make it possible to coalesce the disparate social forces necessary to address them. Human survival can provide the broadest and most compelling reason for social transformation and concerted action.

We can make a comparison to the conditions in which nation-states formed in the eighteenth and nineteenth centuries. People faced many distinct problems in spheres such as economic development, military security, law, and governance. These problems all had roots in the combination of small, despotic principalities and duchies with sprawling, poorly organized imperial dynasties. And all led to the same institutional change—the formation of nation-states—to solve them.

The formation of nation-states did not abolish separate parochial interests. But most individuals and groups came to pursue their more parochial interests within the emerging national framework. They sought to have their aspirations included in national policies. National rulers, conversely, tried to keep parochial interests from turning to separatism by ensuring that many of their aspirations could be pursued as part of a broader national interest. In the case of the United States, such a unification arose out of thirteen independent and rancorous former colonies. A similar process at a later time brought together the states of Europe—at war with each other for a millennium—into the European Union.

Since the 1992 Rio Earth Summit, the question of a viable human future has often been discussed in terms of "sustainability" and "sustainable development." Sustainable development was defined at the Earth Summit as development that "meets the needs of the present without compromising the ability of future generations to meet their own needs."[1] A movement for human survival could perhaps be thought of as a further development of the movement for sustainability. Why then talk as well of survival? One reason is that sustainability might seem to imply that the world is in an acceptable state and that all we need to do is maintain it. But sustaining the status quo is not an option—either we radically transform it or we face doomsday threats to our very survival. Another reason is that the status quo is so unjust that sustaining it can hardly be a reasonable objective for most of the world's people. Further, the threats of mutual destruction require fundamental structural changes that are often disregarded in the current discourse of sustainability. Finally, the threat to survival entails a far greater immediacy and universality and therefore a more universal and compelling motivation for action. Let's call the human preservation movement sustainability on steroids.

The goal of a movement for human preservation would be to provide a vehicle through which people can pursue their interests and responsibilities for the survival of our species. Such a movement can be powerful because it represents the most profound common interests of individual human beings and groups, and of humanity as a whole. It therefore has the potential to initiate a broad global consensus and mobilize very large social forces on behalf of the changes needed for common survival.

The identity of the human preservation movement might resemble that of what is generally called—and calls itself—the peace movement. The peace movement encompasses a wide array of issues, campaigns, and organizations pursuing nuclear and conventional disarmament, test bans, prevention of and resistance to particular wars, ending of occupations, international conciliation, regional demilitarization, nuclear-free zones, amelioration of war-causing injustice, and many other specific policies and objectives. It also includes a variety of organizations and movements around the world, each pursuing its own agenda. Not infrequently there are conflicts within the peace movement on methods, strategies, and immediate objectives. But all share a common goal of reducing war and militarism and all cooperate across a wide spectrum of issues and concerns. Someone becomes part of the peace movement primarily by adopting an identity and engaging in activity that he or she defines as part of it. I remember my friend Luc Labelle, a nonprofit co-op developer in Quebec, who said during a staff meeting at the height of the movement against the Iraq war that co-op developers should consider what they do as part of the peace movement because it contributes to creating a world based on social justice and cooperation rather than war-spawning rivalry.

Indeed, human preservation is first and foremost an interpretive frame designed to facilitate cooperation among a wide range of otherwise disparate forces. Such frames are ways that individuals and organizations define a problem, organize their beliefs about the causes of the problem, and develop ideas that inform action to deal with the problem. Frames have been defined as "conscious strategic efforts by groups of people to fashion shared understandings of the world and of themselves that legitimate and motivate collective action."[2]

While developing the frame for a movement for human preservation must be an ongoing process in which many people take part, the following themes are likely elements:

- Survival is a goal that is required to secure all other human goals.
- People have an inherent human right to social self-defense for our common survival and an obligation to act for common human preservation. A human preservation movement seeks to empower people to exercise that right and meet that obligation.
- Survival requires a democratization of national and international institutions that allows people's common interest in survival to reshape human society. Such democratization represents a fulfillment of the principles articulated in the Universal Declaration of Human Rights, other human rights documents, and the obligations of states to their peoples under international law.
- Survival requires the restriction of actions by nations, corporations, and other institutions that threaten common survival.
- Survival requires implementing existing international norms, rules, laws, and principles designed to halt threats to survival, such as the Kyoto agreement and other environmental treaties; the UN Charter prohibitions on aggression; the Nuremberg restrictions on war crimes; and the Nuclear Non-Proliferation Treaty requirement that nuclear powers move rapidly toward nuclear disarmament.
- Survival requires the elaboration of such obligations into a governance regime that eliminates the environmental, military, and other threats to human survival.
- Where governments and international institutions are not taking the actions necessary to ensure a secure human future, it is instead up to the world's people to take those actions through popular rule-making, monitoring, and enforcement.
- The possessors of means of destruction—military and environmental—must be made subject to control by their victims, which means all of us.
- Human survival requires that the world's economy be converted to environmentally sustainable production and consumption. This includes demilitarization and a replacement of environmentally destructive productive techniques.
- Survival requires rapid progress toward a global social justice that reduces the causes of conflict and gives all a stake in creating and preserving a sustainable global social order.

Such a human preservation movement is not a struggle of group against group or nation against nation. It is a global peoples' movement to eliminate threats to human survival, whatever nation, group, or institution may perpetrate them. It is a transnational withdrawal of consent from the war of all against all.

56

EMERGENCE AND CONVERGENCE

૨♠

How might the elements of a human preservation movement draw together? The closest example I know to such an emergence and convergence was the development of the movement against economic globalization in the 1990s. As the effects of globalization became increasingly evident, people's established strategies of addressing their needs in national contexts became less and less effective. The process of developing new, global strategies was polycentric, emerging in different ways in different places around varied issues and utilizing different forms of action. Gradually, though punctuated by sudden leaps, those experimenting with these initiatives began to learn of each other, engage in dialogue, and coordinate common actions. The result was what we know as the global "anti-globalization" or global justice movement—globalization from below.

A similar process of emergence is likely to characterize a movement for human preservation. It will have roots in existing environmental and peace organizations, especially those that are already connected internationally. It will incorporate many of the elements that have already come together worldwide to combat global warming. It will draw on the global justice movement, much of which is now represented in the polycentric World Social Forum process. It will include many who are responding to issues of survival within political systems at all levels. It will involve many organizations like unions and religious congregations whose primary purpose is not to address issues of survival, but which are drawn in by the concerns and interests of their constituencies. These will include many new recruits, such as the evangelical Christians who have begun to shift from a shunning of environmental concerns to a new focus on "stewardship." It will need to find ways to draw in the new democratization movements that have spread from Tunisia and Egypt to countries around the globe.

A human preservation movement will nurture and promote both the emergence and the convergence of these forces. It will link them conceptually by helping them construct a shared frame for understanding and acting on the problems they face. And it will link them organizationally by constructing networks that facilitate coordinated planning and action.

How can we go about drawing such diverse movements into a common frame? One example comes from an organization I work with called the Labor Network for Sustainability (LNS).[1] It was founded by Joe Uehlein, a retired senior official in the AFL-CIO and a founding board member of the environmental group Ceres. LNS is dedicated to "engaging trade unions, workers and our allies to support economic, social, and environmental sustainability." It works through social networking, a website, meetings, publications, and media to argue for the interest of organized labor in joining the broader movement for sustainability; the interest of workers along with everyone else in ensuring sustainability; the interest of other sustainability advocates in supporting the labor movement; and the need for broader social change to ensure sustainability. As Joe articulates it, "For us the idea of sustainability includes but goes beyond the environment to encompass social and economic sustainability as well. The fight against global warming, for example, is really part of a broad shift in society's principles and vision—a shift from honoring greed to honoring what's good for the health of the planet and the people on it first and foremost. That's to the benefit of labor— and it will only happen if labor helps take the lead."[2] Anyone can work in similar ways in any context to draw disparate groups into a human preservation frame.

Why would such disparate forces, movements, and constituencies with such varied goals come together? Because, first, they otherwise cannot escape the impending mutual destruction that threatens us all. Second, they will not be able to realize their own objectives without working with allies to change global political and economic power relations—a change that is most likely to be realized by a movement for human survival.

Consider, for example, the burgeoning movements for national democracy. National regime change will ultimately fail without global regime change. Efforts to establish national democracies are likely sooner or later to be crushed either by foreign militaries or by domestic ones unless both are made subject to demilitarization. And programs for economic development and the reduction of poverty are likely to prove futile unless there is a general limitation of global warming and a democratization of the global economy that allows countries and communities to plan and invest for the things people need. Global demilitarization, decarbonization, and economic cooperation are the necessary complement of national democratization and economic development. Human preservation needs to be part of the program and values of the democracy movement worldwide.

Now consider the movement for climate protection. Many saw climate protection as just one more "environmental issue" and hoped that minor adjustment in markets would accomplish the transition to a low-carbon economy easily and automatically. Unfortunately, if that was ever the case our quarter-century of failure to take precautionary measures against global warming means that it is the case no longer. Climate protection will require imposing massive changes on economies and political systems worldwide. That in turn will require a global mass movement. But such a movement is likely to find only narrow support if it fails to combine protection against the gradually intensifying threat of climate change with a program of greater economic well-being for the world's people as part of a transition to a green economy.

The same is true for many other movements as well. The mass mobilizations in Europe, North America, and elsewhere to resist cuts in public employment, social benefits, and living standards are unlikely to succeed without global cooperation to block the race to the bottom and legitimize public policies that use available human resources to meet human needs. The global justice movement will confront intensified inequality unless it is able to join with others to reduce global warming and shift resources from the military to the reduction of poverty. The protection of oceans will only succeed if nations and enterprises can be forced to reduce greenhouse gas emissions and other forms of pollution and put the need for long-term preservation of fish stocks above short-term economic gain. But that in turn will intensify hunger and unemployment without alternative forms of nutrition and livelihood for those affected.

More broadly, why would people do any more to support a human preservation movement than the separate movements for climate protection, disarmament, economic justice, and the like? The reason is that what people really want is to have their lives and the future of the things and people they care about put on a secure basis. Climate protection, disarmament, and economic justice are, after all, primarily means to that end. A human preservation movement offers what we really want—a future protected against the major looming threats, including the threat from unknown unknowns.

57

CHANGING TO SURVIVE

ﺯﺍ

BEFORE THE EMERGENCE OF GLOBALIZATION FROM BELOW, MANY LOCAL, NATIONAL, and global movements had worked out programs for the changes required to meet their needs and objectives. Anti-poverty movements, for example, had proposals for economic development, social welfare, resource reallocation, and public employment. Food security movements had plans for changes in laws and policies that would provide investment in local farming while encouraging the development of markets for local food.

As these movements began to reach out to each other, engage in dialogue, and experiment with joint action, a common agenda began to emerge, represented not in any single document but in thousands of statements by individual organizations and hundreds of joint declarations, as well as in what people said to each other and themselves. It sought, for example, empowerment of local communities, restrictions on global corporations, and reorientation of international economic institutions to support national and local transition to sustainable development. These changes in turn required changes in the organization of power—for example, by challenging the political power that let global drug corporations use the WTO to prevent poor countries from securing AIDS drugs for their citizens.

The emergence of such a common program inevitably involved disagreements—for example, between workers in poor countries who got jobs that had been "offshored" and those in industrialized countries who feared losing their jobs to lower-wage countries. Such conflicts were ameliorated by dialogue—for example, first and third world trade unionists agreed on a global strategy of full employment and rising labor standards that would counter the race to the bottom that was ruinous for all. The emergence of a common program facilitated mutual aid and joint campaigns that increased the power of each.

The emergence of a movement for human preservation is likely to involve a similar process of mutual assimilation and accommodation of goals and strategies. For instance, the climate-protection movement's goal of reducing carbon in the atmosphere to 350 parts per million has already been adopted by a wide array of organizations whose primary mission is not climate protection. Similarly peace movement proposals for nuclear abolition can be assimilated by diverse constituencies, all of whom have an interest in eliminating such threats to human survival.

Thousands of volumes of reports, studies, and programs by UN agencies, NGOs, and social movements spell out in detail many of the changes that are necessary for human survival. But a program for human preservation must be more than just a laundry list adding together the proposals of various constituencies. It needs to spell out an integrated transition to "another world" that can realize both the common and the distinct needs of those affected. It can thereby help construct a common interest that incorporates the particular interests of different groups. This can allow goals that conflict in the status quo world—for example, between jobs for workers in developing and developed countries—to become compatible or even synergistic.

One core element of such an integration that has already emerged in many movements around the world is to address climate change and other environmental threats by creating millions of green jobs to make the transition to renewable energy, thereby simultaneously creating full employment, reducing poverty, giving countries and communities greater control over their sources of energy, reducing the threat of energy wars, and forestalling oil spills and nuclear reactor meltdowns. This approach, often expressed in terms of a "Global Green New Deal," has been advocated by labor-environmental coalitions within many countries and by international groups like the UN Environmental Program and the International Trade Union Confederation.

Another integrating element is demilitarization. This includes the move toward the abolition of nuclear weapons—backed, astonishingly, by the likes of Henry Kissinger and Brent Scowcroft. But it also includes the reduction of conventional weapons by region and category; the move to military systems designed only for defense of national territory, not power projection; and the protection of people and nations by proactive pursuit of common security, rather than national power. Such demilitarization not only makes war less likely and less destructive, it frees vast resources to meet human and environmental needs; it reduces tyranny and oppression; and it affords significant cuts in greenhouse gasses and other forms of pollution itself. To realize such a change, however, requires a planned conversion to non-military production complementary to the conversion to a renewable energy economy.

A third integrating element is political democratization.[1] At present ordinary people are prevented from enforcing human preservation by political structures that empower others and dis-empower them. The world has been electrified by the democratization movements that have recently shaken the Middle East and spread to many other parts of the world. These movements are seeking not merely the trappings of formal democracy, but the effective empowerment of participatory democracy. Such democratization is synergistic with and necessary for almost all elements of human preservation, from protecting the environment to curtailing military establishments.

Such democratization must be not only national but also global. That requires among other things reducing the power of international institutions like the World Bank, the IMF, and the veto-empowered "permanent members club" in the UN Security Council that represent the global elite. It means increasing the power of those institutions, including the UN General Assembly and other parts of the UN system, that come closer to representing common human interests. Alliances among smaller countries and popular movements, such as the "coalition of the unwilling" during the Iraq war and the coalition supporting climate protection at the Copenhagen summit, may serve as a means and precursor to such institutional power shifts.

A fourth integrating element is economic democratization.[2] The global concentration of wealth gives a disproportionate share of power to those individuals and institutions that stand to make short-term gains from the very things—like pollution and militarism—that threaten human survival. Reducing their power to determine the use of human and natural resources is essential to human survival. For example, human survival requires a massive public investment in a transition to a low-carbon economy; that in turn requires changing the neoliberal global economic rules that restrict public economic activities to rules that encourage grassroots economic planning and investment.

While a human preservation movement will converge first and foremost around the universal threats to humanity as a whole, such as climate change and nuclear weapons, the transformation required to ensure human survival is intimately connected with many of the world's other critical problems. Ensuring food security for billions of people threatened with starvation will be advanced by limiting climate change, reducing desertification, funding small local producers, and making resources now allocated to the military available for food production. Conversely, including food security as part of a human preservation agenda will give billions of people an immediate interest in supporting that agenda. The same synergism holds for safe water, ocean acidification, global economic justice, species extinction, and myriad other concerns.

A human survival program needs to address not only known present threats but also unknown future ones. This requires building the "precautionary principle" into all of social life. Social movements and popular pressure have already instituted this principle in a number of contexts. The 2003 Cartagena Protocol on Biosafety, for example, states that acceptance of new genetically modified organisms can be based on the precautionary principle that they must be proven safe before they are introduced. Laws requiring environmental impact statements apply the precautionary principle to proposed development projects. Laws against human cloning, recently passed in many countries, address unanticipated but potentially catastrophic consequences of this emerging technological possibility. More broadly, epidemiology and other public health strategies are designed to search out possible sources of disease and limit them before they get out of hand. Human preservation requires that such approaches be applied to all aspects of life worldwide.

The changes needed to ensure human survival require changes in power relations. For example, they require restrictions on states and their capacity for war and plunder. They require restrictions on corporations, wealth holders, and markets sufficient to prevent destructive results of economic activity like races to the bottom, downward economic spirals, and destructive externalities—side effects and interaction effects.

Many of those restrictions already exist, but are not enforced. For example, aggressive war is prohibited by the UN charter, and many environmental treaties ban various types of pollution, but violations of these rules are not subject to effective sanction. Additional rules are necessary to make such restrictions more comprehensive. Equally important, human survival requires extending the accountability of governments, corporations, and other institutions for fulfilling their national and international obligations. More effective ways are needed to enforce these rules, especially against the most powerful institutions.

This rule-making and enforcement will entail the redistribution of power from nations and corporations both upward and downward. It will require the empowerment of transnational institutions to define and enforce limits on the destructive behavior of all actors. At the same time it will require a process of democratization in which all institutions become more fully subject to control by those they affect. For example, the rules governing disarmament and pollution reduction might be established through global institutions, but their monitoring and enforcement might be conducted by international inspection teams that included technical experts and grassroots representatives from both inside and outside of the institutions and countries being regulated.

Such new means of inspection and monitoring illustrate the possibility of creating new strategies and institutions to implement human preservation. Such innovations are a characteristic feature of new common preservations; two examples from labor history are union-initiated employer bargaining associations and labor banks, such as the Amalgamated Bank created in 1923 by the Amalgamated Clothing Workers to establish a worker voice in the financial aspects of the clothing industry. The human survival movement might, for example, initiate the formation of courts of human preservation. Such courts could start as civil society institutions like the citizen tribunals that have been used to evaluate the criminality of wars from Vietnam to Iraq. Initially they could help identify and legitimate appropriate targets for civil disobedience against threats to survival. Over time, they could be incorporated in the global and national legal system with injunctive power to halt threats to human survival.

The movement for human survival will emerge into a world that is characterized by vast inequalities and injustices. These include disparities of wealth and income within and between nations; oppression of peoples through imperialism and occupation; exploitation of workers; oppression of women; discrimination based on racial, ethnic, religious, and other differences; and a wide range of other violations of human rights. A movement for human survival can all too easily become a vehicle to help some people survive and prosper at the expense of others. It can only succeed, however, if it instead deliberately pursues the survival and well-being of all.

There will be complex relations between the general struggle for survival and the struggle of poor, oppressed, and exploited people against domination and for justice and equality. The least powerful are in many cases those whose survival is most threatened; global warming, for example, is already having devastating effects on marginalized people in the third world. The perpetrators of environmental and military threats are often also the same individuals and groups who seek to maintain injustices, making them potential common targets. Oppressed groups are potentially key power players in campaigns against threats to survival. Struggles for the interests of the oppressed can make governments and elites shift their resources to the needs of their own people, rather than pursuing the aggrandizement of themselves and their powerful supporters. But the oppressed can also have interests that augment threats to human survival; for example, the hydrocarbon energy resources of third world countries may help them reduce poverty while at the same time increase global warming.

As part of its program, a movement for human survival must aim to create the conditions of survival not just for the species as a whole, but for every human being. It must provide basic human rights—economic, social, and political—for all in order to give all a stake in human preservation and the transformation it requires. All proposals for change should incorporate a "just transition" that provides ways to rapidly establish for all the international human rights standards that define essential minimums for survival. Only such a commitment will provide a direct interest in the human survival movement to each person on earth.

THE POWER OF THE POWERLESS

ã

Such a program for human preservation might create a better world, but where might the power to make it happen come from?

Because human survival is a compelling interest shared by all, persuasion is likely to be unusually effective in pursuing it. Power will nonetheless be necessary because there are individuals, groups, and organizations who oppose—from ideology, greed, and/or the requirements of their institutional role—the policies that are necessary to ensure human survival.

Throughout this book we have seen massive evidence that governments, corporations, and other powerful institutions are dependent on the people who cooperate or acquiesce in their power by providing labor, resources, civility, and consent. Social movements can be powerful because they embody the possibility that people may withdraw their acquiescence and consent, undermining the "pillars of support" that governments and institutions need to survive and realize their goals. Social movements can present a significant threat to those who hold power—and thereby compel them to change.

In the case of the labor movement and mass strikes, we saw that workers may be powerless as individuals, but they are not alone in this condition. They share it with their coworkers and the great majority of other people who are also workers. When workers discover common interests at local, national, or global levels, they may turn from individual to collective strategies. Then they discover they have far greater power together than they have alone because their employers, indeed all the institutions of society, depend on their labor. By withdrawing their labor and refusing to cooperate with established authorities in other ways, they can bring any workplace, community, or country to a halt.

The same underlying reality has recently been re-revealed by the people-power democratization movements in Tunisia, Egypt, and elsewhere. Dictatorships that had lasted for decades with the backing of foreign powers and huge military and police forces crumbled in the face of popular refusal to acquiesce in their rule.

But can people power force global change?

Consider the movement that arose in response to the threat of nuclear holocaust. Millions of people worldwide, I among them, talked, wrote, organized, voted, marched, and sat-in to demand the reduction and elimination of nuclear weapons. While we were marching and protesting, we generally believed that our movement was having little impact, and many of us lived in a state of chronic despair. Only when I discovered Lawrence Wittner's magisterial three-volume history *The Struggle Against the Bomb* did I find out I was wrong.

Wittner himself had started out believing that the struggle against the bomb had been "ineffectual." But the information he uncovered in the declassified records of the superpower war agencies changed his mind. According to Wittner, "Most government officials—and particularly those of the major powers—had no intention of adopting nuclear arms control and disarmament policies. Instead, they grudgingly accepted such policies thanks to the emergence of popular pressure." Confronted by a "vast wave of popular resistance, they concluded, reluctantly, that compromise had become the price of political survival. Consequently they began to adapt their rhetoric and policies to the movement's program."[1]

Occasionally high government officials acknowledged the effect of public opinion and the anti-nuclear movement on policies such as the treaty to ban nuclear testing. Atomic Energy Commission (AEC) Chair Glenn Seaborg admitted that, thanks to "popular concern" about nuclear testing, "persistent pressure was brought to bear on the nuclear powers by influential leaders and movements throughout the world." In 1988 US National Security Advisor McGeorge Bundy wrote that he agreed with Seaborg that "what produced the treaty was steadily growing worldwide concern over the radioactive fallout from testing." The atmospheric test ban "was achieved primarily by world opinion."[2]

Ultimately peace movement action led to the test ban treaty, détente, the end of the Cold War, and an 80 percent reduction in strategic nuclear weapons. Whatever its limitations, it provides an example of a successful reconfiguration of the global system initiated by a global social movement. If we have avoided mutual nuclear destruction until now, it is largely due to this movement's achievements.

How can people power force the changes that are necessary to ensure human survival? We can see new answers emerging in the movement against global warming. The globally coordinated campaign for a climate-protection agreement that focused on the Copenhagen summit provides one example. The shutdown of coal-fired power plants by nonviolent direct action in many places around the world provides another. The massive global days of protest organized by 350.org provide a third. While globally coordinated social movements go back at least to the abolitionist struggle against slavery, they have been significantly facilitated by the rise of social networking and other new communication technologies, and the ways to use these most effectively are only now being invented.

Finding ways to use people power for human preservation will require experimentation with diverse kinds of action by millions of people around the globe. It takes creativity to parlay the actions ordinary people are in a position to take into effective pressure on those who have power. Because the powerful are ultimately dependent on the rest of us, our organized withdrawal of our support, acquiescence, and consent can be a force they have to reckon with.

The taming of the powerful can take a number of forms. Sometimes it happens tacitly, as when even the most powerful nations accepted global norms that made the use of nuclear weapons unacceptable. It can be done by pressure for mutual agreement, as illustrated by the test ban treaty, the Cartagena Protocol, and the Kyoto agreement. It can be done by undermining or disrupting the power of the powerful to act, as was done at the Battle of Seattle. It can be done by establishing a higher power, as was done by the formation of the UN or the EU. These processes can be mutually reinforcing.

Mass direct action is likely to be an essential element of the struggle for human survival. It is illustrated by the dramatic action of environmental and peace groups in interfering with nuclear testing, whale hunting, carbon-promoting airport construction, and power plant expansions. It is likely to use a wide range of pressure techniques, such as shunning, shaming, boycotts, strikes, occupations, embargoes, and the like, that make use of targets' vulnerabilities and dependencies. Where such campaigns are successful, the new patterns they impose can then be generalized to establish new norms, rules, and eventually law.

Such action will be strengthened by cooperation between those inside and outside of nations, corporations, and other institutions. The defeat of apartheid, for example, combined internal movements using strikes and community economic pressure with worldwide support involving, for example, divestment from investment in South Africa. Many labor strikes are won by combining the direct effect of the withdrawal of labor power and the indirect effect of popular pressure on the targeted company and its allies.

Such a collaborative strategy is particularly important for dealing with superpowers. Right now that primarily means the United States, which often serves as a stumbling block to common human preservation, but given the declining power of the United States it might include China or other powers in the not-so-distant future.

The United States is currently a poster child for the failure of self-preservation. Despite half of all the world's military expenditures, repeated wars, bases and military operations around the world, and a policy of asserting national power, the United States is the largest debtor in history, with decades of falling real incomes, growing class division, massive intractable unemployment, political paralysis, decaying infrastructure, threatened human rights, climate deadlock, and plummeting international prestige. Sooner or later such problems will establish the conditions for a people-power movement demanding a shift to a strategy of global cooperation for human preservation.

Notwithstanding its pretenses that it can go-it-alone, the United States in fact is extremely—and increasingly—dependent on the rest of the world. Its economy depends on inflows of hundreds of billions of dollars every year. Its energy system is overwhelmingly dependent on foreign oil. Its security relies on a vast array of alliances, bases, and propped-up regimes and on less and less effective threats against those who not do its bidding. This dependency is likely to grow as a result of the energy, dollar, debt, resource, and climate crises. There have been efforts to exploit these dependencies in the competitive global power game—for example, by challenging the dollar's monopoly of trade in petroleum and by threats to dump dollars held by foreign central banks. A global human preservation movement could instead take advantage of such dependencies to pressure the United States to cut greenhouse gases and begin to demilitarize.

Farfetched? According to Lord Nicholas Stern, former chief economist of the World Bank and author of the British government's Stern Report on the Economics of Climate Change, by 2020 the United States will be banned from selling goods to many countries if it continues to shirk on its promises to cut greenhouse gas emissions.[3]

59

GUIDELINES FOR HUMAN PRESERVATIONISTS

ða.

IF YOU AND I AND OTHERS DECIDED WE WANTED TO BUILD A MOVEMENT FOR HUMAN preservation, how would we do it? Here are some possible guidelines based on the experience of past social movements and of the elements of a human survival movement already in motion:

Advocate human preservation wherever you are. Every milieu can be a cell unit of the shift to common preservation. That's where the construction of a common human interest has its roots. Reach out to others, no matter how much resistance you meet, in the faith that sooner or later they will be able to grasp the futility of mutual destruction and the necessity for common preservation.

Don't be afraid to be a messenger of the truth. It's not always popular to be a bearer of inconvenient news. Often people would simply rather not hear about the dangers of climate change or mass starvation or nanotechnology. But facing up to bad news that people have disregarded or denied can give courage and hope, especially if it is joined with practical action that people can take. It demonstrates that we do not have to be paralyzed. And sharing such knowledge with others shows that we do not have to face these perils alone.

Work for concrete objectives while defining your work as part of the human preservation movement. Human preservation will result from efforts to achieve such specific objectives as reduction of greenhouse gasses, food security, and nuclear-free zones. But by articulating such disparate efforts as elements of a movement for human preservation, we can make them part of a broader strategy for human survival. That can be done in conversations, presentations, organizational statements, and media. For example, a 2011 demonstration in Adelaide, Australia, called primarily to demand cuts in greenhouse gas emissions, nonetheless billed itself as "The First March for Survival."[1]

212

Promote convergence. Dialogue: Listen to others and share your thoughts with them. Support the struggles of others and integrate their goals into the objectives of the movements in which you take part. Seek ways to realize the objectives of groups you are part of within the context of a path to mutual survival.

Remember that the real power of the movement lies in people's capacity for self-organization. Organizations are important, but organizations can come and go while the movement lives on. The ability to construct links with others, whether in a local community or around the world, whether through a basement meeting or global Internet networking, is what ultimately allows people to form common goals and coordinate actions.

Maintain the movement's independence. One reason the worldwide anti-nuclear movement was able to force global change was that it could not be controlled by one country or one side of the Cold War. It therefore could hold up a single standard of what countries had to do for peace and stigmatize bad actions by either side—creating a "bidding war" among the powers. While we should welcome support from governments, businesses, and political leaders, we should not let them control or co-opt the movement. They all share the long-term common interest in preventing global catastrophe, and we should do what we can to encourage them to act on that interest. But their short-term special interests in power and profit make them unreliable advocates for long-term common interests. We should look first and foremost to each other, to those who will pay the price of mutual destruction without benefitting from the policies and practices that are bringing it about.

Experiment. Keep in mind that faced with a historically unprecedented reality, none of us knows all the answers. Social action is an enterprise whose consequences are hard to predict. Much of the time you don't know what is going to work. You have to be willing to try things out, observe the consequences, and modify your strategy.

Ensure that those who suffer most from today's mutual destruction, and those who may suffer from the process of transition away from it, have their rights and needs protected. Don't let the human survival movement become a vehicle for some humans to survive at the expense of others!

Don't let the movement give birth to new dominations and disorders. Movements can go wrong. Organizations and leaders can become undemocratic, even tyrannical. They can pursue their own interests instead of common ones. They can bog everyone down in intractable conflicts that perpetuate rather than solving problems. Governments, even democratized ones, can misuse powers given to them for valid purposes to pursue conflict and domination. International institutions can become unaccountable bureaucracies or new bases of domination for themselves or those who control them. The French Revolution led to war, empire, and renewed monarchy. The Egyptian popular uprising, in which men and women of different religions demonstrated side by side, was followed within weeks by brutal and lethal attacks on women and religious minorities. Make sure the movement's own organization and action stay within the norms you are trying to establish for the world. Build in ways to keep organizations accountable to their participants and open to change. Be prepared to join with those who have been adversaries to establish new forms of common preservation.

Act up. The basic capacity that allows people to contest the powerful is the refusal to acquiesce. Disobeying authority—whether through blocking a polluting electrical utility or planting a community garden on private property—is a necessary part of changing unequal power. The movement for human survival is ultimately the withdrawal of consent from mutual destruction. Each action by which you express your refusal to acquiesce can be a blow for human survival. Just be sure you do it in a way that builds, rather than undermines, support for common preservation in the long run.

Undermine the pillars of support for mutual destruction. Global warming denialism, water privatization, foreign invasions, and all other such manifestations of mutual destruction are initiated by specific individuals, groups, and institutions. They in turn are dependent for their power and well-being on other specific individuals, groups, and institutions who themselves are dependent on others, and so on. Many of those in the chain will be subject to persuasion in the interest of common preservation. And many will be vulnerable to pressure from those who refuse to acquiesce in their business as usual. Just because strategies are indirect doesn't mean they are ineffective.

Be in it for the long haul. It took half a century for the nuclear disarmament movement to achieve a test ban treaty, a non-proliferation agreement, and an 80 percent reduction in strategic nuclear weapons, and full nuclear disarmament is still far from achievement now. But in the meantime the movement managed to so stigmatize nuclear weapons that no country dared to use them. Movements can prevail, but it is often a victory just be able to stand up and fight in the face of repression and abuse. Movements need to persist through defeats, schisms, and wild fluctuations in strength and support. A sense of urgency is important, but so is a commitment to human preservation that can persevere through frustration and adversity.

Keep your eyes on the prize. The goal of a human preservation movement is to make a shift from mutual destruction to common preservation sufficient to ensure the survival of our species and its members. While that entails fighting to halt particular threats, it ultimately means imposing the requirements of common human preservation on the institutions and processes that generate the threats to survival. Might that goal justify a lifetime of struggle?

60

A PROTRACTED STRUGGLE
IN AN ERA OF TURMOIL

ક્ર

WE KNOW THAT IN THE PAST, SOCIAL MOVEMENTS HAVE SOMETIMES MADE RAPID AND often unexpected change that countered apparently immutable social problems.

The international abolitionist movement in the course of a few decades virtually eliminated slavery, one of the oldest and most widespread of human institutions, from the face of the earth. The sit-down strikes of the 1930s forced the mightiest US corporations to come to the table to bargain with their employees. The civil disobedience campaigns led by Gandhi won India's independence from the world's greatest imperial power.

The worldwide anti-nuclear ban-the-bomb movement helped secure a nuclear test ban treaty, US-Soviet détente, and international agreements restraining the arms race. The US civil rights movement brought about the abolition of legal racial segregation in the American South. The antiwar movement helped force the withdrawal of half a million US troops from Vietnam. The women's liberation movement turned the subordination of women from a generally accepted inevitability to something contested in every sphere of life and every country in the world. The gay rights movement, ever multiplying since the Stonewall confrontations of 1969, has won rights long denied to sexual minorities.

The Solidarity movement and its general strikes led to the fall of Communism in Poland and helped bring about its demise throughout Eastern Europe and the USSR. People-power movements have brought about the overthrow of authoritarian dictatorships from the Philippines to South Korea to Argentina. The Battle of Seattle and the global justice movement prevented the writing of corporate-dominated globalization into international law. The nonviolent popular uprisings in Tunisia, Egypt, and elsewhere are changing the face of the Middle East in ways that we cannot yet even begin to characterize.

Even these accomplishments are a far cry from the worldwide social transformations we need to assure human survival against threats such as global warming and nuclear proliferation. But they embody patterns of social change that may help us envision what kind of movement can help us make progress toward human survival.

The shift to common human preservation will no doubt take a protracted struggle lasting an era at least as long as the era of mutual destruction. It is not likely to be a smooth transition. It will be marked by unpredictable and uneven development in different spheres. An era of turmoil is likely to be necessary to teach the world the necessity of common preservation. One role of the movement for human preservation is to grasp and teach those lessons.

The shift to human preservation is not likely to look much like past revolutions or social reforms. It is likely to involve changes on many different time scales, from glacial changes in underlying attitudes and beliefs, to sudden crystallizations like the Arab Spring, to whole periods of rolling, roiling, cascading people-power upheavals that present, as Rosa Luxemburg said of periods of mass strike, "a ceaselessly moving, changing sea of phenomena." Success will require a general process of shifting to common preservation, but will be manifested at different rates with leads and lags in different spheres.

Human preservation will involve small-scale local and sectoral actions, massive regional and national peoples' power mobilizations, and global Seattle- and Copenhagen-style protests. It will include self-organization on a micro-level, social movements, and global networks like the World Social Forum and 350.org. A task of the human preservation movement will be to make all these efforts synergistic.

Ultimately, human preservation must become an irresistible force. How that will happen is unpredictable. The path between today's starting points and the ultimate destination will have to be created by those who travel it.

Part 5 represents a bare sketch of what a human preservation movement might be. Filling it in is a task for hundreds, and eventually millions, of people. It is for them to debate, test, correct, and revise.

The human preservation movement could be viewed as the self-organization of humanity. It represents a cumulative, synergistic process of withdrawal of consent from doom. If humanity has a future, it will be a future of common preservation.

This proposal for a human preservation movement grows out of my own background, study, and experience. I know it may not provide the best approach to the problem of human survival or of constructing a movement to secure it. There may well be good reasons to reject the very idea. I only ask that if you reject it you devise and act on your own approach to solving the problems it addresses. I ask you to recognize that to stand by in critical detachment is to acquiesce in collective suicide—and in the destruction of whatever you hold dear.

A human preservation movement will be an uncertain venture into the unknown. But as scientist and novelist C. P. Snow said in 1960 of the risk of trying to limit nuclear weapons compared to the certainty of a global catastrophe: "Between a risk and a certainty, a sane man does not hesitate."[1]

Indeed, a human survival movement might echo the closing words of the *Port Huron Statement:* "If we appear to seek the unattainable, as it has been said, then let it be known that we do so to avoid the unimaginable."[2]

COMMON PRESERVATION

28.

SIXTY YEARS AFTER THE FIRST APPEARANCE OF THE *BULLETIN OF THE ATOMIC SCIENTISTS'* famous Doomsday Clock indicating how close humanity is to catastrophic destruction, the clock continues to hover close to midnight, while the sources of possible doom multiply. The drift toward doom continues unabated year after year, decade after decade, despite our knowledge of the threats, and despite the semblance of official action to combat them.

What has come to be known as the Serenity Prayer appeals for "the serenity to accept the things we cannot change, courage to change the things we can, and wisdom to know the difference."[1] If the question is whether any of us as individuals can halt global warming or remove the threat of nuclear warfare, we had better start praying for serenity.

But what we can or cannot do individually is not the measure of what we can do together. If the question, conversely, is whether all of us acting together could reverse the drift to doom, the answer is just as clearly yes. We could do so in a day. But that doesn't mean it will just happen. It depends on what people determine to do.

While people make use of their established strategies, they also change them. And so how they will respond to new situations is never fully predictable. The most terrible events may be taken as a cause for despair or as a spur to change. The close encounter with nuclear holocaust in the Cuban Missile Crisis unexpectedly led both the United States and the USSR to back off from the mad pursuit of nuclear superiority and move toward a strategy of détente and arms control. There is no guarantee that the Katrinas of the future will have a similar effect—but there is no guarantee that they won't.

The condition for human survival is a new strategy based on the cooperation of all to ensure the survival of all. Common preservation is now the necessary condition for self-preservation. None of us can count on survival, let alone well-being, for ourselves and the people and things we care about unless we take concerted action to transform the current patterns of human life. Self-preservation for individuals and groups can now only be ensured through common preservation of our species and its environment as a whole.

Doom sends out its harbingers. It was the discovery of fallout from nuclear testing that made the threat of the nuclear arms race real to millions of people who had previously experienced nuclear Armageddon as only a remote and hypothetical threat. Hurricanes, heat waves, wildfires, dust storms, and floods provide an almost Biblical harbinger of the approaching catastrophe of climate change.

Is it already too late? We know that something is already lost. But there is no way to be sure that all is lost. There is no way to know for certain in advance what a collective response may yet achieve. We are in the position of parents who may already have lost a child and now must choose whether to give up or to fight for their other children who are threatened but still alive.

We may be tempted to respond to our condition with the dying words of the labor poet Joe Hill: "Don't mourn for me—organize." But the truth is we have to mourn. We have to mourn for the victims of Katrina and for the way of life that it destroyed. We have to mourn for the many other Katrinas that have already occurred in Bangladesh and Indonesia and more that are fated to occur, despite whatever we may do. We have to mourn for the polar bears whose habitat has been destroyed. We have to mourn for the victims of the nuclear meltdown at Fukushima. We have to mourn for each cherished piece of our own environment: a certain kind of winter day or the songbirds who no longer visit an altered clime. We have to mourn for what we will lose—what we must sacrifice—to do what is necessary to ward off doom. Our grief is the only way to keep faith with the things which—and the people who—have already been sacrificed to our folly.

And yet, if all we do is mourn, are we not colluding in the condemnation of additional peoples, cities, and habitats to destruction?

Let us say rather, paraphrasing Mother Jones, "Mourn for the dead; fight like hell for the living."

Or, in the words of the African American spiritual embraced by the civil rights movement:

> We are soldiers in the army
> We've got to fight, although we've got to cry.
> We've got to hold up that bloodstained banner;
> We've got to hold it up till we die.

The attempt to solve our problems by self-preservation at the expense of others now threatens the survival of all. Conversely, the preservation of all has become the condition for the self-preservation of each.

Let us then try what common preservation can do.

L'ENVOY

&

OUR ERA HAS BEEN HAUNTED BY WALTER BENJAMIN'S IMAGE OF THE ANGEL OF History.[1] The angel, looking toward the past, sees "one single catastrophe" that "keeps piling wreckage and hurls it in front of his feet." The angel would like to "make whole what has been smashed." But "a storm is blowing in from Paradise." The storm "irresistibly propels him into the future" while "the pile of debris before him grows skyward." This storm, Benjamin concludes, "is what we call progress."

Much of what has been called "progress" is undoubtedly a continuing catastrophe. But it cannot be blamed on a storm blowing from beyond the earth. History is made by living people interacting in the world. If a storm is piling up wreckage, that storm is the product of our own action. And we are not irresistibly propelled anywhere. We can stop, look, and listen. We can see what it is we are doing. We can share our understandings of what we see. And we can agree to change it.

Shall we try?

NOTES

❧

PROLOGUE

1. Jeremy Brecher, "In the Shadow of the Pyramids," http://www.jeremybrecher.org/labor/in-the-shadow-of-the-pyramids/, and "Egyptian Textile Worker Strike: The Story Behind the Story," http://www.jeremybrecher.org/labor/egyptian-textile-worker-strike-the-story-behind-the-story/.

2. Matthew Taylor, "Anti-Cuts Campaigners Plan to Turn Trafalgar Square into Tahrir Square," *The Guardian*, March 22, 2011.

3. "Rep. Luis V. Gutierrez Denounces Civil Rights Violations in Puerto Rico," Hispanically Speaking News, February 17, 2011, http://www.hispanicallyspeakingnews.com/notitas-de-noticias/details/rep.-luis-v.-gutierrez-denounces-civil-rights-violations-in-puerto-ric/5345/.

4. "Call for a Peaceful Civil Insurgency in Mexico," Demotix, January 31, 2011, http://www.demotix.com/news/576102/call-peaceful-civil-insurgency-mexico.

5. Jordan Fabrian, "Rep. Ryan: Wisconsin Protests like Egypt," *The Hill*, February 17, 2011.

6. Pat Simms, "Union Busting in Wisconsin Prompts Mass Protest," *AFP*, February 17, 2011, http://www.google.com/hostednews/afp/article/ALeqM5iQ7tj4fE3EtfLOaDnaIOnuXISyUw?docId=CNG.2feda1c6289a29f15f093bf828524495.1031.

INTRODUCTION

1. Albert Einstein, *Telegram*, May 24, 1946.

2. Jordan Lite, "Earth's Days Are Numbered, Hawking Says," *Daily News*, June 14, 2006.

3. The Doomsday Clock is a symbolic clockface maintained since 1947 by the *Bulletin of the Atomic Scientists*. Sources of doom, in addition to nuclear war, include climate-changing technologies and new developments in the life sciences and nanotechnology that could inflict irrevocable harm. The clock was advanced at the start of 2007 to five minutes to midnight. On January 14, 2010, it was set back to six minutes to midnight to reflect worldwide cooperation to reduce nuclear arsenals and limit the effect of climate change. For background on the clock and documentation of the threats that inform it, see http://www.thebulletin.org/minutes-to-midnight/.

4. "350.org's Call to Action," *CNN*, October 29, 2009.

5. George H. Sabine, ed., *The Works of Gerrard Winstanley* (New York: Russell & Russell, 1965), pp. 536–37.

CHAPTER 2

1. Historical research indicates that the world indeed came close to nuclear war during the Cold War, notably in the Cuban Missile Crisis. See for example, Michael Dobbs, *One Minute to Midnight: Kennedy, Khrushchev, and Castro on the Brink of Nuclear War* (New York: Knopf, 2008).

2. The story is told in Norman Cousins, *Present Tense: An American Editor's Odyssey* (New York: McGraw-Hill, 1967), and Rodney Barker, *The Hiroshima Maidens* (New York: Viking, 1985).

3. When President George W. Bush addressed the UN General Assembly in 2002 in the lead up to the attack on Iraq, the United States insisted that a reproduction of *Guernica* be removed from the hall.

4. In the 1990s my Japanese friend Muto took me to the place where one hundred thousand people were killed in one day by the "conventional" Allied bombing of Tokyo—about as many as in Hiroshima. See Howard W. French, "100,000 People Perished, but Who Remembers?" *New York Times,* March 14, 2002.

CHAPTER 3

1. I later confirmed this story through family oral histories I conducted.

CHAPTER 5

1. For a recent journalistic account of the Mountain People, see Ben McGrath, "Strangers on the Mountain," *The New Yorker,* March 1, 2010, p. 50.

CHAPTER 6

1. Erich Fromm, *Marx's Concept of Man* (New York: Frederick Ungar, 1961). I later learned that Fromm's book is an object of derision for some subsequent scholars of Marxism.

CHAPTER 7

1. Andy Newman, "In Baby Teeth, a Test of Fallout," *New York Times,* November 11, 2003.

CHAPTER 9

1. Ernest Schachtel, *Metamorphosis: On the Development of Affect, Perception, Attention, and Memory* (New York: Basic Books, 1959).

CHAPTER 10

1. "I Come and Stand at Every Door," written by Hikmet/Waters. The original Turkish poem was by Nazim Hikmet. The English translation was by Jeanette Turner. Adaptation was by Pete Seeger (1962). Text copyright © 1966 by Stormking Music, Inc. An excerpt can be heard at http://www.folkways.si.edu/albumdetails.aspx?itemid=388.

2. The Fort Detrick biological warfare program is widely believed to have been the original source of the anthrax that killed postal workers and contaminated the US Capitol in 2001.

3. Long afterward I discovered in the Connecticut State Library a once-secret 1954 Civil Defense document titled "Mass Burial Annex" revealing that Hartford, only fifty miles from my home and then a center of military industry, was regarded by the Defense Department as a probable target for any nuclear attack. It predicted 125,000 fatalities for Hartford and East Hartford—equal to the majority of their entire population. "Mass Burial Annex," Connecticut Office of Civil Defense, May 1, 1954. "Plan A: Hartford Is Attacked," Connecticut State Library.

4. The history of these struggles is recounted, based on massive research, in the three volumes of Lawrence S. Wittner, *The Struggle Against the Bomb* (Stanford: Stanford University Press, 1993–2003).

CHAPTER 11

1. Lewis F. Richardson, *Statistics of Deadly Quarrels* (Pacific Grove, CA: Boxwood Press, 1960).

2. Today they might also be related to the most effective solutions to games theory's Prisoner's Dilemma, in which moves are used to encourage other players to adopt cooperative rather than apparently self-interested but actually self-defeating behavior. See Robert Alexrod, *The Evolution of Cooperation* (New York: Basic Books, 1984).

3. E. P. Thompson, ed., *Out of Apathy* (London: Stevens, 1960).

CHAPTER 12

1. See Michael S. Sherry, *In the Shadow of War: The United States since the 1930s* (New Haven: Yale University Press, 1997).
2. C. Wright Mills, *The Causes of World War III* (New York: Simon and Schuster, 1958).
3. Connecticut was one of the states most dependent on military production, most affected by its fluctuations, and perhaps the one most devastated by the arms cutbacks that followed the end of the Cold War.
4. Seymour Melman, *Our Depleted Society* (New York: Holt, Rinehart and Winston, 1965).

CHAPTER 13

1. "Talking Union," on *Talking Union,* currently available from Smithsonian/Folkways. Written by Millard Lampell, Lee Hayes, and Pete Seeger. An excerpt can be heard at http://www.folkways .si.edu/albumdetails.aspx?itemid=965.
2. "Solidarity Forever" was written by Ralph Chaplin in 1915.
3. Paul Buhle, *Taking Care of Business* (New York: Monthly Review Press, 1999), p. 172.
4. C. Wright Mills, *The New Men of Power* (New York: Harcourt Brace, 1948).

CHAPTER 14

1. "Keep your eyes on the prize," words by Alice Wine, copyright © 1963, 1965.
2. See, for instance, the three volumes of Taylor Branch's series on *America in the King Years* (New York: Simon & Schuster, 1998–2006).
3. Gene Sharp, *The Politics of Nonviolent Action,* volumes 1–3 (Boston: Porter Sargent, 1973).

CHAPTER 15

1. See Kirkpatrick Sale, *SDS* (New York: Random House, 1973), for the history of the Inter-collegiate Socialist Society and its successors.
2. Students for a Democratic Society, *The Port Huron Statement,* 1962.
3. C. Vann Woodward, *Reunion and Reaction* (Boston: Little, Brown, 1951).

CHAPTER 16

1. Robert Michels, *Political Parties* (London: Jarrold and Sons, 1915).
2. For a detailed account, see Sale, *SDS,* p. 210ff.
3. See, for example, the discussion of cross-border participatory democracy in Muto Ichiyo, "For an Alliance of Hope," in *Global Visions,* eds. Jeremy Brecher, John Brown Childs, and Jill Cutler (Boston: South End Press, 1993).

CHAPTER 17

1. Sale, *SDS,* p. 357, gives a partial list of women in the formal leadership of SDS.
2. Many of these practices are described in Marge Piercy, "Grand Coolie Dam," in *Sisterhood Is Powerful,* ed. Robin Morgan (New York: Random House, 1970).
3. Casey Hayden and Mary King, "A Kind of Memo," 1965, http://www.cwluherstory.com/ a-kind-of-memo.html. A version appeared in the April 1966 edition of *Liberation Magazine.*
4. Sale, *SDS,* p. 252. According to Sale, it was the first workshop on this topic in any left organization in the 1960s.

CHAPTER 18

1. Sale, *SDS,* pp. 183–84.
2. Ibid., pp. 185–86.
3. Jeremy Brecher, Jill Cutler, and Brendan Smith, eds., *In The Name of Democracy: American War Crimes in Iraq and Beyond* (New York: Metropolitan Books, Henry Holt, 2005).

CHAPTER 19

1. William James, *Varieties of Religious Experience* (New York: Longmans, Green, 1905). See also Francesco Alberoni, *Movement and Institution* (New York: Columbia University Press, 1984) regarding the "nascent state" that often precedes joining or forming a movement.

2. Interview with Charles Sherrod, "Eyes on the Prize: America's Civil Rights Years (1954–1965)," December 20, 1985.

CHAPTER 21

1. E. P. Thompson, *The Making of the English Working Class* (New York: Vintage, 1963).

2. Robert V. Bruce, *1877: Year of Violence* (Indianapolis: Bobbs-Merrill, 1959).

3. Irving Bernstein, *Turbulent Years: A History of the American Worker 1933–1941* (Boston: Houghton Mifflin, 1970), p. 217.

CHAPTER 22

1. Jeremy Brecher and Stanley Aronowitz, "Notes on the Postal Strike," *Root & Branch* 1 (June 1970): 1–5; reprinted in *Root & Branch: The Rise of the Workers' Movements.* See also Jeremy Brecher, *Strike!,* revised edition (Cambridge, MA: South End Press, 1977), pp. 257–61.

2. President's Commission on Postal Organization, headed by Frederich R. Kappel, quoted in *Wall Street Journal,* March 19, 1970.

3. *Washington Post,* March 22, 1970.

4. Alan Whitney, Executive Vice-President, National Association of Government Employees, radio interview cited in *Strike!,* 1997 revised edition, p. 260.

5. Ad Hoc Committee of Government Employees to Support the Strike, "If They Did It, Why Can't We?" Flyer in author's possession.

CHAPTER 23

1. Jeremy Brecher, "The Vietnam Moratorium," *Liberation Magazine,* December 1969, http://www.jeremybrecher.org/peace/the-vietnam-moratorium/.

CHAPTER 24

1. George F. Addes and R. J. Thomas, "Introduction," in *The Many and the Few,* Henry Kraus (Los Angeles: Plantin Press, 1947).

2. "Trade Unions in the United States." *Microsoft® Encarta® Encyclopedia 2001.* Copyright © 1993–2000 by Microsoft Corporation.

CHAPTER 25

1. Maurice Sugar, "Sit Down," *United Automobile Worker,* Detroit, January 1937.

2. Louis Adamic, *My America, 1928–1938* (New York: Harper, 1939).

3. Ruth McKenney, *Industrial Valley* (New York: Harcourt Brace, 1939).

4. Henry Kraus, *The Many and the Few* (Los Angeles: Plantin, 1947).

5. McKenney, *Industrial Valley,* pp. 261–62.

6. Adamic, *My America, 1928–1938,* p. 309ff.

7. "Unauthorized Sit-Downs Fought by CIO Unions," *New York Times,* April 11, 1937.

8. Herbert Harris, *American Labor* (New Haven: Yale University Press, 1939), p. 291.

CHAPTER 26

1. Stephan Thernstrom, "Urbanization, Migration, and Social Mobility in Late Nineteenth-Century America," in *Towards a New Past: Dissenting Essays in American History,* ed. Barton J. Bernstein (New York: Vintage, 1969), pp. 172–73.

2. Rosa Luxemburg, "The Mass Strike, the Political Party and the Trade Unions," in *Rosa Luxemburg Speaks* (New York: Pathfinder Press, 1970), p. 182.

3. Anton Pannekoek, *Workers' Councils* (Melbourne, Australia: Southern Advocate for Workers Councils, 1948); reprinted (Oakland, CA: AK Press, 2003).

4. See Paul Mattick, *Anti-Bolshevik Communism* (White Plains, NY: M. E. Sharpe, 1978). See also Jeremy Brecher, "Review of Paul Mattick, *Anti-Bolshevik Communism*," *Our Generation* 15, no. 3 (Fall 1982).

5. Paul Mattick, *The Inevitability of Communism* (New York: Polemic Publishers, 1936).

6. Much of Glaberman's writing has been collected in Martin Glaberman, *Punching Out and Other Writings* (Chicago: Charles H. Kerr, 2002).

7. Stan Weir, "USA—The Labor Revolt," first published in the *International Socialist Journal* (Rome, Italy), April and June 1967; reprinted in *American Labor Radicalism*, ed. Staughton Lynd (New York: Wiley, 1973).

8. Commission of Inquiry, Interchurch World Movement, *Report on the Steel Strike of 1919* (New York: Harcourt, Brace, and Howe, 1920), p. 147.

CHAPTER 27

1. *Strike!*, 1977 edition, p. vii.

2. *Strike!*, 1997 revised edition, p. 238. For a fuller discussion of issues of class, see Jeremy Brecher, "Book Review: *The Fall of the House of Labor: The Workplace, the State, and American Labor Activism, 1865–1925*," *Review of Radical Political Economics*, December 1988.

3. Terence V. Powderly, *Thirty Years of Labor, 1859–1889* (Columbus: Excelsior Publishing House, 1889), pp. 26–27. The actual course of capitalist development was of course different in different countries.

4. Gabriel Kolko, *Wealth and Power in America* (New York: Praeger, 1962), p. 51.

5. In 1989 the top 1 percent of US families owned 48 percent of net financial assets while 54 percent of American families had zero or negative net financial assets. Lawrence Mishel, Jarred Bernstein, and John Schmitt, *The State of Working America, 1996–1997* (Armonk: M. E. Sharpe, 1997), pp. 278, 280. In 2011 the wealthiest 1 percent of US households had net worth that was 225 times greater than the median or typical household's net worth in 2009. This is the highest ratio on record. Sylvia A. Allegretto, "The State of Working America's Wealth, 2011," Economic Policy Institute, March 23, 2011, http://epi.3cdn.net/002c5fc0fda0ae9cce_aem6idhp5.pdf.

CHAPTER 28

1. *Strike!*, 1977 edition, p. viii. This passage illustrates the unconscious reduction of the very broad category "activity" to the economic one of "work" and the reduction of "society" to "the country."

2. *Strike!*, 1977 edition, p. viii. "People directing their own action cooperatively toward common purposes" is very close to what I now term common preservation. This quote indicates the utopian aspirations that colored *Strike!* without entirely shaping it.

3. Ruth Allen, *The Great Southwest Strike* (Austin: University of Texas, 1942), p. 30.

4. Alfred P. Sloan, Jr., January 5, 1937, Kraus Papers, Box 9, cited in Sidney Fine, *Sit-Down: The General Motors Strike of 1936–37* (Ann Arbor: University of Michigan Press, 1969), p. 182.

CHAPTER 29

1. Stan Weir, "The Informal Workgroup," in *Rank and File: Personal Histories of Working-Class Organizers*, eds. Alice and Staughton Lynd (Boston: Beacon Press, 1973).

2. Elton Mayo, *The Human Problems of an Industrial Civilization* (Cambridge: Harvard University Press, 1946), pp. 226–27.

3. Donald Roy, "Making Out: A Counter-System of Workers Control of Work Situations and Relations," in *Industrial Man*, ed. Tom Burns (Baltimore: Penguin, 1969).

4. Orvis Collins, Melville Dalton, and Donald Roy, "Restriction of Output and Social Cleavage in Industry," *Applied Anthropology* (Summer 1946): 4.

5. Powderly, *Thirty Years of Labor, 1859–1889*, pp. 26–27.

6. *Wall Street Journal*, August 6, 1970.

7. See "Keep on Truckin'," Mac Brockway (pseudonym for Tim Costello), *Root & Branch* no. 2 (1971); reprinted in *Root & Branch: The Rise of the Workers' Movements*, ed. Root & Branch (Greenwich, CT: Fawcett Publications, 1975). See also the memorial website for Tim Costello at http://www.globallaborstrategies.org/?cat=18.

8. *Strike!*, 1972 edition, p. ix.

CHAPTER 30

1. John R. Commons, *History of Labour in the United States*, Volume II (New York: MacMillan, 1918), p. 366.

2. Bruce, *1877*, pp. 128–29.

3. *Strike!*, 1977 edition, pp. 82–83. *U.S. Strike Commission Report*, Senate Exec. Doc. No. 7 53d Cong., 3d Sess. (Washington: GPO), submitted to President Cleveland on November 14, 1894, p. 140.

4. Commons, *History of Labour in the United States*, Volume II, pp. 373–74.

5. Powderly, *Thirty Years of Labor, 1859–1889*, p. 496.

6. Alexander M. Bing, *War-Time Strikes and Their Adjustment* (New York: E. P. Dutton, 1921), p. 262.

CHAPTER 31

1. Mac Brockway (Tim Costello), "Keep on Truckin'."

2. Clayton W. Fountain, *Union Guy* (New York: Viking Press, 1949), pp. 28–29.

3. Commons, *History of Labour in the United States*, Volume II, p. 370.

4. Cited in Henry David, "Upheaval at Homestead," in *America in Crisis*, ed. Daniel Aaron (New York: Knopf, 1952), p. 167.

5. *U.S. Strike Commission Report*, p. 76.

6. Commons, *History of Labour in the United States*, Volume II, pp. 373–74.

7. *Strike!*, 1977 edition, pp. 237–38.

8. Eugene Victor Debs, *Public Opinion*, July 5, 1894.

9. Clarence E. Bonnett, *History of Employers' Associations in the United States* (New York: Vantage Press, 1956), p. 282.

10. Hugh D. Graham and Ted R. Gurr, *The History of Violence in America, A Report to the National Commission on the Causes and Prevention of Violence* (New York: Bantam Books, 1969), p. 380.

11. Leon Wolff, *Lockout. The Story of the Homestead Strike of 1892: A Study of Violence, Unionism and the Carnegie Steel Empire* (New York: Harper & Row, 1965), p. 228.

CHAPTER 32

1. Alvin W. Gouldner, *Wildcat Strike: A Study in Worker-Management Relationships* (New York: Harper & Row, Torchbooks edition, 1965), p. 66.

2. For "extended authority," see Charles Lindblom, *Politics and Markets: The World's Political-Economic Systems* (New York: Basic Books, 1977). For Gandhi and the Russian Revolution of 1905, see Gene Sharp, *Gandhi as a Political Strategist* (Boston: Porter Sargent, 1979), p. 29 and *Indian Opinion*, November 11, 1905.

CHAPTER 34

1. History Committee of the Seattle General Strike Committee, *The Seattle General Strike* (Seattle: The Seattle Union Record Publishing Company, 1920). Original report drafted by Anna Louise Strong. See Anna Louise Strong, *I Change Worlds* (New York: Henry Holt, 1935), p. 68.

CHAPTER 35

1. *Strike!*, 1977 edition, p. 238.

2. Ibid., p. 240.

3. Ibid., p. 239.

4. *Strike!*, 1997 revised edition, pp. 274–75. For a similar formulation of class equilibrium and its disruption see E. P. Thompson's essay "Revolution": "The countervailing powers are there, and the equilibrium (which is an equilibrium within capitalism) is precarious. It could be tipped back towards authoritarianism. But it could also be heaved forward, by popular pressures of great intensity, to the point where the powers of democracy cease to be countervailing and become the active dynamic of society in their own right. This is revolution." E. P. Thompson, "Revolution," in *Out of Apathy*, ed. E. P. Thompson (London: Stevens, 1960).

5. *Strike!*, 1997 revised edition, p. 303. To my surprise, my current perspective on revolution as only one of a variety of forms of social change echoes a position of John Dewey's. In a debate with Trotsky, Dewey did not rule out revolutionary class struggle as a means to human freedom, but refused to endorse it as the consequence of a fixed law of social development. He observed that "the belief that a law of history determines the particular way in which the struggle is to be carried on certainly seems to tend toward a fanatical and even mystical devotion to the use of certain ways of conducting the class struggle to the exclusion of all other ways of conducting it." Quoted in Robert B. Westbrook, *John Dewey and American Democracy* (Ithaca, NY: Cornell University Press, 1991), p. 472. If this be pragmatism, make the most of it!

6. *U.S. Strike Commission Report*, p. 121.

CHAPTER 36

1. Steven Sapolsky, "*Strike!*: A Review," *Root & Branch* no. 4 (1973). For a retrospective view of the non-reductionist approach to the complexity and diversity of working-class experience that Steve's teacher David Montgomery was developing at the University of Pittsburgh at the time, see James R. Barrett, "Class Act: An Interview with David Montgomery," *Labor: Studies in Working-Class History of the Americas* 1, no. 1 (Spring 2004).

2. *Strike!*, 1997 revised edition, p. 6.

3. *Strike!*, 1977 edition, p. viii.

4. See, for instance, Alberto Melucci, *Challenging Codes: Collective Action in the Information Age* (Cambridge: Cambridge University Press, 1969).

CHAPTER 38

1. Jeremy Brecher, Jerry Lombardi, and Jan Stackhouse, eds., *Brass Valley: The Story of Working People's Lives and Struggles in an American Industrial Region* (Philadelphia: Temple University Press, 1982). See also Jeremy Brecher, "A Report on Doing History from Below: The Brass Workers History Project," in *Presenting the Past: Essays on History and the Public*, ed. Susan Porter Benson, Stephen Brier, and Roy Rosenzweig (Philadelphia: Temple University Press, 1986); Jeremy Brecher, "How I Learned to Quit Worrying and Love Community History: A 'Pet Outsider's' Report on the Brass Workers History Project," *Radical History Review* 28–30 (1984): 187–201; Jeremy Brecher, *History from Below: How to Uncover and Tell the Story of Your Community, Association, or Union* (New Haven: Advocate Press/Commonwork, 1986); Lynne Williamson, Jeremy Brecher, Ruth Glasser, and Jean J. Schensul, "Using Ethnography to Enhance Public Programming," in *Ethnographer's Toolkit: Volume 7: Using Ethnographic Data: Interventions, Programming, and Public Policy*, eds. Jean J. Schensul, Margaret D. LeCompte, et al. (Lanham, MD: AltaMira Press, 1999). Accounts of the project are also given in Dolores Hayden, *The Power of Place: Urban Landscapes as Public History* (Cambridge, MA: MIT Press, 1995), and James Green, *Taking History to Heart: The Power of the Past in Building Social Movements* (Amherst: University of Massachusetts Press, 2000). See also the video documentary *Brass Valley* produced by the Brass Workers History Project and distributed by Cinema Guild, New York, NY.

CHAPTER 39

1. *Brass Valley* video documentary.

2. Brecher, Lombardi, and Stackhouse, *Brass Valley*, p. 230.

CHAPTER 40

1. I believe the first time I ever saw the phrase "global assembly line" was in Barbara Ehrenreich and Annette Fuentes, "Life on the Global Assembly Line," *Ms.* magazine, January 1981.

2. Jeremy Brecher and Tim Costello, *Global Village or Global Pillage: Economic Reconstruction from the Bottom Up,* second edition (Cambridge, MA: South End Press, 1998), p. 67ff.

3. Ibid., pp. 68–69.

CHAPTER 41

1. Bennett Harrison, *Lean and Mean: The Changing Landscape of Corporate Power in the Age of Flexibility* (New York: Basic Books, 1994), pp. 125–26.

2. Brecher and Costello, *Global Village or Global Pillage,* p. xvii.

3. David C. Ranney, *The Evolving Supra-National Policy Arena* (Chicago: University of Illinois at Chicago, Center for Urban Economic Development, 1993).

4. Details are spelled out in Jeremy Brecher, Tim Costello, and Brendan Smith, *Globalization from Below: The Power of Solidarity* (Cambridge, MA: South End Press, 2000), pp. 6–9.

5. Ibid., pp. 9–10.

6. Ibid., p. xiv.

CHAPTER 42

1. See Saskia Sassen, *Territory, Authority, Rights: From Medieval to Global Assemblages* (Princeton, NJ: Princeton University Press, 2006).

2. Susan George, "Network Guerillas," *Financial Times,* April 30, 1998.

3. Charles Lindblom, *Politics and Markets: The World's Political-Economic Systems* (New York: Basic Books, 1977).

CHAPTER 43

1. Joseph Stiglitz, "Worker Rights Key to Development," *Reuters,* January 8, 2000.

2. Ginger Thompson, "Fallout of U.S. Recession Drifts South into Mexico," *New York Times,* December 26, 2001.

3. Bloomberg News, "Taiwan: Economy Slumps," *New York Times,* February 23, 2002.

CHAPTER 44

1. The classic analysis of this corporate structure is Alfred Chandler, *The Visible Hand* (Cambridge, MA: Harvard Belknap, 1977).

2. Bennett Harrison, *Lean and Mean: The Changing Landscape of Corporate Power in the Age of Flexibility* (New York: Basic Books, 1994), is the classic analysis of the transformation from vertical and horizontal integration to the core/ring structure of networked production.

3. Ibid., pp. 9, 171.

CHAPTER 46

1. Samuel Gompers, *Seventy Years of Life and Labor* (New York: E. P. Dutton, 1957), p. 280.

2. The subservience of the US Communist Party is documented in Theodore Draper, *American Communism and Soviet Russia* (New York: Viking Press, 1960) and has been confirmed by subsequent scholarship, especially since the opening of Soviet archives after 1991.

3. See Beth Sims, *Workers of the World Undermined: American Labor's Role in US Foreign Policy* (Boston: South End Press, 1992). Ironically enough, the AFL-CIO's International Affairs Department was long dominated by former Communist internationalists like Jay Lovestone.

4. Jeremy Brecher and Tim Costello, "Labor Internationalism," *Z,* November 1988.

5. Ibid. The National Labor Committee on El Salvador, which led labor criticism of US policy in Central America, eventually evolved into the National Labor Committee, a pioneer of the campaign against international sweatshops. See Andrew Ross, *No Sweat* (London: Verso, 1997), p. 64.

6. Peter Waterman, ed., *The Old Internationalism and the New: A Reader on Labour, New Social Movements and Internationalism* (The Hague: International Labour Education, Research and Information Foundation, 1988).

7. Brecher and Costello, "Labor Internationalism," p. 104.

8. Ibid., p. 103.

9. Brecher and Costello, *Global Village or Global Pillage*, p. 96.

10. Ibid., p. 97.

11. Naomi Klein, "Rebels in Search of Rules," *New York Times*, December 2, 1999.

12. Jeremy Brecher and Tim Costello, "Labor Goes Global I," *Z*, January 1991.

13. Michael Mann, *The Sources of Social Power, Volume I: A History of Power from the Beginning to AD 1760* (Cambridge: Cambridge University Press, 1986), p. 16.

CHAPTER 47

1. The lines are an excerpt from Bertolt Brecht's *Deutsche Kriegsfibel* (*German War Primer*), which appears in Bertolt Brecht, *Gesammelte Werke* vol. IV (Berlin: Suhrkamp, 1967), p. 638. The literal translation quoted here was provided to me in personal correspondence by the Brecht scholar Martin Esslin. It was published on page 240 of Jeremy Brecher and Tim Costello, *Common Sense for Hard Times* (Boston: South End Press/Institute for Policy Studies, 1976) with thanks to Mr. Esslin.

2. Donald G. McNeil, Jr., "As Devastating Epidemics Increase, Nations Take on Drug Companies," *New York Times*, July 9, 2000.

3. Esther Kaplan, "The Mighty Act Up Has Fallen: The Philadelphia Story," *POZ*, November 2001.

4. Rena Singer, "Drug Firms Yield to Cry of the Poor," *Christian Science Monitor*, April 20, 2001.

5. Geoff Dyer, David Pilling, Vanessa Valkin, and Frances Williams, "US Climbs Down Over Brazil's Patent Law," *Financial Times*, June 26, 2001.

6. "How to Save Lives Without Even Trying," *Frontline* (India), November 24–December 7, 2001.

7. Gene Sharp, *The Politics of Nonviolent Action* (Boston: Porter Sargent, 1973). Sharp's approach to "indirect strategy" drew heavily on the ideas of military theorist Liddell Hart.

CHAPTER 48

1. Walden Bello, "Reforming the WTO Is the Wrong Agenda," in *Globalize This!*, eds. Kevin Danaher and Roger Burbach (Monroe, Maine: Common Courage Press, 2000), p. 177ff.

2. David Korten, *When Corporations Rule the World* (Bloomfield, CT: Kumarian Press, 2001).

3. United Nations Human Development Program, *Human Development Report 1992* (New York: Oxford, 1992), pp. 78–79.

CHAPTER 49

1. Brecher, Costello, and Smith, *Globalization from Below*, p. xiv.

2. The White House, *The National Security Strategy of the United States of America* (Washington, D.C., September 2002).

3. Jeremy Brecher, "Terminating the Bush Juggernaut," *Foreign Policy in Focus* (May 2003): 10.

4. Patrick E. Tyler, "Threats and Responses: News Analysis; A New Power in the Streets," *New York Times*, February 17, 2003.

5. See, for example, Chuck Morse, "Theory of the Anti-Globalization Movement," *New Formulation* 1, no. 1 (November 2001): 22–31. Morse writes that the authors' "basic theoretical commitments are fundamentally antagonistic to the goal of revolutionary transformation" and that the authors "do not want such a transformation" (p. 51). See also Jeremy Brecher, "Reply to Chuck Morse," *New Formulation* 2, no. 1 (February 2003).

6. Brecher, Costello, and Smith, *Globalization from Below*, p. 122.

ACKNOWLEDGMENTS

This book reflects what I've learned from innumerable friends and colleagues over the past half century. I thank them all, especially those who have led me to question my own ideas. As William Blake said, "Opposition is true friendship."

Jill Cutler has sustained me through the long travails of making this book, as well as providing me the luxury of an in-house editor. Without Michael Pertschuk's faith in it this book might never have seen the light of day. Essential support also came from Anthony Arnove, Nando Fasce, Charles Lindblom, Michael Ferber, Francis Fox Piven, and Frieder Otto Wolf. My editor Jennifer Knerr's vision was essential to the realization of this project.

My colleagues Becky Glass, Brendan Smith, and Joe Uehlein at the Labor Network for Sustainability have provided a context of thought and action that has informed the final shaping of the book.

Thanks to those who have read part or all of the manuscript at one stage or another, including Michael Ames, Michael Athay, Jill Cutler, Josh Dubler, Sharon Hammer, Charles Lindblom, Peter Marris, Brendan Smith, Dan Sofaer, Michael Pertschuk, and Frieder Otto Wolf.

Many of the ideas in this book were worked out over four decades in collaboration with the late Tim Costello.

INDEX

❧

233

Diamond, Jared, 184
Diggers, 7–8
direct democracy, 63
disorder, globalization and, 176–178, 186
Dixiecrats, 61
Doctors Without Borders, 172
Doha round, 172–173
domination, globalization and, 174–176,
    177–178, 186
Doomsday Clock, xv–xvi, xvii, 5, 219
draft, antiwar movement and, 73, 75
draft resisters, 75
"Drug Firms Yield to Cry of the Poor"
    (article), 172
Durr, Clifford, 20, 52, 54
Durr, Lulah, 52
Durr, Virginia, 52

ecological shift, 9, 137, 141, 190–192
ecology, 28–30
Economic and Philosophic Manuscripts
    (Marx), 27
economic democratization, 205. *See under*
    democratization economic globalization,
    10, 142, 144, 169, 183, 200; alternatives
    to, 174–178. *See also* globalization
    economic nationalism, 179
Economic Research and Action Project
    (ERAP), 60, 65
economics, of war, 46–47
economy: pre-globalization, 150;
    unregulated global, 192
Egypt: democracy movement in, 2, 3, 4, 7,
    85, 138, 193, 200, 208, 214, 216; strikes
    in, 1–2, 3
1877: Year of Violence (Bruce), 86
Einstein, Albert, 5, 184
Eisenhower, Dwight D., 39, 45, 46
elites: American power, 46, 50; bureaucratic
    power, 63–64; concentration of wealth
    and power among, 108; Leninist and
    social democratic party, 103
El Salvador, 164
emergent properties, labor and social

struggles and, 136–137
Encarta Encyclopedia, 97
END. *See* European Nuclear Disarmament
    (END)
The End of History (Fukuyama), 59
"The End of Ideology as Ideology" (Haber),
    59
The End of Ideology (Bell), 59
environmental degradation, globalization
    and, 157
environmental holocaust, 184
environmentalism, 28–30
environmental movement, rise of, 190
ERAP. *See* Economic Research and Action
    Project (ERAP)
Esparza, Martin, 4
European Nuclear Disarmament (END), 44
European Union, social dimension of, 177
externalities, 29

Facing Reality, 111
factory committees, 125
factory councils, 103
fallout shelter program, 37–38
FBI (Federal Bureau of Investigation), 55, 77
Federal Communications Commission, 20
feedback loops, social action and, 141–142
Fellowship of Reconciliation, 52
Ferber, Michael, 75
Fifth Avenue Peace Parade Committee, 40
financial deregulation, 156
financial destabilization, globalization and,
    156
Financial Times (periodical), 155, 172
"fix it or nix it" slogan, 171
Flacks, Richard, 59–60
food security movements, 203, 205
Ford workers, 161
Foster, Charles, 119
Fountain, Clayton, 117
frame, 198; for human preservation
    movement, 199
France, 89, 137, 138, 171
Freedom Budget, 47

ABOUT THE AUTHOR

JEREMY BRECHER HAS PARTICIPATED IN MOVEMENTS FOR NUCLEAR disarmament, civil rights, peace, international labor rights, global economic justice, accountability for war crimes, climate protection, and many others. He is the author of fifteen books on labor and social movements, including the national best seller *Strike!* He has received five regional Emmy awards for his documentary film work. He is currently policy and research director for the Labor Network for Sustainability. His "Commentaries on Solidarity and Survival" appear regularly on the LNS website at "Strike! Jeremy Brecher's Corner. https://www.labor4sustainability.org/strike/.

PM Press is an independent, radical publisher of books and media to educate, entertain, and inspire. Founded in 2007 by a small group of people with decades of publishing, media, and organizing experience, PM Press amplifies the voices of radical authors, artists, and activists. Our aim is to deliver bold political ideas and vital stories to all walks of life and arm the dreamers to demand the impossible. We have sold millions of copies of our books, most often one at a time, face to face. We're old enough to know what we're doing and young enough to know what's at stake. Join us to create a better world.

PM Press
PO Box 23912
Oakland CA 94623
510-658-3906
www.pmpress.org

PM Press in Europe
europe@pmpress.org
www.pmpress.org.uk

FRIENDS OF PM

These are indisputably momentous times—the financial system is melting down globally and the Empire is stumbling. Now more than ever there is a vital need for radical ideas.

In the many years since its founding—and on a mere shoestring—PM Press has risen to the formidable challenge of publishing and distributing knowledge and entertainment for the struggles ahead. With hundreds of releases to date, we have published an impressive and stimulating array of literature, art, music, politics, and culture. Using every available medium, we've succeeded in connecting those hungry for ideas and information to those putting them into practice.

Friends of PM allows you to directly help impact, amplify, and revitalize the discourse and actions of radical writers, filmmakers, and artists. It provides us with a stable foundation from which we can build upon our early successes and provides a much-needed subsidy for the materials that can't necessarily pay their own way. You can help make that happen—and receive every new title automatically delivered to your door once a month—by joining as a Friend of PM Press. And, we'll throw in a free T-shirt when you sign up.

Here are your options:
- $30 a month: Get all books and pamphlets plus 50% discount on all webstore purchases
- $40 a month: Get all PM Press releases (including CDs and DVDs) plus 50% discount on all webstore purchases
- $100 a month: Superstar—Everything plus PM merchandise, free downloads, and 50% discount on all webstore purchases

For those who can't afford $30 or more a month, we have Sustainer Rates at $15, $10, and $5. Sustainers get a free PM Press T-shirt and a 50% discount on all purchases from our website.

Your Visa or Mastercard will be billed once a month, until you tell us to stop. Or until our efforts succeed in bringing the revolution around. Or the financial meltdown of Capital makes plastic redundant. Whichever comes first.

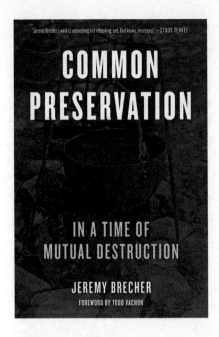

Common Preservation
In a Time of Mutual Destruction

Jeremy Brecher
Foreword by Todd Vachon

ISBN: 978-1-62963-788-4
$26.95 • 6x9 • 448 pages

As world leaders eschew cooperation to address climate change, nuclear proliferation, economic meltdown, and other threats to our survival, more and more people experience a pervasive sense of dread and despair. Is there anything we can do? What can put us on the course from mutual destruction to common preservation? In the past, social movements have sometimes made rapid and unexpected changes that countered apparently incurable social problems. Jeremy Brecher presents scores of historical examples of people who changed history by adopting strategies of common preservation, showing what we can we learn from past social movements to better confront today's global threats of climate change, war, and economic chaos.

In *Common Preservation*, Brecher shares his experiences and what he has learned that can help ward off mutual destruction and provides a unique heuristic—a toolkit for thinkers and activists—to understand and create new forms of common preservation.

> "Chapter by chapter, I learn from it; and I admire its ambition. When I sampled it, it engaged me so much that I set aside other work until I finished it. Overall, a fine manuscript. Rich in content. Also engaging. Is it not all or part of a philosophy or worldview?"
> —Charles Lindblom, Sterling Professor Emeritus of Political Science and Economics at Yale University; author of *The Market System*

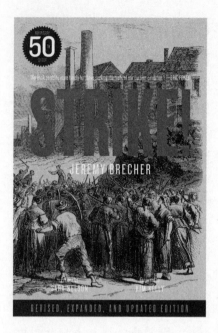

Strike!
50th Anniversary Edition

Jeremy Brecher
Preface by Sara Nelson
Foreword by Kim Kelly

ISBN: 978-1-62963-800-3
$28.95 • 6x9 • 640 pages

Jeremy Brecher's *Strike!* narrates the dramatic story of repeated, massive, and sometimes violent revolts by ordinary working people in America. Involving nationwide general strikes, the seizure of vast industrial establishments, nonviolent direct action on a massive scale, and armed battles with artillery and tanks, this exciting hidden history is told from the point of view of the rank-and-file workers who lived it. Encompassing the repeated repression of workers' rebellions by company-sponsored violence, local police, state militias, and the U.S. Army and National Guard, it reveals a dimension of American history rarely found in the usual high school or college history course.

Since its original publication in 1972, no book has done as much as *Strike!* to bring U.S. labor history to a wide audience. Now this fiftieth anniversary edition brings the story up to date with chapters covering the "mini-revolts of the twenty-first century," including Occupy Wall Street and the Fight for Fifteen. The new edition contains over a hundred pages of new materials and concludes by examining a wide range of current struggles, ranging from #BlackLivesMatter, to the great wave of teachers strikes "for the soul of public education," to the global "Student Strike for Climate" that may be harbingers of mass strikes to come.

> "Jeremy Brecher's *Strike!* is a classic of American historical writing. This new edition, bringing his account up to the present, comes amid rampant inequality and growing popular resistance. No book could be more timely for those seeking the roots of our current condition."
> —Eric Foner, Pulitzer Prize winner and DeWitt Clinton Professor of History at Columbia University

Against Doom

A Climate Insurgency Manual

Jeremy Brecher

ISBN: 978-1-62963-385-5
$12.95 • 8x5 • 128 pages

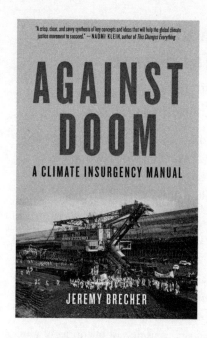

Before the election of Donald Trump the world was already speeding toward climate catastrophe. Now President Trump has jammed his foot on the global warming accelerator. Is there any way for the rest of us to put on the brakes?

Climate insurgency is a strategy for using people power to realize our common interest in protecting the climate. It uses mass, global, nonviolent action to challenge the legitimacy of public and corporate officials who are perpetrating climate destruction.

A global climate insurgency has already begun. It has the potential to halt and roll back Trump's fossil fuel agenda and the global thrust toward climate destruction.

Against Doom: A Climate Insurgency Manual tells how to put that strategy into action—and how it can succeed. It is a handbook for halting global warming and restoring our climate—a how-to for climate insurgents.

> "*Against Doom* lays out key elements of a far-reaching, global-scaled, pragmatic, people-powered strategy to topple the power of the fossil fuel industry and the institutions behind it."
> —David Solnit, author of *Globalize Liberation: How to Uproot the System and Build a Better World*

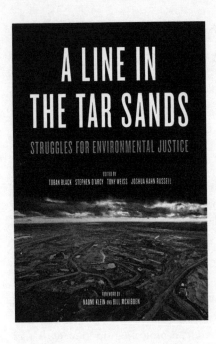

A Line in the Tar Sands

Struggles for Environmental Justice

Edited by Joshua Kahn, Stephen D'Arcy, Tony Weis, Toban Black • Foreword by Naomi Klein and Bill McKibben

ISBN: 9781629630397
$24.95 • 9x6 • 392 pages

Tar sands "development" comes with an enormous environmental and human cost. In the tar sands of Alberta, the oil industry is using vast quantities of water and natural gas to produce synthetic crude oil, creating drastically high levels of greenhouse gas emissions and air and water pollution. But tar sands opponents—fighting a powerful international industry—are likened to terrorists; government environmental scientists are muzzled; and public hearings are concealed and rushed.

Yet, despite the formidable political and economic power behind the tar sands, many opponents are actively building international networks of resistance, challenging pipeline plans while resisting threats to Indigenous sovereignty and democratic participation. Including leading voices involved in the struggle against the tar sands, *A Line in the Tar Sands* offers a critical analysis of the impact of the tar sands and the challenges opponents face in their efforts to organize effective resistance.

Contributors include: Greg Albo, Sâkihitowin Awâsis, Toban Black, Rae Breaux, Jeremy Brecher, Linda Capato, Jesse Cardinal, Angela V. Carter, Emily Coats, Stephen D'Arcy, Yves Engler, Cherri Foytlin, Sonia Grant, Harjap Grewal, Randolph Haluza-DeLay, Ryan Katz-Rosene, Naomi Klein, Melina Laboucan-Massimo, Winona LaDuke, Crystal Lameman, Christine Leclerc, Kerry Lemon, Matt Leonard, Martin Lukacs, Tyler McCreary, Bill McKibben, Yudith Nieto, Joshua Kahn Russell, Macdonald Stainsby, Clayton Thomas-Muller, Brian Tokar, Dave Vasey, Harsha Walia, Tony Weis, Rex Weyler, Will Wooten, Jess Worth, and Lilian Yap.

The editors' proceeds from this book will be donated to frontline grassroots environmental justice groups and campaigns.

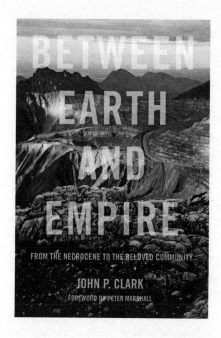

Between Earth and Empire
From the Necrocene to the Beloved Community

John P. Clark
Foreword by Peter Marshall

ISBN: 978-1-62963-648-1
$24.95 • 6x9 • 384 pages

Between Earth and Empire focuses on the crucial position of humanity at the present moment in Earth history. We are now in the midst of the Necrocene, an epoch of death and mass extinction. Nearing the end of the long history of Empire and domination, we are faced with the choice of either continuing the path of social and ecological disintegration or initiating a new era of social and ecological regeneration.

The book shows that conventional approaches to global crisis on both the right and the left have succumbed to processes of denial and disavowal, either rejecting the reality of crisis entirely or substituting ineffectual but comforting gestures and images for deep, systemic social transformation. It is argued that a large-scale social and ecological regeneration must be rooted in communities of liberation and solidarity, fostering personal and group transformation so that a culture of awakening and care can emerge.

Between Earth and Empire explores examples of significant progress in this direction, including the Zapatista movement in Chiapas, the Democratic Autonomy Movement in Rojava, indigenous movements in defense of the commons, the solidarity economy movement, and efforts to create liberated base communities and affinity groups within anarchism and other radical social movements. In the end, the book presents a vision of hope for social and ecological regeneration through the rebirth of a libertarian and communitarian social imaginary, and the flourishing of a free cooperative community globally.

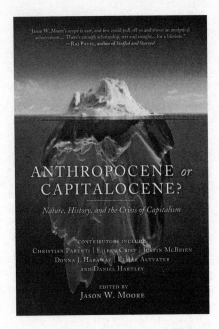

Anthropocene or Capitalocene?

Nature, History, and the Crisis of Capitalism

Edited by Jason W. Moore

ISBN: 978-1-62963-148-6

$21.95 • 9x6 • 240 pages

The Earth has reached a tipping point. Runaway climate change, the sixth great extinction of planetary life, the acidification of the oceans—all point toward an era of unprecedented turbulence in humanity's relationship within the web of life. But just what is that relationship, and how do we make sense of this extraordinary transition?

Anthropocene or Capitalocene? offers answers to these questions from a dynamic group of leading critical scholars. They challenge the theory and history offered by the most significant environmental concept of our times: the Anthropocene. But are we living in the Anthropocene, literally the "Age of Man"? Is a different response more compelling, and better suited to the strange—and often terrifying—times in which we live? The contributors to this book diagnose the problems of Anthropocene thinking and propose an alternative: the global crises of the twenty-first century are rooted in the Capitalocene, the Age of Capital.

Anthropocene or Capitalocene? offers a series of provocative essays on nature and power, humanity, and capitalism. Including both well-established voices and younger scholars, the book challenges the conventional practice of dividing historical change and contemporary reality into "Nature" and "Society," demonstrating the possibilities offered by a more nuanced and connective view of human environment-making, joined at every step with and within the biosphere. In distinct registers, the authors frame their discussions within a politics of hope that signal the possibilities for transcending capitalism, broadly understood as a "world-ecology" that joins nature, capital, and power as a historically evolving whole.

Contributors include Jason W. Moore, Eileen Crist, Donna J. Haraway, Justin McBrien, Elmar Altvater, Daniel Hartley, and Christian Parenti.